Thought Reform of the Chinese Intellectuals

大陸知識分子思想改造

Thought Reform of the Chinese Intellectuals

by

THEODORE H. E. CHEN

Professor of Asiatic Studies
University of Southern California

HONG KONG UNIVERSITY PRESS

OXFORD UNIVERSITY PRESS
1960

THE OXFORD UNIVERSITY PRESS, AMEN HOUSE, LONDON, E.C.4
AND 417 FIFTH AVENUE, NEW YORK 16, ARE THE EXCLUSIVE
AGENTS FOR ALL COUNTRIES EXCEPT ASIA EAST OF BURMA

香 港 印
Printed in Hong Kong by
CATHAY PRESS
153 Island Road at Aberdeen

To

WEN-HUI

My Partner in Work and Play

PREFACE

REPORTING on the work of his government at the Fourth Session of the First National People's Congress on June 26, 1957, Chou En-lai, Communist China's prime minister and then also foreign minister, summarized the record of the Communist regime in consolidating its power and using it to lead the country into socialism. The consolidation of state power, he said, was achieved by dint of 'five major campaigns': (1) the agrarian reform to destroy feudalism and the landlord class; (2) the 'Resist-America Aid-Korea' campaign against American imperialism; (3) the suppression of counter-revolutionaries to eliminate opposition to the people's democratic dictatorship; (4) the 'three-anti' and 'five-anti' campaigns against the bourgeoisie; and (5) ideological remoulding to change the outlook, the thought patterns, and the basic loyalties of the people.

These five campaigns, he said, paved the way for what he called 'the three big transformations'. These were: (1) the socialist transformation of agriculture into co-operatives and collectives; (2) the socialist transformation of individual handicraft production into co-operative production; and (3) the socialist transformation of private capitalist industry and commerce into joint state-private enterprises.

Chou En-lai pointed out that of the five major campaigns two were specially directed towards the intellectuals. The Resist-America Aid-Korea campaign had for its object the uprooting of the pro-American attitudes and habits of thought so common among intellectuals while the campaign of ideological remoulding had for its object their ideological indoctrination and thought reform.

In actuality, thought reform is basic to every one of the five campaigns and three transformations. The land reform was considered an important means by which the intellectuals as well as the entire rural population learned the significance of the class struggle; the suppression of counter-revolutionaries meant, in part, the elimination of persons ideologically opposed to the new rulers; and the 'three-anti' and 'five-anti' were campaigns directed against 'bourgeois ideology' as well as the bourgeoisie as a class. Finally, the Communists have laid stress on 'socialist education' and the development of a 'socialist ideology' as a prerequisite to the socialist transformation of agriculture, the handicrafts and private capitalism.

Thought reform clearly constitutes a major policy of the Chinese Communist regime. Its importance has been further underscored by the happenings of 1956 and 1957. Such developments as the policy of the 'Hundred Flowers', the rectification campaign, and the drive against Rightists are only the most recent phases of this broad and continuous programme.

When this study was first formulated a few years ago, it was the author's intention to deal only with the thought reform and the 'confessions' of intellectuals in the 1950–1952 period. Recent developments made it worthwhile to expand the study in order to tell a continuous story of this Communist programme from the early period to the present day. The early phase of the thought reform is therefore summarized in the first nine chapters, and the last ten chapters are devoted to the developments of 1956 and 1957. The thought reform of Chinese intellectuals will continue for many years, and a study of past methods and their results may therefore help readers to understand the events that are yet to come.

Who are the intellectuals? The literal translation of the Chinese term *chih-shih fen-tzu* 知識份子 is 'knowlegeable elements', or 'elements with knowledge', which in the press is frequently rendered as 'intelligentzia' in the collective. It is in the general sense that we use in our discussion the term 'intellectuals'.

In actuality the term *chih-shih fen-tzu* applies to all the educated people or all who have had some schooling. The students constitute a very important part of the intelligentzia, but in the treatise we shall not discuss their problem except when we refer to indoctrination agencies set up for the intelligentzia. Our attention is focussed on the professional people—the scholar, the teacher, the writer, the artist and others of the professional groups.

'The Party' in the Chinese Communist terminology refers specifically to the Chinese Communist Party, and is spelt with a capital 'P' in this study.

THEODORE H. E. CHEN

Los Angeles, California
January, 1958

ACKNOWLEDGEMENTS

GRATEFUL acknowledgements are due to Mr William L. HOLLAND, Secretary-General of the Institute of Pacific Relations, who first saw the value of such a study and encouraged the author to pursue it; to Dr Frederick Teh-chi YÜ, Associate Professor of Journalism, Montana State University, who offered helpful suggestions in the initial stage of the study; to Dr Sin-ming CHIU, Assistant Professor of History, Centenary College of Louisiana, who rendered valuable assistance in looking up sources of data pertaining to the 'confessions' of 1951–1952; and to my wife Wen-hui for helping to scan Chinese Communist publications for pertinent information concerning the 'Hundred Flowers' policy and the anti-Rightist campaign. I am of course solely responsible for the views expressed in the book.

THEODORE H. E. CHEN

Los Angeles, California
January, 1958

CONTENTS

Contents

CHAPTER I

THE POLICY OF
ABSORB AND REFORM

1. THE FIRST RESPONSE OF SOME INTELLECTUALS

IN the autumn of 1948 the Chinese Communists were making steady progress in their military conquest of the country. Some months were still to pass before Peking fell into their hands, but the general feeling in China was that the Nationalist Government would not be able to halt their advance. A group of college professors were asked how they felt about the political change. One of them spoke as follows:

> . . . We intellectuals have gone through three phases in our thinking. At first, most of us supported the government, recognizing its many faults, but hoping it would reform. Then we became increasingly discouraged with reform prospects, but saw no feasible alternatives. Though the present government, we felt, was bad, what might take its place would be even worse. During this second phase intellectuals were uncertain and bewildered. Then came the present, third phase. We have become so completely convinced of the hopelessness of the existing government that we feel that the sooner it is removed the better. Since the Chinese Communists are obviously the only force capable of making this change, we are now willing to support them as the lesser of two evils. We ourselves would prefer a middle course, but that is no longer possible.[1]

On October 1, 1949, the People's Republic of China was proclaimed. One of the major policies of the new regime was to carry out a nation-wide programme of agrarian reform, at the heart of which was a fierce and bitter class struggle against the landlords. Intellectuals were required to participate in it in order to learn at first hand the significance of the class struggle. One of them, Wu Ching-ch'ao, wrote about his experience as follows:

> After I joined the ranks of the peasants, I came to realize that the land reform is a bitter struggle which heightens my consciousness. The first step of the agrarian reform is to organize a broad anti-feudal united front to wage a class struggle against the landlords. . . . Between the two battle fronts, where do you stand? . . . Whom do you support? Whom do you oppose? . . . Every person must make an unequivocal answer.[2]   *JMJP* April 1, 1951

When in June 1950 came the Korean war, the anti-American campaign was intensified. Intellectuals were called upon to renounce their past connections with the United States, to denounce 'Imperialist America', and to express their newly acquired admiration for the Soviet Union. Huang Chia-te, an editor who had studied in the United States, found it wise to state his position as follows:

I had blindly worshipped the 'material civilization' of European and American imperialism and especially the 'science' and 'culture' of American imperialism. . . . Not until the 'Resist-America, Aid-Korea' campaign was underway did I awaken . . . to realize the decadent nature of American imperialism and the ugliness of American cultural aggression. . . . The criminal use of bacteriological weapons in Korea and the Northeast further proves that the American imperialists are the deadly enemy of the Chinese and of all the peace-loving peoples of the world.[3]   KMJP July 11, 1952

Another, T'eng Ta-ch'un, wrote:

I now understand that to hate America and to love the Soviet Union are two sides of the same coin. After I began to hate America, I naturally came to see that the Soviet Union is lovable and worthy of respect and admiration. As a matter of fact the Soviet Union is giving us unreserved guidance with its own revolutionary and constructive experience, Soviet specialists are selflessly helping us, and the Soviet Union is unconditionally lending us support in world affairs. I feel ashamed that I have in the past stood on the same ground with the reactionary elements.[4]   KMJP Dec. 31, 1951

As the new rulers extended and consolidated their control, they demanded that the intellectuals reform themselves in order to make themselves acceptable and useful to the new society. Recantations and confessions were considered necessary prerequisites to reform. The intellectuals vowed to break away from their reactionary past. Here are the repentant words of Lo Ch'ang-p'ei, a scholar who happens to be of Manchu origin:

When I was eighteen years old, I worked as a secretary to support myself and my family. Although I later taught in middle schools and universities, I was still a plain citizen owning neither a home nor a piece of land. Three generations of my ancestors were public-supported members of the army, but none had held any high position in government. By any definition of class, I thought, I could very well be classified as a mental labourer. My later and relatively pleasant life as a professor should make me a petty bourgeois at the worst. Certainly I could not have had the consciousness of the exploiting class. However, a more objective analysis would reveal otherwise. . . . While the farmers were always worried about droughts, floods and locusts, we Manchus received our allowances regularly in good years or bad. This is proof that my ancestors lived on others' labour. The ideas of the exploiting class that still survive within myself are traceable to this.[5]

Then came the 'ideological remoulding'. The intellectuals pledged themselves to study Marxism-Leninism and the 'thought of Chairman Mao'. This is how Yü Te-yüan expressed himself on May 19, 1952.

I feel extremely grieved to realize how much harm has been done to the people because of my failure to use faithfully the ideology of the proletariat as a yard-stick in my work. . . . Henceforth I will redouble my efforts to study Marxism-Leninism and the thought of Chairman Mao, with the hope of reforming fundamentally. I will steadfastly hold to my position with the working class in order to serve the people better.[6]

Gradually the intellectuals accepted the new order and adjusted themselves to the new ideology. To what extent was there inner rebellion in spite of the overt adjustments, it was then impossible to tell. The intellectuals bowed to the inevitable when there was no alternative. Their frustrations and the great stress under which they lived burst out in open criticism only when at a later date the rulers were compelled to correct excesses in their measures of control and suppression. Even when they did have this chance to speak their mind, it behoved them to be cautious and stay within the limits allowed by the authorities.

Describing the personal problems of the intellectuals, Professor Feng Yu-lan said:

> Generally speaking the professors are much better off now than before. But if many of them did not have savings before . . . they would still be hard pressed. Many still have to do housework at home. . . . Many lack the money to buy books. . . . Even if they can afford to buy . . . they do not have room to store them.[7]   *JMJP* Jan. 15, 1956

Chi Hsien-lin, another intellectual, said:

> Before liberation, the professors were free to teach anything they liked, in any way they liked. They were university professors and respected figures in society. . . . Things are different today. Intellectuals, like other labourers, all work for the collective well-being of the people. They must have plans and organization. They teach according to outlines of instruction. If anything wrong is found in their work, they have to face criticism and self-criticism.[8]
> *JMJP* Jan. 13, 1956

When during the first five-year plan the intellectuals were called upon to fill new needs and adjust themselves to the movement of the 'high tide of socialism' promoted by the Party, this is what one of the intellectuals wrote:

> I feel honoured and excited as an intellectual in New China. Through education and the assistance of the Party I became aware of the great signi-ficance of my work . . . The more I visualize the bright future of socialism, the stronger and more confident I become. Therefore, I am willing to contribute all I possess to the Party and to the people in this epoch-making period of socialist construction.[9]   Chang Wei in *JMJP* Jan. 18, 1956

2. THE 1939 RESOLUTION

The problem of the Communists has been how to absorb and treat the intellectuals whom they needed and yet distrusted. Long before reaching nation-wide victory they were quite aware of the important role of the intellectuals in the history of China and their strategic leadership in the various reform movements. The reform movement at the close of the 19th century and the revolu-tionary movement under Sun Yat-sen had been spearheaded by China's awakened intelligentzia. The Kuomintang under Chiang Kai-shek, in its beginning, depended on the support of students and intellectuals.

The Communists knew that if they could win over the intellec-tuals they would have gone a long way towards capturing the support of articulate public opinion in and outside China. As early as 1939 Mao declared that 'the intellectual elements are indispensable' and to 'win over all progressive elements is one of our most important tasks'.[10] The Communists knew that it was in the universities and in the early 'study circles' organized by China's intellectuals that the Marxist movement in China had originated and not in the factories or the proletariat.

The Resolution on the absorption of intellectuals passed by the Chinese Communist Party in 1939 reaffirmed, in its first paragraph, the importance of the intellectuals in China:

> . . . In its glorious struggle to build a new China, the Communist Party must know well how to attract the intellectual elements before it will be able to organize the tens of millions of the peasant masses, and to promote the revolutionary cultural movements as well as develop the united front. Without the participation of the intellectuals, victory in the revolution will be impossible.[11]

The Resolution criticized Party members who had 'a mentality of fear and rejection towards intellectuals' and who failed 'to enlist young students *en masse*'. Affirming that 'a correct policy towards the intellectuals is one of the prime conditions for the success of the revolution', it specified the following measures for the 'absorption of intellectual elements':

> (a) All Party units in combat areas and in the Communist armies should strive to induce large numbers of intellectuals and semi-intellectuals to join our army, enter our schools, and work in our government. . . .
> (b) In the adoption of this policy of absorbing intellectuals *en masse*, we should undoubtedly reject completely those sent over to us by the enemy or the bourgeois political party, and disloyal elements should also be rejected. . . .
> (c) Intellectuals and semi-intellectuals who are useful in various degrees and who are more loyal should be given appropriate work, trained adequately, and led gradually to correct their weaknesses in the course of our sustained struggle, in order to enable them to revolutionize themselves. . . .
> (d) Those cadres who are opposed to the participation of intellectuals in their work . . . should be persuaded to realize the necessity of absorbing intellectuals to participate in such activities. . . .[12]

The Communists were then in control of only a very small area in the Northwest of China. They wanted the intellectual elements to leave the areas under the Kuomintang and join their side. Their efforts met with some success after 1932, when the Japanese conquered Manchuria. A considerable number of intellectuals, especially students, had become dissatisfied with the appeasement policy of Chiang Kai-shek's government and responded favourably to the Communist slogans of 'no civil war' and 'resist Japanese aggression'. To these intellectuals who came over the Communists extended a hearty welcome and offered them an opportunity to serve a patriotic cause.

But the Resolution showed the policy of 'absorbing the intellect-uals' did not consist of merely enlisting their services but of remoulding them into 'revolutionaries' after the Communist pattern. While needing the intellectuals the Communists were suspicious of them.

The Resolution stipulated that the intellectuals should be led to 'correct their weaknesses' and should be helped 'to revolutionize themselves, to adopt a truly mass point of view, and to get along harmoniously with the veteran Party members and cadres as well as with the Party members of worker or peasant stock'. At the same time it spoke of 'cadres who are capable of handling the intellec-tuals'. In other words, the reform of the intellectuals was already a thought-out policy at this time.

3. YENAN 1937-1942

When the Sino-Japanese war broke out in 1937, the Communists stepped up their activities to persuade students and intellectuals to go to Yenan, their new base in northern Shensi province. The intellectuals were absorbed into the People's Anti-Japanese Milit-ary and Political University, *K'ang-ta* for short, the successor of the Red Army Academy in Kiangsi.[13] Later, as the influx of students and other intellectuals increased, the Yenan Academy *(Shan-pei kung-hsüeh)* was opened and almost at the same time two other institutions were founded. In 1939, these institutions were amalgamated to become the North China Associated University with German-trained Ch'eng Fang-wu as president.

After living at close quarters with intellectuals for some time, the Communists became alarmed by the spread of the 'bourgeois ideology' which the intellectuals had brought with them. By 1942 they had inaugurated an 'ideological remoulding campaign' to combat the various forms of 'unproletarian ideology' such as 'liberalism' and 'idealism'. In May of that year a special conference of writers and artists was called at Yenan to determine the course to be followed in literature and art. At that conference, Mao Tse-tung made his famous speech on literature and art which the Chinese Communists still uphold as an important guide-post for intellectuals engaged in these fields.[14] His basic thesis is that litera-ture and art must serve political purposes and that writers and artists must be close to the masses and produce for the benefit of the broad masses of workers, peasants, and soldiers rather than for the minority petty bourgeoisie.

> Politics, whether revolutionary or counter-revolutionary, represent the struggle between opposing classes, not the behaviour of a few individuals. Ideological warfare and the warfare in art and literature, especially revolutionary ideological warfare and revolutionary warfare in art and literature, must be subordinate to political warfare.

In other words, intellectuals must constitute a 'cultural army' to wage war on the cultural front of the proletarian revolution. Partly to ridicule the intellectuals and partly to underscore his insistence that intellectuals must learn 'the viewpoint of the working class', Mao said:

> Whenever I compare unreformed intellectuals with workers, peasants and soldiers, I feel that not only there are many unclean things in the mind of the intellectuals but their bodies are also unclean. The cleanest people are the workers and peasants, even though their hands may be soiled and their feet smeared with animal excreta. Anyway they are still cleaner than the bourgeoisie and the petty bourgeoisie.[15]

On another occasion, at the opening day ceremony of the Party School at Yenan on February 1, 1942, Mao said:

> There are many intellectuals who consider themselves knowledgeable and who assume an insolent attitude, not knowing that such an attitude is harmful and impedes their own progress. They should know this truism: a great many so-called intellectuals are oftentimes the most unenlightened, and sometimes workers and peasants are even more knowledgeable.[16]

He decried 'book knowledge' in the following words:

> . . . Look at those students who have graduated from schools completely shut off from society. . . . First, they do not know how to farm; second, they cannot work; third, they do not know how to be soldiers; and fourth, they know nothing about administration. They have not an iota of knowledge in these practical matters. All they have is book knowledge. Can these people be considered intellectuals? I think they can only be half-intellectuals.[17]

It is thus clear that the two-fold policy of 'absorbing' and 'reforming' the intellectuals grew out of the Communists' two-faced attitude towards them: while they need win over the intellectuals, they were fundamentally distrustful of these products of bourgeois society and capitalist culture.

CHAPTER II

CORRECT THOUGHT THE CURE-ALL

1. THE PRODUCTS OF BOURGEOIS SOCIETY

WHEN in 1948 the power of the Chinese Communists was expanding fast and national victory within their reach, the problem of dealing with the intellectuals became more complicated and more urgent. Not only were they confronted with much larger numbers of intellectuals in the areas under their control but their need for their services had increased. Under the comparatively simple conditions in the 'caves' and rural areas it had been possible to get along with Party members and cadres who, in the main, had had little formal education, and still less technical training. Now to take up the manifold tasks of city administration, of teaching in all levels of schools and colleges, of engineering, medicine, business management, etc. it became necessary to enlist the services of the intelligentzia.

To cope with this situation the Central Plain Bureau of the Chinese Communist Party issued on December 18, 1948 a special directive instructing all Party members to 'win over, unite with, reform and cultivate the intelligentzia'.[1] It was one of the Party's major policy statements with regard to intellectuals at that time, and charted the course of action to be followed throughout the country during the early months of the regime. It recommended the following procedure for absorbing and reforming the intelligentzia:

i. All our agencies in position of leadership should recognize the importance of this task (of winning over and reforming the intellectuals) from the political point of view. They must make use of all kinds of opportunities, such as lectures, reports, cultural and recreational activities, through various media, such as newspapers, posters, bulletins, handbills, cartoons, etc., to carry out propaganda in oral and written form, explaining our Party's policy towards the intellectuals, pointing out the way for them to follow, alleviating their worries about us, so that they may understand and turn to us.

ii. Organize short-course schools and training classes; call on and mobilize them to *hsüeh-hsi* (study) and to receive training. In these schools and training classes. . . giving courses at least three to four months in duration, political study must precede occupational study. Political study is to be primarily concerned with current affairs, basic problems of the Chinese revolution, and our Party's major policies.

iii. The people's government on all levels should convene various discussion meetings for intellectuals . . . to enable them to understand why the Kuomintang is doomed to fail and why Communist victory is inevitable, so that they may know the road to follow.

iv. Maintain, reopen, or establish regular schools, especially in newly-liberated cities, to cultivate more intellectuals from the long-range point of

view and simultaneously to enable university and school teachers to remain
at their jobs. At present, however, emphasis should still be placed on winning
and reforming the intellectuals now available.

This Party directive was more specific about the need of
reforming the intellectuals than the Resolution of 1939. It expressed uneasiness over the bourgeois background of the intellectuals.

> ... Most of the intellectuals come from families of landlords, rich peasants,
> and the bourgeois and petty bourgeois classes, and have long been con-
> taminated by bourgeois education. Though the possibility exists that the
> majority of them may lean towards the revolution, they generally look down
> on the workers and peasants and stay away from the masses. Therefore, to
> enable them 'to serve the people', and 'to identify themselves with the workers
> and peasants' . . . it is incumbent upon us to carry on propaganda among
> them and to reform them ideologically.[2]

A Chinese Communist writer recently summarized the weaknesses of China's intellectuals as follows:

> *i.* Because of their close association with the landlord class and the
> bourgeoisie, most intellectuals are disdainful of the labouring people.
>
> *ii.* Since most intellectuals have not participated in the hard struggle for
> production or in the bitter national and class struggles, they can only rely on
> book knowledge and consequently commit such ideological errors as sub-
> jective thinking, reformism, utopian socialism, and equalitarianism.
>
> *iii.* They lack courage in combating reactionary forces. . . . They are
> eager to participate in the revolution when it is successful, but become
> pessimistic when it suffers reverses.
>
> *iv.* The petty bourgeoisie are accustomed to a libertine and individualistic
> way of life . . . and are averse to organization and discipline.[3]

Whenever we read Communist statements about serving the
'people' and the 'ideology of the working class', we should remember
their logic which argues that the Communist Party is the 'organized
vanguard of the working class' and is the only true guardian of the
interests of the 'people'. Only the Communist Party knows what
the interests of the 'people' and the 'working class' are and how
they should be served. To say that intellectuals must 'follow the
working class' and learn 'the ideology of the working class' is
tantamount to saying that they must follow the Communist Party
and accept the ideology of Marxism-Leninism.

Politicians in non-Communist countries usually have paid little
attention to intellectuals who take no interest in politics. They
even find it convenient to leave alone the intellectuals who prefer
to stay aloof of politics, and consider them harmless when they
pursue knowledge for its own sake.

The Communists, however, do not look at the intellectuals in
this light, and do not follow the traditional respect of the Chinese
for scholars. To them, it is not enough that the intellectuals should
be competent in their respective fields of study or service; the more

important requisite is that they must have the 'correct' ideological 'viewpoint' or political outlook. If they do not, however eminent they may be in their chosen fields, they must undergo reform before they can be accepted. This applies not only to the social scientists or the university teachers who exert a decisive influence on the young, but also to the engineers, physicians, scientists and technicians. From all of them, the Communists demand a high degree of 'political consciousness'.

The Communists lay great emphasis on mass support and the Party Constitution elaborates on the importance of the 'mass line'. In all that they do, they demand the support of public opinion and solicit mass participation. Whole-hearted participation requires an understanding of why people must work and what they work for; in other words, an appreciation of the political objectives. Not only must all intellectuals participate with everyone else in the new society, but they must also lead public opinion and set a good example to the masses. Hence the importance of a new political and ideological orientation for all intellectuals.

But there is another and more important reason for Communist insistence on ideological correctness. The Communist revolution is a 'total revolution', which aims to bring about radical changes in the entire social structure and in the pattern of human behaviour. It sets out to replace the old way of life with a new 'working style', to substitute new allegiances for old loyalties, and to introduce a new code of personal and social ethics. While economic reform, political reform, social reform, educational and cultural reform are all important to their programme, the most fundamental of all is the ideological reform. An ideologically correct person, according to them, is likely to overcome old habits of thought and action and to become a successful worker for the proletarian revolution; whereas a person committed to bourgeois and reactionary ideology is bound to fall into serious deviations in action and in thought.

'The Communist Party of China', declares the Party Constitution, 'takes Marxism-Leninism as its guide to action. Only Marxism-Leninism correctly charts the path leading to the achievement of socialism and communism'. Communist leaders say that the most important weapon which has helped them in their revolutionary struggle is their ideology. Mao Tse-tung said at the threshold of national victory in 1949:

> Our Party has passed through twenty-eight years. As everyone knows, these have been difficult years. We had to fight against enemies within the country

and abroad, and within as well as outside the Party. Our thanks are due to
Marx, Engels, Lenin and Stalin for having given us weapons. These weapons
are not machine-guns, but Marxism-Leninism.[4]

2. THE IDEOLOGICAL WEAPON

To be effective, the ideological weapon must be kept sharp all
the time. It must be protected from the corroding influences of
reactionary ideologies. Its sharpness and effectiveness can be
insured only by a never-relaxing 'ideological struggle' or 'thought
struggle'. This 'struggle' against 'unproletarian ideologies' or
'impure ideas' constitutes the essence of the 'ideological remoulding
campaigns' or 'reform movements' of the Chinese Communist
Party through the decades of its growth. Launching an attack on
liberalism and other bourgeois ideas, Mao said in 1937, 'We
advocate a positive thought struggle because it is the weapon for
attaining the solidarity between the Party and other revolutionary
organizations. . . . Every Communist Party member and every
revolutionary must take up this weapon'![5]

Before the Communists assumed power on a national scale,
thought struggle was carried on within the ranks of Party members and Party workers. Emphasis was then on 'inner-party'
struggle, which, according to Liu Shao-ch'i, who wrote a special
treatise on this subject in 1941,[6] is 'an ideological struggle against
all kinds of hostile and non-proletarian influences inside the
Party'. As early as 1929, Mao Tse-tung was waging a 'thought
struggle' against petty bourgeois ideologies which had infected the
infant Red Army. The ideas under attack included ultra-demo-
cratism, absolute equalitarianism, idealism and individualism.
Through the years a vigorous 'thought struggle' (*ssu-hsiang tou-
cheng* 思想鬥爭) was one of the chief methods of forging the unity
and maintaining the rigid discipline of the Chinese Communist
Party.

After 1949, there arose the need of extending the thought
struggle to the entire population. It was necessary to consolidate
the military victory with 'victory on the ideological front'. To this
end, a nation-wide 'study (*hsüeh-hsi* 學習) movement' was inaugurated to indoctrinate the population with Marxism-Leninism and
to promote 'the self-education and ideological remoulding of the
liberated people'.[7] This 'political education' was carried on not
only in the regular schools, but by an extensive system of institutes
and training classes which drew into the thought reform movement
housewives, merchants, workers and peasants as well as the school

population and the professional people. Its object was to enable the people to 'reform their bad habits and thought derived from the old society'.[8]

Since then 'correctness of thought' has become an expression of daily use. All success in personal and collective effort are attributed to proper ideological guidance while the least failure or weakness is invariably explained by 'incorrectness of thought'. Hesitancy to accept the new regime, lack of enthusiasm to join the anti-American campaign or any other mass movement, tendencies to question the absolute altruism and indispensable leadership of the Soviet Union—in brief, any shortcoming is considered remediable by the sure-fire cure-all of ideological conversion or thought reform. If the land reform meets with difficulties, the trouble probably lies in the incorrect thought of peasants or landlords or cadres, and the obvious solution is an intensified effort in 'thought struggle'. If co-operatives are badly managed, it is probably due to such heresies as 'equalitarianism' or 'individualism' or 'adventurism'. If production lags behind schedule, the cause is likely to be the ideological backwardness of the workers or the ideological mistakes of the personnel in charge. Errors in national planning are to be remedied by a more careful study of Marxist dialectics and the past experience of the Soviet Union. The cure is always to be found in thought reform, in a more positive effort to combat deviations in thought and to establish firmly the proletarian-socialist veiwpoint.

The reform of the intellectuals is thus essentially a reform of their thought or their ideology, in Chinese *ssu-hsiang kai-tsao*. It is specially important for the intellectuals because they are more likely than the uneducated population to resist indoctrination and propaganda. Immersed in unproletarian ideas and nurtured in a bourgeois culture, they cannot be swayed so easily by the emotional appeals which are effective with the uncritical masses. They are more likely to question the new ideology they are asked to accept. Consequently their thought reform is of primary concern to the new regime.

This line of reasoning is well reflected in Mao Tse-tung's statement in a session of the National Committee of the Chinese People's Political Consultation Conference on October 23, 1951: 'Thought reform, especially the thought reform of the intellectuals, is one of the most important prerequisites for the realization of democratic reform and industrialization'.

CHAPTER III

EARLY REFORM MEASURES

THE Communists are terribly class conscious and view their revolution as a class revolution with the Party as the organized vanguard of the working class. To them none can escape the influence of his class and to deny this influence merely betrays one's unprogressive thinking. The fundamental need is the rise of a new-type intelligentzia free of bourgeois class influence; the urgent need of the moment, however, makes it necessary to use the old-type intellectuals and try to reform them.

To avoid undue harshness at the beginning for fear of arousing violent reaction, the Communist method is to introduce changes gradually. Later, moderation gives way to more stringent measures, and 'methods of persuasion' assume a coercive character. Increasing pressure is brought to bear on individuals to 'persuade' them to conform 'voluntarily'.

In 1949 and 1950 the methods of reforming the intellectuals were mild. They were encouraged to form study groups or join classes for 'self-remoulding'.

1. THE MASS STUDY MOVEMENT

The mass 'study' *(hsüeh-hsi)* movement started as soon as the Communists came into power; it was nation-wide, involving the entire population. It set out to impart to all the ideology of the new regime, and had for slogan Mao Tse-tung's injunction: 'study, study and again study'.[1]

No one was to be left out of the movement: workers, peasants, housewives, old men and women and the unemployed. In all government offices the personnel were convened daily for at least an hour of political 'study'. Government workers had to report at their offices an hour earlier than usual: at 6.30 a.m. in the summer and at 7 a.m. in spring and spend an hour and a half in 'study'; in the winter months, the 'study' period was reduced to one hour, starting at 7.30 a.m.[2] A famous hospital in Peking closed its out-patient department on Friday mornings to allow its staff members to 'study'.[3]

The 'study' programme was especially important for the intellectuals. They not only had to study the theory and organization of the new regime and current events according to the viewpoint of the new rulers, but also the principles of Marxism-Leninism and 'the thought of Mao Tse-tung'. This 'study' was taken up by students and faculty in the schools and universities, and by other intellectuals within their own professional groups or organizations they were associated with.

In the universities and other higher educational institutions, joint committees of faculty and staff members were established as an expression of the new 'democratic' spirit of the day. They were composed of professors, instructors, assistants, clerks and janitors, and all had a voice in the administration of the higher institutions. In co-operation with the student body organizations, these committees became the channel through which the Communists directed the programme of political re-education. In the University of Peking, the Joint Committee of Faculty and Staff members was organized on October 16, 1949. According to Professor Lo Ch'ang-p'ei, its chairman, its three major tasks were: *i.* to unite with the masses; *ii.* to establish the standpoint of the proletarian class; and *iii.* to strengthen political study.[4]

Before the end of October, 1949, the Union of Educational Workers was established in Peking.[5] Its membership included professors, teachers, and staff members of universities, colleges, middle schools and elementary schools; janitors, servants and school police were all invited to join. One of its major tasks was to promote the *hsüeh-hsi* movement.[6] The Union is one of many 'people's organizations' through which the Communist Party carries out its policies. By placing trusted cadres or 'activists' in key positions, the Party directs the activities of such organizations from behind the scenes, while it maintains that the people are 'mobilized' by their 'voluntary organizations'. At the end of 1949, at the National Conference of Educational Workers held in Peking, the vice-minister of Education, Ch'ien Chün-jui, clearly revealed the intentions of the Party when he said in his address:

> The most important task in all schools in the newly liberated areas is to engage systematically in political and ideological education among teachers and student youth. The main objective is to establish gradually a revolutionary outlook in their minds.[7]

2. POLITICAL STUDY

Among the early changes in the educational institutions was the so-called 'political class' or 'the big class', which everybody, janitors included, was required to attend. It was not unusual for

a Party official to talk for five or six hours at a stretch. One of the
most authoritative lecturers was Ai Ssu-ch'i, who has been called
China's 'Number One Brainwasher'.[8] At the request of the Minister
of Education, he wrote the syllabuses for such topics of 'political
study' as 'historical materialism', 'history of social development',
'materialism' and 'dialectic'. He spoke before a microphone and
four loudspeakers broadcast his words even to learning groups
elsewhere.[9] After attending the 'big class', the learners engaged in
informal discussions and organized their notes, incorporating their
comments and personal reactions. Such notes were required by
the 'study committees' for them to criticize. Finally every person
had to submit his 'thought conclusions' as a personal testimony
of his ideological change.[10]

'Political study' in Tsinghua University was inaugurated in
October 1949, in a dramatic way. The first 'political lesson' or
'big class' was a show staged by a troupe of cultural workers from
the North China Revolutionary University.[11] It was a five-act play
called *ssu-hsiang wen-t'i* (The question of thought).[12] It described
how different persons with different class and educational back-
grounds tried to 'reform' themselves while attending the North
China Revolutionary University.

The plot of the play is briefly summarized as follows:

A group of intellectuals with unwashed brains are brought together. One
is naively pro-American; another is a landlord's son. There is a former
Kuomintang army officer, a subdued clerk, and a pretty girl whose head is
full of frills and boy friends. There's sex, intrigue and everything that Holly-
wood demands. Through the medium of democratic group discussions alone,
this diverse group goes through varying periods of agonizing conversions
until in the grand finale, all have become true Communists, full of hatred for
the United States and of eagerness to go to war against it—particularly the
disillusioned former friend of America. They are full of love for the Soviet
Union and fully indoctrinated with the conviction that the highest patriotism
that a Chinese can show his own country is to support and defend Moscow.[13]

After watching the play, the professors and students broke up
into small groups for informal discussion and to draw the lesson
from the play. Thus the junior class of the Department of Electrical
Engineering of the University divided up into seven groups to
discuss the following problems: *i*. What are the important types
of personalities in the play? *ii*. What type of personalities are
found in Tsinghua? *iii*. What mistakes have we (the participants
in discussion groups) committed? *iv*. How are we going to correct
our mistakes? *v*. What attitudes to take in the thought reform?[14]

In the study of dialectical materialism and historical materialism, the 'big class' dealt with such themes as 'labour as the creator of the world', 'class struggle and class differentiation', and 'the state as an organ of oppression'. A sub-topic under 'labour' was the evolution of man from the ape by dint of labour, which led to the conclusion that 'labour creates man and the world'. History was studied from the standpoint of the class struggle and an important objective of political study was to enable students to analyse the classes in Chinese society and to make a clear differentiation between (class) friends and (class) enemies. Mistakes in the 'ideology of the petty bourgeoisie' were severely criticized. Such concepts as the 'new democracy' and the 'people's democratic dictatorship' were given a prominent place in the indoctrination. And, of course, the 'advanced experience of the Soviet Union' was constantly held up as a model and a source of inspiration for the Chinese revolution. According to an official report on the first year of political study in institutions of higher learning in Peking and Tientsin, among 1,190 students in Peking University, more than half held erroneous views on the Soviet Union at the beginning, but by the end of the year their numbers had been reduced to a mere hundred.[15]

Another report dealt with political study in Wuhan University in Hankow. Seven objectives of thought reform were listed: *i.* To know the difference between revolution and counter-revolution, the difference between the Chinese Communist Party and the Kuomintang; *ii.* to know the situation of our victorious revolution and to have faith in its future; *iii.* to establish the standpoint of serving the people; *iv.* to establish the standpoint of labour; *v.* to develop the collective spirit and the concept of belonging to the organization;[16] *vi.* to learn the standpoint of the masses and the democratic way; and *vii.* to foster internationalism and friendship for the Soviet Union. According to the report, six months of political study produced tangible results. Faculty and students learned to trust the Party members and youth leaguers in their midst and to turn to the Party for guidance in all matters. They changed their way of life and abandoned such bad habits as extravagance, waste, corruption, gambling, etc. They became appreciative of labour and the benefits of collective living. They got rid of their anti-Soviet sentiments and became ardent Soviet supporters. They came to like the motion pictures from the Soviet Union and to dislike those from the United States.[17]

Nevertheless, the re-education of the intellectuals was meeting with some resistance, for the report on political study in Peking and Tientsin universities contained the following statement:

> In the study of the two topics, 'Socialism and the New Democracy' and 'The State and Politics', the students raised questions which betrayed the continued existence of a narrow nationalism. They were prejudiced against the Soviet Union. They were muddled in their thinking in regard to the stripping of factories (in Manchuria) and the independence of Outer Mongolia. They also misunderstood the meaning of the united front of the people's democracy. . . . After learning about the class nature of the state and the difference between socialism and capitalism, and after participation in such practical activities as the celebration of Stalin's birthday, they acquired a preliminary solution of this problem. But it is not possible yet to establish completely the ideology of (proletarian) internationalism.[18]

The 'big classes' were systematically directed; the study was organized in 'units', with each unit devoted to the elimination of certain 'erroneous ideas' or 'enemies'. Professor Fei Hsiao-t'ung reported:

> When we were studying the standpoint of labour, we naturally encountered such erroneous ideas as the standpoint of exploitation and the sense of superiority of the intellectuals. When we took up the unit on the standpoint of class, we had to deal with such hostile ideas as supra-class mentality or middle-of-the-road mentality. We tried to win every battle in every unit. In every unit we tried to lay our hands on the definite enemies—certain hostile ideas existing in our minds—and hit hard at them.[19]

The 'examination' was an important part of the study. Each person had to grade his own examination paper and then submit it to the study group to which he belonged. The group discussed every paper to see whether it had been properly graded by the writer.[20] This is where criticism and self-criticism were given a real test.

About eight months after the establishment of the Peking regime in 1949, vice-premier Kuo Mo-jo gave an optimistic report at the Chinese People's Political Consultative Conference in June, 1950. He jubilantly listed the 'accomplishments' of the nation-wide political study programme as follows:

> *i.* By studying the three documents adopted by the Chinese PPCC, especially the Common Programme, the fundamental differences between old and New China have become clear to the broad masses of the people . . . Self-criticism is practised by many old-style intellectuals, and government personnel engage in self-criticism of their old erroneous ideas. The influence of the fallacious idea of a so-called 'middle road' has, in the main, been eradicated.
>
> *ii.* The broad masses of the people have also gained a better understanding of the two great camps in the world; the camp of world peace and world democracy headed by the U.S.S.R., and the camp of imperialist aggression headed by the U.S.A.
>
> *iii.* The concept that labour is the creator of civilization has been decisively established among the broad masses of the working people and the intellectuals. . . .

iv. The idea of serving the people has become prevalent among intellectuals and government personnel. After political study, many intellectuals and young students have taken part in the work of revolution and construction. The great majority of them are very industrious and have displayed initiative in their work.[21]

While one may discount the accuracy of such official reports, there is little doubt that these are the results which the Communists sought to achieve in their indoctrination programme.

3. SHORT-TERM POLITICAL TRAINING

It has been mentioned that short-term institutes and special classes were also important agencies of political indoctrination. Such institutes were especially important for the teachers. It was obviously impossible to send all teachers to the 'revolutionary universities', not only because there were not enough universities to accommodate them, but also that the teachers could not be spared by the schools. Consequently, the teachers were asked to remain at their posts, and to engage in political study on the side. In addition to the regular mass-study movement which all teachers and students had to participate in, the teachers were enlisted for intensive indoctrination during the summer and winter vacations.

During the summer of 1949, about 5,800 elementary and secondary teachers in Peking were brought together for concentrated 'study'; in August 1949, all its secondary teachers were organized into discussion groups for political study; and from September 10 to October 8, 1949 the teachers and staff members of elementary schools in Peking and suburban areas started their 'autumn study programme'. The study was directed by central authorities, but conducted in different areas.

According to incomplete figures released by Kuo Mo-jo, during the early part of 1950 about 470,000 intellectuals participated in political study either in political universities or short-term political classes.[22]

4. ESTABLISHMENT OF REVOLUTIONARY UNIVERSITIES

Equal in importance to the mass study programme was the establishment of special 'universities' for the 're-education' of intellectuals in the early period of the Communist regime. These were known as 'revolutionary universities'. One was set up in every 'military-political region'. The North China People's Revolutionary University in Peking and the East China University of Political

Science and Military Studies in Shanghai are examples. In the
provinces or smaller areas, the re-education of the intellectuals
was carried on in 'political training classes', in 'off-hours study
associations', and by a system of 'intensive training of teachers by
rotation'. Their purpose was to 'help' the intelligentzia to build up
a revolutionary attitude on life and an ideology of dialectical
materialism and historical materialism.[23] According to one report,
about 500,000 intellectuals of different professions participated in
the 'revolutionary universities' and 'political training classes' before
the end of 1949. An equal number of teachers in elementary and
secondary schools also received such training. These figures did
not include the large number of government employees who were
required to 'study' on their jobs.[24]

The first of the 'revolutionary universities' was the North China
People's Revolutionary University in Peking. It opened its doors
as early as March 1949, only a couple of months after the 'liberation'
of the old capital city. It provided an intensive six-month course
in political indoctrination to 'weed out non-proletarian or anti-
proletarian ideology', and turn out a new type of intellectual
'devoted to the welfare of the masses'. Intellectuals were sent here
to be remade and to have their thinking reconstructed. 'The college
is turned into a battleground of ideas, in which the first casualties
are "pure" theory and empiricism. Superstition and idealism
wage a losing struggle with the theory of evolution and historical
materialism'.[25] In the first year, this 'university' graduated 18,000
students to serve as builders of the new order.

Another institution of this type was the Southwest People's
Revolutionary University in Chungking. According to its president Liu Po-ch'eng, the famous one-eyed general, the studies in
the institution may be grouped under three headings: *i*. historical
materialism; *ii*. fundamental problems of the Chinese revolution;
and *iii*. current affairs and government policies.[26] It was reported
that the various 'revolutionary universities' produced as many as
200,000 graduates in the first year of the new regime.[27] In all of
them the new methods of collective learning were group study in
brigades, 'democratic grading' by the group, and criticism and
self-criticism. Students were assigned labour duties on the campus
so that they might 'reform themselves through labour'. Each
student belonged to a group and the members of the group studied,
ate and lived together. If he did not fully conform to the new
pattern of living, he was submitted to the inquisition of 'mass

struggle meetings' in which the recalcitrant was denounced as inimical to the revolution and 'the people'.[28]

At the termination of the indoctrination period, each student was to submit a report on his 'thought conclusions'. Again, group pressure was brought to bear on the individual. Before the individual reports were prepared, the whole student body was called together in a mass meeting, in which the students were asked to challenge one another in the spirit of criticism and self-criticism so that each might learn 'to use political theoretical study as a weapon for analysing and criticizing his own thought'. One student vividly described his experience as follows:

> It took us ten days (to complete the thought conclusions), . . . in the course of which we did not even have a recess on Sunday. During this period, the students were engaged in meditation and writing day and night, each person endeavouring to scrape out, to expose, to analyse, and to criticize his personal history and thought. If there was any part of the ugly past which had not been brought into the open, here was the last chance to report to the organization . . . in order to complete the final and thorough reform.[29]

5. NEW-TYPE PROLETARIAN INTELLIGENTZIA

Brief mention may be made in passing of the Communist plan to produce a new-type intelligentzia who are specifically trained to meet the demands of the proletarian-socialist revolution and are unhampered by a bourgeois past. The candidates for the new-type intelligentzia must come mostly from the worker-peasant class. Hence the importance of worker-peasant education. To produce this new-type proletarian intelligentzia, the Chinese People's University was established in Peking in March 1950 as the model of a 'university of the working class'. Its students were recruited from workers and cadres of 'worker-peasant origin' who had proved their ideological reliability and rendered valuable service to the proletarian cause either in production or in 'revolutionary work'. Academic qualification was deemed less important than political outlook. Among the 3,000 students enrolled in the autumn of 1950, sixty per cent were cadres of worker-peasant origin and six per cent were 'advanced industrial workers'. Moreover, 1,733 of the students were members of the New Democratic Youth League.

The original plan for the People's University stipulated that it must be guided by the 'progressive experience of the Soviet Union'. Soviet advisers helped organize the curriculum and Soviet scholars occupied key positions on the faculty. Soviet models served in the preparation of text-books and teaching material. Soviet theories were accepted in all fields of study.

To meet the problems of producing a proletarian intelligentzia when there are few cadres and 'activists' academically qualified for collegiate work, the Communists have established special secondary and elementary schools for workers and peasants. For workers and cadres capable to benefit from higher education, they have set up short-term middle schools providing an accelerated course in which six years of secondary education are condensed into three years. They are known as worker-peasant short-term middle schools and their graduates are given preferential treatment when they apply for admission to higher institutions.

Obviously, it is not easy to turn out a new intelligentzia required for the manifold needs of a new society. The task will require many years. In the meantime, the service of the old-type intelligentzia is still indispensable and their reform is of imperative importance.

CHAPTER IV

PARTICIPATION IN MASS MOVEMENTS

THE Chinese Communists love to say that 'Marxism is not a dogma, but a guide to revolutionary action'. Their slogan is 'the integration of knowledge and action'. Their theorists explain that knowledge must be based on action and tested in action, that theory must grow out of revolutionary experience so that it may serve as a guide for future revolutionary action. In the reform of the intellectuals, the Communists do not rely entirely on theoretical study; they demand that the intellectuals identify themselves with 'the masses' in action as well as in thought and that they 'heighten' and 'sharpen' their political consciousness by taking part in the mass movements or the various forms of class struggle.

1. THE LAND REFORM

It is hardly necessary to say that the land reform in Communist China is far more than an economic programme. It suffices to quote Teng Tzu-hui, a prominent Communist leader, who made many authoritative pronouncements on Communist China's agricultural policy. He said in 1950: 'Some comrades look upon the agrarian reform as simply the distribution of land . . . or merely as means of developing production. This view is incorrect. . . . The basic mission of the Chinese revolution is to oppose imperialism and feudalism. The present Resist-America Aid-Korea campaign is carried on to oppose imperialism. The agrarian reform is, on the other hand, the last and fiercest battle in the series of systematic class struggles to eradicate feudal influences'.[1]

In view of the political significance of the land reform, the Communists believed that participation in the 'land-reform struggle' would be of great value in the reform of intellectuals, among whose major faults was their inability to see the importance of the class struggle. In the winter of 1949–1950, thousands of students and intellectuals were organized into work teams to go to the villages under the direction of trained cadres to become a part of the 'bitter class conflict' and to be given 'a practical initiation into the social structure and class alignments of the areas'.[2] In December, 1951, more than 16,000 intellectuals went out from Canton alone to learn the 'class struggle' by actual participation.

The Communists say that political consciousness is, in essence, class consciousness. To be 'progressive' is to be an alert and courageous class warrior. In their study of the 'history of social development', the intellectuals had been taught to re-interpret all history in terms of the class struggle. Now, they were to re-enforce their learning by direct participation in a class struggle. They were to take part in mass meetings waging a 'fierce struggle' against the landlords, the class enemies of the 'people'. No longer were they onlookers; they were to become a part of the mass movements against fuedalism.

> They took part in mobilizing the peasants and explaining land reform policies to them; they joined in the work of classifying the peasant and landlord families; they went to the fields to measure the land and they helped the peasants work out an equitable and democratic distribution of land, farm tools and equipment; and they also drew up the new title-deeds. On the side, they helped the peasants to organize their own cultural activities, put on entertainment performances for the villages and conducted short winter-study classes.[3]

What the Communists expected from the intellectuals after their participation in land reform comes out clearly in the statement:

> This participation of intellectuals in the land reform had a special significance in Peking, the main cultural centre of old China. Here a large proportion of the intellectuals, particularly in the case of the professorial staffs, were returned students from England, America or other capitalist countries and they passed on their fundamentally bourgeois education and outlook to their students. Many were 'non-political', if not reactionary. . . . If they hated the landlord system, it was in many cases from a vague sense of equalitarianism. They had no direct contact with the brutalities of the feudal system as it embittered the day-to-day life of the poor peasants or hired labourer. Now, in the countryside around their familiar Peking, they found that, all unknown to them, landlords had been literally squeezing the peasants to death.
>
> The intellectuals returned to the city with a new feeling of comradship with the peasants. . . . The intellectuals had helped to reform the age-old feudal land system of China. This in turn helped them to reform themselves. It had given them a clearer insight into the historic tasks of the revolution, in wiping out the terrible exploitation to which the majority of the Chinese people, the peasants, were subjected; a clearer understanding of their own role in the transformation taking place in China. It had helped to make them better citizens of the People's China.[4]

The students and professors of the universities were not the only people who had to participate in the land reform. Even government workers had to take time off to learn this 'lesson of struggle'. For instance, in May 1950, all workers in the administrative and judicial departments of the government went to the suburban areas of Peking to take part in the land reform as part of their 'study' programme. When they returned from the countryside they declared they had learned the following lessons: *i.* understanding the problems of the revolution, that is, the meaning of struggle, *ii.* understanding themselves, *iii.* having a desire to participate in the revolution, *iv.* realizing the importance of practical experience, *v.* learning how to analyse problems, *vi.* learning not to be influenced by their petty bourgeois mentality or sentimentalism.[5]

It could not, of course, have been a pleasurable experience for the intellectuals. They were supposed to overcome their 'sentimentalism' and their 'bourgeois notions' of kindness and humaneness and learn to be ruthless toward the class enemies of the revolution. They were to acquire the emotions of class warriors by plunging themselves into the thick of the class war; under the leadership of the cadres they were to denounce the feudalistic landlords, and to watch without wincing the brutal treatment, even the physical liquidation, of 'village despots' in the mass accusation meetings or struggle meetings. On their return each person had to write his 'thought conclusions' or his 'impressions'. Conclusions acceptable to the Party were published in the press for propaganda purposes. At one time when the land-reform movement was in full swing, the Communist newspapers and magazines were practically flooded with articles written by professors, scholars, and men of note reporting their experience of the class struggle. Many of these articles were edited and compiled into books or booklets.[6]

An example of ideological conversion that was supposed to result from participation in the land reform is the experience of Professor Lei Hai-tsung of Tsinghua University. Before Peking fell to the Communists in 1949, in an article he labelled the Communists as 'fanatics' and described the Communist revolution as 'an adventurist act of hunger-stricken peasants', and the Communist Party 'a semi-secret fanatic sect'.[7] In January 1950, Lei, after joining the large number of professors and students in land-reform work, was quoted as saying: 'This was the turning point of my life. It was only then that I understood the bitter class conflict and cruel oppression that poisoned the life of these seemingly peaceful and harmonious villages'.[8]

On another occasion he related in greater detail:

During the whole of my past, I was completely at sea. But I never realized that I was drifting aimlessly and that my academic research work, carried on only for its own sake, was futile. Had it not been for the liberation, I would have spent all my life in this manner, and, what is worse, I would have remained smug and contented. After liberation, I began to accept the new way of life intellectually. But it was as if I were looking at the new society from a long distance away. Emotionally, I was reluctant to plunge into the new life.

But a sudden change came over me during my close contact with actual life in the course of my recent land-reform work. Although I did not realize exactly when it happened, I discovered that I had entered the new society.[9]

Hsiao Ch'ien, one of the more popular modern novelists, had the following to say after he returned from a land-reform trip:

> To participate in land reform is the most intensive type of study of revolutionary experience, because land reform is the most complete reflection of the struggle of revolutionary truth against feudalism. . . . I realized, after my participation, that I had been at the forefront of the battle against feudalism fighting a relentless ideological war. . . .[10]

He related that during his trip a militia woman, a poor peasant, had heard of the escape of a landlord and insisted on getting him back. With two other persons, she trailed him along snow-covered mountain paths to an inn, and she caught him when he was about to flee again. Though bitten by the landlord, she held on until her two companions arrived and the three of them finally brought him back to the village. 'When I saw the grim determination of the poor peasants in their struggle against landlordism', Hsiao concluded, 'I became even more confident of the leadership of the working class in alliance with the peasants'.

2. THE RESIST-AMERICA AID-KOREA CAMPAIGN

Mao Tse-tung had in earlier years stated that the twin enemies of the Chinese revolution were imperialism and feudalism and that the immediate tasks of the revolution must be to attack these two.[11] In 1950, the Chinese Communists launched two nation-wide mass movements to achieve these objectives: the land reform to liquidate feudalism, and the Resist-America Aid-Korea campaign against imperialism, now symbolized by the United States of America.

The Resist-America Aid-Korea campaign was officially launched after the 'Chinese Volunteers' entered the Korean War. Actually the intellectuals had been thrown into the fight against imperialism, notably 'American imperialism', long before Communist China was involved in the Korean War. As early as 1947, the Communists were attacking American intrigue and espionage in China and accused the United States of intervention and exploitation by means of the Hurley Mission, the Marshall Mission, and other forms of 'aid' and 'co-operation'. In August and September 1949, before the establishment of the Communist government in China, professors in Peking, already then occupied by the Communists, were being pressured into anti-American activities. The publication of the *White Paper* by the U.S. Government in August caused violent reactions in Communist-controlled areas. The New China News

Agency released several editorials published by *Jen-min jih-pao* denouncing it.[12] At that time, the mass study programme had already been inaugurated in Peking, Tientsin, and other Communist cities, and for several weeks the 'White Paper', or 'opposing the White Paper', was the central theme of the 'study' sessions. At Yenching University, one of the Christian colleges established under American auspices, 124 faculty and staff members signed a statement denouncing the 'White Paper'.[13] At Peking University, four hundred professors and staff members placed their signatures to a protest against American imperialism exposed in the 'White Paper'.[14]

Following the outbreak of the Korean War, anti-American activities were conducted on a nation-wide basis. On July 1, 1950, Mao Tse-tung issued an appeal calling on all lovers of peace and freedom to unite against the new American aggression in the Far East. On July 17 was inaugurated the 'National Campaign Week against U.S. Aggression in Taiwan and Korea'. In all parts of China there were accusation meetings in which people of different walks of life, with tears in their eyes, were reported to have cited case after case of oppression and exploitation by American imperialists. The 'crimes' of American imperialism covered a wide range, including 'criminal acts' in hospitals, orphanages, and schools founded by American missionaries. All these were denounced and 'exposed' as exploitation in disguise. Pressure was exerted on the intellectuals, especially those who had been educated in American schools in China or in the United States, to renounce their past relations with American imperialism. Not only were they expected to join in accusing 'Imperialist America' of various crimes of oppression and aggression, but they also had to admit their own errors in their association with American imperialism.

It would be unnecessary to list all the various activities of the Chinese intellectuals in the Resist-America Aid-Korea Movement. An idea of the nature of the campaign may be obtained from the reports in the *Kuang-ming jih-pao* in Peking, in November and December 1950. They are as follows:

November 1, 1950: 260 agricultural scientists signed a petition of protest against American aggression in Korea and Formosa.

November 4: An anti-aggression evening rally was held in the Peking Normal College.

376 professors in Peking University wrote to Chairman Mao denouncing the crimes of the American imperialists.

November 5: Professor Feng Yu-lan published an article entitled 'To aid Korea and to fight for peace'.

November 16: Professors in Peking took action in the Resist-America Aid-Korea movement; professors of Tsinghua University went to work in the countryside; professors of the Peking Normal College decided to take up work in factories.

November 20: Professors in Tsinghua Uinversity opposed listening to the Voice of America programmes.

Journalism students in Yenching University held a meeting against listening to the Voice of America.

December 14: Geology and mining students in Tsinghua University encouraged fellow students to enroll in military activities.

December 16: Over 3,000 professors in Shanghai sponsored demonstration parades against America.

December 23: Religious groups, medical people, and American-returned students in the Wuhan area held accusation meetings.

All anti-America activities were directed by the Resist-America Aid-Korea Association, a branch or committee of which was organized in every city and in almost every university, school, factory and farm. Each branch received orders from a higher organ directing the activities to be pursued in a given period. The branches in the universities worked in close co-operation with the 'study committees' of both professors and students. Anti-American activities were thus integrated with the thought reform programme.

A few months after the Resist-America Aid-Korea campaign was initiated, *Jen-min jih-pao* in an editorial on the gains the Communists had made in the campaign, said that the students in universities and high schools had enthusiastically studied current affairs, held parades, demonstrations and many meetings. In Peking alone, it added, more than 30,000 college and high school students had gone to factories and farms to engage in propaganda. Many university presidents and professors had signed statements denouncing American imperialism. In religious circles, more than 26,700 Christians had signed statements making known their decision to sever their connection with imperialism, and members of the medical profession had organized field teams to serve on the Korean front.[15]

In some schools and universities, regular classes were suspended for two or more weeks to make possible an 'intensive study' of American imperialism. The starting point of the 'study' was a specially prepared handbook entitled 'Know America'. It told the story of American exploitation of the Chinese people through the years. It described the tyranny and decadence of the capitalist class in America. It explained at great length why the United States was to be hated and despised, not feared or admired. To supplement the content of this handbook, students and faculty were assigned special topics for intensive study and report. In the Peking Normal College, for example, students and faculty reported on such topics as 'The reactionary character of American education', 'How the United States helped the corrupt Manchu government to suppress the T'aip'ing Rebellion', 'America and the atom-bomb', etc. In all cases, the progressive individual was supposed to point out the reactionary character of American society and the menace of American imperialism.

3. THE CHINESE CHRISTIANS

The Chinese Christians deserve brief mention at this point because they, in the Communist view, had been poisoned by the baneful influence of American imperialism. The Christian Church, the Communists charged, had been used as an instrument of American influence and must sever all ties with imperialism before it could be of service to the 'people' in the New Democracy. Christians must purge themselves of the reactionary ideologies to which they had been long exposed by close association with American missionaries, many of whom were imperialist agents under the cloak of religion.

Here again the 'mass movement' was chosen to be the medium for thought reform. It was known as the 'Three-Self Movement'. Its declared objective was to make the Chinese Christian Church self-governing, self-supporting, and self-propagating.[16] The first step in the campaign was the issuance of a manifesto on September 30, 1950, bearing the signatures of 1,527 'progressive' Christians who had pledged themselves to support the new regime. It promised that Christian churches and organizations would 'give complete support to the Communist programme and, under the leadership of the government, oppose imperialism, feudalism, and bureaucratic capitalism, and engage in a struggle to build an independent, democratic, rich and powerful New China'.[17] 'The most important task at the present moment', said Wu Yao-tsung,[18] 'is to resist American aggression and aid Korean resistance'.[19] Christians from all over the country were asked to add their signatures to those of the 1,527 original sponsors of the September Manifesto. Those who hesitated to join were considered as reactionaries and out of step with the spirit of the times. Half a million Protestant Christians were reported to have signed the manifesto. A similar campaign, with a manifesto and mass signatures, was started among the Catholics.

It is not within the purview of this treatise to discuss the religious and educational consequences of the Three-Self Movement. The movement coincided with the nation-wide anti-American campaign and set out to stamp out the influence of 'Imperialist America' not only in institutions but in the hearts and minds of people who had had close associations with Americans. Missionary schools and colleges were taken over and transformed into government schools and colleges. Speaking of the nationalization of Christian institutions formerly subsidized by American organizations, a prominent Communist leader called upon all Chinese Christians to get rid of their 'fear-America, worship-America and love-America mentality' and to adopt the new 'progressive' attitude of hating and despising America.[20]

The methods of thought reform in this instance were essentially the same as those employed in the reform of intellectuals in general. Christians had to reform themselves by 'study' as all other people did. Their 'study materials' on the New Democracy and government policies were supplemented by documents bearing directly upon the Three-Self Movement. Group discussions, criticism and self-criticism, and various forms of group pressure instigated by 'progressive elements' and 'activists' were as important here as elsewhere. Accusation meetings were recommended as an effective weapon in this 'ideological struggle'.

The *Jen-min jih-pao* editorialized:

> The accusation campaign among Christians is the best and most important method to develop and intensify the Three-Self Movement among Christians. It is a self-education campaign in which the Christians themselves report on the crimes committed by American imperialists against the Chinese people.[21]

Christian intellectuals were subjected to a two-fold pressure to join the accusation campaign. As intellectuals they were already expected to take part in the Resist-America Aid-Korea campaign; as Christians, they were to take additional action to denounce the harmful influence of American imperialism on Chinese religion and education. The closer a person's past relation with the United

States, the more he was under suspicion, and the more necessary it became for him to make loud and sweeping accusations of America in order to avoid being branded an 'enemy of the people'. It is no wonder then that some of the most violent denunciations of America came from the Chinese Christian colleges and universities. The Communists were especially eager to push such a campaign in the Christian colleges and universities not only because they considered these institutions as strongholds of American influence and the students and faculty as people in the greatest need of cleansing themselves of American ideas and American ideology, but also because they wanted to create an atmosphere and a 'public opinion' favourable to the seizure of these institutions and turning them into government institutions under state control.

CHAPTER V

TIGHTENING THE VICE

1. THE RISE OF TERRORISM

IN 1951, the Communists passed from the early and mild forms of 'study' to more severe methods in a concentrated effort to remould the intellectuals in the various professional groups. Group pressure, always manipulated from behind the scenes, became more coercive in nature; public confessions were demanded and given wide publicity. The pledges hitherto made by the 'progressive' and the opportunist elements were now expected of all the intellectuals.

The Communists had now consolidated their power and had greater confidence in their ability to extend and intensify their control of the people. The Korean war gave them a unique opportunity to achieve this; in the name of the national emergency, they asked the people to give unreserved support to their government. They were in a position to punish the non-conformists as unpatriotic, even as enemies of the state.

The Chinese Communist intervention in the Korean War was not greeted with general approval in China; the people had grown sick and tired of war, and they were even more opposed to a foreign war. Despite the intense anti-American propaganda many were sceptical and in the winter of 1950 opposition expressed itself in sabotage acts and armed uprisings. To cope with this the government adopted on February 20, 1951, the 'Regulations for the Suppression of Counter-revolutionary Activities' punishable by death or life imprisonment.[1] This period of terrorism in China was marked by 'public trials', mass arrests and executions, and a horrible system of mutual spying and informing which penetrated into the intimate circles of the family. Thus the general trend was for more severe methods of thought reform.

2. INCREASED PRESSURE ON THE TEACHERS

The new stage in the reform of the intellectuals was ushered in by a stepped-up programme of ideological remoulding—another Communist term for thought reform—for the teachers, because by the latter part of 1951 the Communists were ready to revamp the entire educational system. In 1949, the general moderation policy of the initial period was applied to education, and school teachers were urged to remain at their posts and assured that no radical changes were being contemplated.[2] In 1950, the Communists were satisfied with the gradual introduction of new institutions and new methods without scrapping the old school system. On October 1, 1951, however, the government promulgated a new school system which bore a striking resemblance to the Soviet system. The reasons for this move were summarized by an editorial of the *Jen-min jih-pao*, on October 3, which says, in part:

> A school system is the reflection of the development of production and science in a given society. . . . The school system of the capitalist states is a reflection of capitalist production and serves the purpose of the monopolistic economy of the capitalist class. The school system of the socialist states, on the other hand, is a reflection of the advanced methods of socialist production and meets the needs of the ever-expanding socialist and Communist construction. The school system of the old China was an imitation of the system of the capitalist states and *reflected the reactionary ideology of landlords, bureaucrats, and the compradore class of semi-colonial semi-feudal society*. . . .[3]

It was estimated at that time that national construction in the ensuing five years would require the service of 150,000 technologists, 500,000 technicians, 10,000 teachers of institutions of higher learning, 100,000 secondary school teachers, 1,500,000 elementary school teachers, and 200,000 medical and health workers.[4] This needed personnel not only must be competent in their respective fields but must be thoroughly rooted in Marxism-Leninism. To make sure that the students acquire the proper ideological outlook, the teachers must be put through a thorough-going process of ideological reform.

3. THE UNIVERSITY PROFESSORS

Teachers in institutions of higher learning were chosen to be the first targets. In September 1951, more than 3,000 teachers[5] from twenty higher institutions in Peking and Tientsin were ordered to undertake four months of 'reformative study' *(kai-tsao hsüeh-hsi)*. Directed by the ministry of Education, this intensive thought reform was the beginning of a 'study campaign' which spread all over the country. The necessity of a stepped-up campaign, the vice-minister of Education frankly admitted, was that earlier 'study' programmes and participation in mass movements had not given the desired results, and that the teachers of the higher institutions had not yet got rid of their reactionary ideology; they had 'failed to carry out true reform', thus endangering the entire programme of educational reform.[6] He specifically mentioned three 'incorrect

trends of thinking and working style' which must be attacked and
liquidated:

> *i.* Quite a few teachers in higher institutions still retain the ideology of
> the European-American capitalist class. They stubbornly worship the
> so-called 'American way of life'.
>
> *ii.* There still exist a strong individualism and subjectivism in thought
> and in attitude among the teachers. They enthusiastically pursue their
> personal interests but ignore the urgent demands of the people and of
> national construction.
>
> *iii.* The teachers are guilty of doctrinairism, which divorces theory from
> practice. They teach the old stuff they learned in England and America
> ten, twenty or thirty years ago. They even lecture in English and ask their
> students to take notes and prepare exercises in English.[7]

An experimental project of intensive indoctrination of university
professors had been tried in the summer of 1951 at Peking University, where its president Ma Yin-ch'u, well-known economist and
one of the first intellectuals to accept the new regime and its
ideology, organized his faculty for summer 'study' and ideological
reform. Pleased with his accomplishment, he recommended a
nation-wide 'study campaign' for all teachers of higher institutions.
His proposal was promptly accepted by the ministry of Education,
and thus began a campaign which meant for the teachers months
of merciless inquisition and sophomoric 'study' of Communist
ideology with nerve-racking soul searching under the direction of
half-baked cadres and humiliating confessions.

In each higher institution a local unit of the special committee
of the ministry of Education in charge of the thought reform of
college teachers was organized. At the start of the campaign, Chou
En-lai, in a long address on the aims and methods of systematic
'study' by college teachers, called on the teachers to strive for the
development of a 'revolutionary standpoint, viewpoint and method'.
Teng Tzu-hui, a prominent member of the Central Committee of
the Chinese Communist Party, later elaborated on this when he
spoke of the 'standpoint of serving the people, the viewpoint of
materialism, and the method of dialectics'.[8]

The methods of study in this campaign may be grouped under
three headings: (a) the study of Communist documents, (b) reports
and speeches by leading Communists and government officials,
and (c) criticism and self-criticism. University presidents, deans,
professors, as well as young instructors and staff members diligently
'studied' the works of Marx, Lenin and Stalin, as well as the
writings of Mao Tse-tung. They listened for hours at a time to
preachments and 'reports' by the big names in the Party and

government. Finally, under the watchful eyes of the cadres, they practised criticism and self-criticism by which they were expected to tear apart their wonted thought patterns, to recognize the reactionary nature of their ideas, and to declare their new stand and ideological conversion.[9]

The harrowing experience of the intellectuals may be inferred from a *Jen-min jih-pao* editorial, laying down the tasks of the 'reformative study':

> College teachers of the new era must boldly criticize their erroneous and incorrect thoughts. On the one hand they must examine themselves and oppose the attitude of self-complacency and self-delusion, and, on the other hand, they must boldly criticize each other, discarding the hypocritical politeness which tries to offend nobody. (October 23, 1951)

4. OTHER EDUCATIONAL WORKERS

The campaign was next extended to the lower schools. Early in November 1951, teachers of elementary and secondary schools in the Wuhan area were organized for 'thought reform study'. A few months later all teachers of higher and secondary schools in other areas were involved in the campaign.[10]

Even village school teachers were not neglected by the Communists, although their work was hardly more than the teaching of a few hundred elementary characters and some elementary arithmetic. In November 1951, all the 'winter school'[11] teachers were called on by Ma Hsü-lun, then minister of Education, to engage in 'political study' and to pay particular attention to the study of current affairs. 'The main tasks of the teachers in the winter schools', he said, 'is to explain the Resist-America Aid-Korea campaign, the land reform, the agricultural producers co-operatives, the marriage law, etc. The cultural teaching programme must be tied in with political propaganda'.[12]

The methods were not essentially different from those used for the college teachers. Thus early in 1952, more than 1,100 teachers from more than fifty secondary schools in Chungking embarked on 'systematic study' which was described as follows:

> Their study was divided into three units: *i.* to understand clearly the purpose of political study and to engage in preliminary criticism and self-criticism; *ii.* to criticize the reactionary thoughts existing in each school, and to learn to differentiate clearly between [class] friends and [class] enemies; and *iii.* to criticize thoroughly the corrupt and decadent ideology, and to establish the standpoint and viewpoint of serving the people. The study methods consist of listening to reports, perusing selected documents, group discussions, democratic argumentation, educational movies, etc.[13]

Speaking at a conference of educational workers on January 30, 1952, Ai Ssu-ch'i said that as they had been reared in the old society and many of them had been born in the families of the landlord class, they needed reform. 'However energetic they may be in their work, they still would have many shortcomings, mainly because their thinking is more or less erroneous'. 'An educational worker who comes from a landlord family', he continued, 'must resolutely break away from his original class and take a stand in opposition to the class from which he came. . . . Those who come from the families of rich peasants and middle peasants must [also] give up the ideology of the bourgeoisie and the petty bourgeoisie'.[14]

5. WRITERS AND ARTISTS

'Workers in literature and art'—poets, novelists, playwrights, musicians, painters, actors, actresses, film directors and others—are another group of intellectuals whose reform was required by the Communists. Since their work affects the thought of people, their own thinking must be free from ideas unfavourable to the proletarian-socialist revolution. An intensified campaign for the reform of writers and artists began with a 'mass meeting for the mobilization of literary and art circles in thought reform and study', which was held in Peking late in November 1951. One of the chief speakers was Hu Ch'iao-mu, deputy director of the Propaganda Department of the Chinese Communist Party and Director of the Information Administration of the Central People's Government. Quoting Stalin and Mao Tse-tung, Hu Ch'iao-mu emphasized that literature and art should serve the masses, particularly the proletarian class. He censured writers for 'non-Marxist viewpoints' and for failure to look upon their work as an essential phase of the class struggle.[15] He asked them to take up the following tasks:

   i. To follow the directive of Mao Tse-tung, to pursue earnestly thought reform study, to study Marxism, and to unite with workers, peasants, soldiers and the masses.

   ii. To publicize fully the Marxist ideas on literature and art.

   iii. To reorganize the leadership in the field of literature and art; to oppose liberalism and careerism [or occupationalism].

   iv. To reorganize the literature and art groups in the country, so that every group may be a fighting unit, actually helpful to literary and art workers and really uniting with the working masses. Those groups that cannot meet such requirements must be disbanded.

   v. To rectify the publications in the field of literature and art.

   vi. Communist Party members among writers and artists should set good examples in the above activities.[16]

Reference has been made to the Communist contention that thought reform must be integrated with revolutionary action and that an effective means of reforming the intellectuals is to plunge them into the 'mass struggles for liberation'. Close contacts with 'workers, peasants, soldiers and the masses' were considered particularly important for writers and artists. How could they portray the class struggle in their works if they did not have direct experience in the struggle? Hence in March 1952, 'with the co-operation of the Central Committee of the Chinese Communist Party, the All-China Federation of Literary and Art Circles organized the first group of writers to go to Korea, to the factories and rural districts'.[17] In mid-November 1952, the Federation 'organized the second group of writers, several scores of them, for work among the masses. They gathered from many parts of the country in Peking for a month's study and to work out their plans for several months or years, depending on the need'.[18]

> Many other writers in the liberated areas went to the countryside. But it was not just 'to collect materials' in the ordinary sense. They worked as clerks or assistants to the county or district governments or in similar capacities. Being mostly city intellectuals of the old society, they found it difficult at first to establish close contact with the village folk. But with the help of Communist activists in the villages, they were finally able to create a warm understanding with the peasants and thus developed the insight and knowledge to create excellent new works about the revolutionary changes in China's countryside. . . . For any writer, the extent to which he loves the masses of workers, peasants and people's fighters represents the extent to which he has reformed himself ideologically, and also the extent to which his work is educative.[19]

6. OTHER INTELLECTUALS

After 'mobilizing' the teachers, the writers and the artists, the Communists turned to intellectuals in other professions. In a number of cities, 'reform classes' were held for lawyers for indoctrination in the new concepts of law and justice. Recalcitrant lawyers were severely attacked for having charged exhorbitant fees and thus exploited the people. In September 1952, some 1,700 judges and lawyers in Central and South China were reported to have been accused of faulty ideology and of failure to take the proper class viewpoint in distinguishing between class friends and class enemies.[20]

The physicians also came under the thought reform programme. At first, to answer the need for medical personnel on the Korean war front, the Communists launched a drive to enlist physicians for 'voluntary' service in Korea. While many physicians saw no alternative but to yield to the 'persuasion' to volunteer, others resisted. The latter were then subjected to various kinds of vexations which in some cases amounted to persecution. At the same time, Western-trained physicians were carefully watched to see if they reflected too much of their bourgeois ideology. A number of physicians were persecuted or imprisoned for what Communist propagandists built up to be cases of malpractice or for alleged negligence or manslaughter. Political training classes were also organized for physicians to facilitate their 'ideological reform'.

Although research scientists would appear to be far removed from the political whirlpool, they have not been overlooked by the Communists. Science and technology are indispensable to China's industrialization and national construction, and Marxism claims to be a scientific ideology. Shortly after the birth of the new regime in 1949, the Chinese Academy of Sciences was established 'to direct and promote the development of science in China'. It was constantly stressed that science must now 'serve the people'.

In the 'study campaign' of 1951, the scientists were told that they needed thought reform as much as other intellectuals. Among the 'erroneous ideas' they must cast away were their liberalism, individualism, aloofness from politics, and aloofness from class distinctions. Kuo Mo-jo, who was president of the Academy of Sciences as well as a deputy Premier, told the scientists in a 'mobilization meeting' in December 1951, that it was common for scientists to say 'you do your part as revolutionaries and we do our part as scientists', but this view was wrong, and scientists needed political study to change their ideas.[21]

CHAPTER VI

PERSONALIZING THE TARGETS

A METHOD commonly used in the 'thought struggle' is to choose ideologically reprehensible persons as 'types' to serve as targets for criticism and attack. The person's name then stands for a certain pattern of thinking, and all 'progressive' people are asked to join in the fight against this ideological enemy. For example, in the early days, Li Li-san-ism represented 'left opportunism' as expressed in hasty and premature mass revolutionary action. Li Li-san, when leader of the Communist Party, was directly responsible for the policy of seizing urban centres with the peasant Red Army, a policy which ended in failure and was branded as putschism. Since then, Li Li-san-ism became a regular Communist term, used even by Li Li-san himself, to describe a dangerous 'ideological deviation' which the Party must combat.

In recent years, the big guns of the ideological war have been aimed at such personalized targets as the 'Li Ssu-hsi mentality' or the 'Chin Shan-hai mentality'. Li Ssu-hsi was a rural cadre who had an outstanding 'revolutionary' record during the land reform. After the reform, however, he decided that he should settle down on his land to bring up a family. The Party organization charged him with forgetting the revolution and made him a symbol of the evils of relaxation and 'idle enjoyment' arising out of the false notion that the revolution had been accomplished. In the autumn and winter of 1951, the Chinese Communist press waged a concerted campaign against the 'Li Ssu-hsi mentality'.

Chin Shan-hai was the type of an esteemed Party member whose weaknesses were revealed in the period following national victory. His immediate offence was 'disobedience to the organization' for refusing to accept the tasks assigned to him by the Party; the overall charge was that he put personal interests above the Party's and that he had joined the Party for self-advancement and not primarily to serve the revolution.

Inasmuch as the thought patterns of the intellectuals had more or less been influenced by China's history, the Communists chose their types from among the dead as well as the living. In the thought reform of 1951, the criticism of Wu Hsün, a historical figure, was given much publicity and with official support it became a nationwide campaign in which numerous intellectuals took part.

1. WU HSÜN

'Wu Hsün the Beggar' was born of a poor family in Shantung in 1839. His father died when he was only five, leaving seven children, of whom Wu Hsün was the youngest. The family had no resources and only managed to eke out a living by begging. Wu Hsün tried at the age of seven to enter a village school but was turned down because of the low social status of his family. Deprived of schooling, he became even more acutely aware of its importance and he early resolved to open his own school so that other poor children would be given the opportunity he had missed. He failed in all the odd jobs he did for one relative after another and at the age of sixteen was driven to begging again. His slogan was 'Beg in order to found a school'. In the ensuing years he tried all manners of soliciting, even clowning acts which bordered on the ridiculous. In time, he acquired some land and became a moneylender. By 1888, he had accumulated enough money to establish his first school. More schools were opened in the following years until Wu Hsün the Beggar became a famous person widely praised for his interest in education. The Manchu government recognized his public spirit by bestowing posthumous honours and titles on him. Later governments, including the Nationalist Government, also hailed him as an exemplary figure.

Such a man as Wu Hsün, whose selflessness made it possible for children without means to receive an education, seemed to many the personification of the down-trodden man who makes good and devotes himself to service to his fellowmen. In the 1940's, left-wing writers including T'ao Hsing-chih, a well-known educator, were acclaiming Wu Hsün as a hero worthy of a niche among the unsung heroes of the exploited class. Even the Chinese Communists themselves had in earlier years joined in paying tribute to Wu Hsün. As late as December 5, 1949, there appeared an article in *Kuang-ming jih-pao* extolling the 'greatness of Wu Hsün'. The paper even published an editorial entitled 'To learn from Wu Hsün' in memory of his 110th anniversary.

Before the Communist conquest of China, a Chinese motion-picture director who had been educated in America saw the possibility of a successful screen play based on the story of Wu Hsün. Though the story was ready in 1947 the picture was not completed till late in 1950. Little did the director or the producer suspect that it would become a storm centre and would threaten to bring an inglorious end to their careers.

The release of the picture in December 1950 for months caused no alarm. Either the Communists were then unaware of the ideological implications of the film or they were not at that time looking for a whipping boy in the thought reform campaign. The picture got a very favourable reception by film viewers and critics. It drew large crowds all over the country and was rated by the semi-official magazine *Popular Film* as one of the ten best pictures of 1950. At least forty-seven articles and three books were published eulogizing the picture and Wu Hsün the man.[1] Praise came from Communist officials as well as Communist writers.

In April and May 1951, a couple of articles appeared in the *Wen-yi-pao* (Journal of Literature and Art) questioning the value of the story of Wu Hsün and challenging the current evaluation of the film. On May 16, 1951, the *Jen-min jih-pao* reprinted one of the articles with an editor's note that the article should encourage more discussion of the film. Four days later came the big blow. The authoritative and much feared *Jen-min jih-pao* (People's Daily) published an editorial on May 20 condemning the current acclamation of the film as evidence of the ideological confusion of intellectuals and of the deep infiltration of reactionary bourgeois ideologies even among the Party members. It condemned Wu Hsün for his failure to challenge the culture and economic structure of feudal society and for courting the favour of the feudal ruling class. Instead of being a praiseworthy educator, Wu Hsün became a 'propagator of feudal culture'. The authors who had reviewed favourably the film were reprimanded for paying tribute to a historical figure who, instead of attempting to overthrow the reactionary ruling class by violent struggle, had surrendered to it in abject shame. To tolerate such 'shameful deeds' as those of Wu Hsün, said the editorial, 'was to condone "open slander" of the Chinese people'.

On the same day, *Jen-min jih-pao* issued a call to all Communists to join in criticism of the film and the story of Wu Hsün, and 'to participate voluntarily in this ideological struggle' against the infiltration of 'reactionary bourgeois ways of thinking'. Party members were asked to 'rise and fight'. Realizing the serious nature of the approaching storm, producers of the picture hastened to withdraw it from circulation. The studio publicized this decision in newspaper announcements and expressed regret for the ideological mistakes of the picture due to 'lack of political study on the part of our staff'; it promised that its staff would now carry out a

thorough 'self-examination'.[2] Subsequently the studio was reorganized into a state concern 'at the request of the owners'.[3]

Sun Yu, the director of the film, found it wise to publish a
confession of his errors: he concurred with the stand of *Jen-min
jih-pao* that the picture was 'harmful to the people'; he pleaded
ignorance and pledged a thorough examination of his work with
the hope that he might henceforth be able to work 'correctly'.[4]

But the Communists had no intention of giving up such a good
opportunity to carry a step further their programme of remoulding
the thinking of China's intellectuals. With the legend of Wu Hsün
alive particularly in educational and cultural circles, on them the
reformers decided to concentrate the campaign. On June 4, 1951,
the ministry of Education issued a directive calling on all educational workers to take up the 'ideological struggle'. Schools and agencies
of educational administration all over the country were to carry
out organized and 'systematic' discussions and criticisms of 'Wu
Hsün the man and the so-called spirit of Wu Hsün'. This 'ideological
movement', said the directive, should be brought to 'every school
and every single educational worker'.

Educational personnel throughout the land took up organized
study and discussion of Wu Hsün. They read officially approved
'reference books' on Wu Hsün and tried to draw correct 'scientific
conclusions' from their study. Kuo Mo-jo, at that time a vice-
premier and concurrently chairman of the Cultural and Educational
Committee of the Government Administration Council, set an
example by publishing an article stating the lesson he had learned
from the 'criticism of Wu Hsün'.[5] This eminent mouth-piece of
the Communist Party in educational and cultural matters confessed
that he had once praised Wu Hsün out of blind ignorance, but
after reading the recent writings exposing the true character of
the man, he had come now to a new understanding of Wu Hsün
as a reactionary, even as a counter-revolutionary.

Even the minister of Education, Ma Hsü-lun,[6] had to come out
with a confession of having praised in his writings Wu Hsün, and,
like Kuo Mo-jo, he professed a new understanding of Wu Hsün,
who, 'in this age, should not be praised, but whose real nature
should be exposed'. He expressed complete agreement with the
newly inspired criticisms of Wu Hsün.[7]

The *Hsüeh-hsi,* in its issue of June 1951, carried fourteen articles
on Wu Hsün. Most of the writers were well-known university professors such as Fei Hsiao-t'ung, Feng Yu-lan, Chin Yüeh-lin and

T'ang Yung-t'ung. Like Kuo Mo-jo, they claimed that the Wu
Hsün episode had been helpful to their thought reform. Sociologist
Fei Hsiao-t'ung said: 'The discussion of the story of Wu Hsün
afforded me an opportunity to reflect and in the process I discovered my incorrect attitude in study. I have not seriously sought
the truth . . . my mind was paralyzed'.[8]

Philosopher Feng Yu-lan wrote:

> The more I read about Wu Hsün, the more strongly I feel that from the
> May Fourth movement till liberation, many academic and educational
> workers . . . helped to maintain the rule of the reactionaries. To a certain
> extent, they all committed the same mistake as Wu Hsün. They differed from
> Wu Hsün only in the period in which they lived. . . .
> If there is such a thing as 'the spirit of Wu Hsün', we need to struggle
> against it, not to learn from it.[9]

To give the campaign an intellectual appearance, *Jen-min
jih-pao* and the ministry of Cultural Affairs organized a 13-man
investigation commission to visit the birthplace of Wu Hsün in
western Shantung province. Led by Yüan Shui-po, editor of the
Peking daily, the commission spent about twenty days interviewing
more than 160 persons of all classes, including a few who had
actually known Wu Hsün. Its findings appeared in the *Jen-min
jih-pao* in instalments in late July; all drew the conclusion that
Wu Hsün was villainous, feudalistic and anti-people.[10]

Writers and artists were also drawn into the campaign. On
May 25, 1951, the literary and art circles in South China held a
discussion meeting on Wu Hsün. The charges made against him
show clearly why the Communists chose this personalized target
for their thought reform. The following is a summary of the
official minutes of the meeting:[11]

> Wu Hsün praised and supported the feudalistic Ch'ing dynasty. He insulted
> the peasants' revolutionary struggles and the entire Chinese nation. . . . Wu
> Hsün completely lost his class consciousness and national sense; his conduct
> was contrary to the interest of the toiling masses. . . . Wu Hsün served the
> interests of the feudalistic landlords and emperors. . . . Wu Hsün was not a
> representative of the proletariat; he himself was not a labourer. Although he
> had the background of a poor peasant, he spent his life as a beggar. Thus he
> was not engaged in production, nor did he lead a normal life. . . . Wu Hsün
> separated culture and education from the class struggle; he isolated culture
> and education from politics.

Why did the motion-picture create such a tempest? According
to a non-Communist writer the hero in the story sang a song:
'The times have changed, the mainland is gradually no more; who
will lift me from ignorance, who'll alleviate my poverty?'[12] The
allusion seemed to be clear; that is why the picture incurred the
Communist wrath. Another report is that at the time the *Story of*

Wu Hsün was publicly acclaimed, the Soviet film, the *Story of Lenin*, was being shown in China. The Chinese picture threatened to displace the *Story of Lenin* in popularity, and the Communists decided to withdraw it from circulation.[13]

A simpler explanation would be that in Wu Hsün the Communists had a personalized target symbolizing major 'ideological mistakes' among the intellectuals. The most important charge was that Wu Hsün had no class consciousness and saw no need for a class struggle. Although he started out in poverty, he ended up as a landlord and a member of the exploiting class. He never worked with his hands and was therefore alien to the working class and its aspirations. At first glance he seemed to have done some good by establishing schools, but he was basically a 'reformist' and not a revolutionary. He believed that he could reform society by compromising with the feudalistic reactionary rulers of his day. In raising funds for his schools, he actually kōtowed to the reactionary rulers, and helped to maintain their position. In this, argued the Communists, he was really insulting the 'people' and the proletarian class.

Another point which the Communists wanted to drive home with their attack on Wu Hsün is that education and culture cannot be separated from politics. Educational and cultural workers must consider their work as an integral part of the revolution and of the bitter struggle against the 'reactionary forces'. In the words of Hsü Te-li, a former teacher of Mao Tse-tung, who was given high honour after the Communists came to power, the education advocated by Wu Hsün taught people to submit and to 'lie down' and was therefore directly opposed to the education of today, which asked people to stand up and fight.[14]

To smash this popular idol of educational and cultural workers was, to the Communists, a step in the destruction of old thought patterns. The Wu Hsün episode appears to have been carefully calculated to serve as a prelude to the next phase of the thought-reform campaign.

2. J. LEIGHTON STUART

To uproot established traditions is not confined to organized attacks on historical figures, but also on outstanding contemporary educators whose names had been closely linked with the established traditions of the leading unversities. In Yenching University, for example, the personalized target was the well-known American educator, J. Leighton Stuart, who was appointed American Ambassador to China in 1946 at the recommendation of General George C. Marshall in an attempt to get the Kuomintang and the Chinese Communist Party to form together a unified government in China. Stuart had built up Yenching University into one of the best known institutions of higher learning in China. He was known as an able educator, not only by his students and faculty members, but by the Chinese public. Now his work at Yenching was mercilessly 'analysed' as the activity of an agent of imperialism.

3. CHANG PO-LING AND MEI YI-CH'I

In Nankai University, a central target of attack was the distinguished educator Chang Po-ling, who built up one of the most famous private schools in China. In Tsinghua University, students and faculty analysed and criticized the thought and activities of its former president Mei Yi-ch'i. A report by the faculty 'study committee' of Tsinghua on this phase of the thought reform reveals the reasons why personalized targets are used in the thought reform:

> Without analysing and discussing concrete examples of people and events of a general nature, centralized leadership would be difficult and discussions would branch off in a complicated manner, resulting on the one hand in empty, doctrinaire, desultory remarks and, on the other, in arriving at simplified conclusions and ascribing everything to 'individualism' without solving the question. That is why we selected four departments and arranged, under unified control, a discussion of Mei Yi-ch'i as a type. The discussion elicited a greater degree of enthusiasm because the Study Subcommittee was well prepared in advance on the methods of discussing Mei Yi-ch'i and because the object of discussion itself was interest provoking. Some said: Mei Yi-ch'i moved Tsinghua to the south during the war of resistance, because he was patriotic. Others retorted: Mei was not patriotic, he had compradorial ideology. With this, the discussion broke wide open, thereby uncovering many problems.
>
> In the discussion of Mei Yi-ch'i, it was discovered that a great number of cadres hurriedly repudiated Mei and denounced him as unpatriotic. Some cadres, however, attempted by various means to reveal their doubts in order to discuss the question from all angles. In this way, it was made clear how Mei Yi-ch'i step by step lost his national standpoint, and this was better than a hurried conclusion by calling him a few names.[15]

4. HU SHIH

The most sustained campaign against a contemporary intellectual and the ideas he stood for was directed against Hu Shih, one of modern China's most eminent scholars. For the prominent role he played in China's 'New Thought Movement' (also known as China's modern renaissance) and the 'Literary Revolution' some forty years ago Hu Shih has been called the 'Father of the Chinese

Renaissance'. The Communists chose this personalized target for several reasons: Hu Shih had been educated in America and did not conceal his admiration of American democracy. As a student of John Dewey he had been greatly influenced by Dewey's pragmatism. To the Communists he was the type of intellectual who ignorantly admired and worshipped 'Imperialist America'. He was all the more dangerous because of his great influence. His appointment by Chiang Kai-shek as Chinese Ambassador to the United States in the early years of World War II was cited to confirm the charge that he lived to serve the cause of reactionary rule at home and American imperialism abroad.

Hu had never been a member of the Kuomintang. He had never accepted a government post until his ambassadorship. He was highly respected in China as a political independent who had courage enough to speak his mind and to criticize the Kuomintang on various occasions. In view of his stature and his national reputation, Chiang Kai-shek heaped honours on him. At the last hour, before the Communists entered the city of Peking, Chiang sent a special plane to bring Hu out of Peking then encircled by the Communists. Thus, in addition to charging Hu Shih with his close association with the reactionary Kuomintang, the Communists directed the students and faculty of Peking University to attack him as a selfish individualist who deserted his university and shirked his responsibilities in order to join the reactionary rulers whom he served.

One important charge against Hu Shih was that his philosophy was anti-Marxist. As a philosopher, he enjoyed great renown among China's educated people and his pragmatic views had influenced many of them. To the Communists, pragmatism and idealism are both 'bourgeois ideologies' and must be extirpated before a Marxist outlook can be implanted. Hu's philosophy was attacked as feudalistic and reactionary, his advocacy of gradual change as 'reformism', and his aloofness from politics as blindness to the class struggle and therefore a betrayal of the 'people's revolution'. He was an egoist who pursued a sterile scholarship to court favour with the reactionary rulers whose position he did not dare challenge.

Hu Shih personified the intellectual heritage that the Communists were determined to destroy. What he believed and stood for was the belief and standpoint of many of China's intellectuals, old and new. The attack on Hu began in the early days of the Communist regime; one of the severest came from his own son. Young Hu was in 1950 a student in the North China Revolutionary University. Either by 'persuasion' or by choice, he offered in holocaust as proof of his ideological conversion a public denunciation of his father, which was printed in newspapers throughout the country. The highlights of his denunciation are summarized below:

> In the old society, I used to consider my father as an undefiled, honest and good man. After the liberation, I was often resentful of the criticisms directed against him. When I heard Premier Chou En-lai say in an address in Peking University, 'Hu Shih fundamentally does not know what imperialism is', I reacted very strongly within myself. . . . After I studied the history of social development my ideas began to change. . . . I realized the reactionary nature of my viewpoint. . . . As a result of my own *tou-cheng* (struggle), I undertook to make an analysis of my father's history.
>
> My father was born in a family of official gentry. . . . He went to the United States in 1910 . . . where he gradually acquired the viewpoint of the bourgeoisie. . . . After 1919, he wandered further into wrong paths. . . . He introduced pragmatism to counteract materialism. . . . He gave first importance to education, secondary importance to politics and economics. . . . He cherished vain hopes of 'reformism', hoping that the reactionary government might adopt his reform ideas. . . . At the same time, he became more intimately associated with the cultural exploitation of imperialism. He was an important pillar of such groups as the Trustees for the Rockefeller and Boxer Indemnity Funds . . . thus willingly serving as an instrument of imperialism. . . . In 1938 he finally became an official in the service of the Chiang Kai-shek gang. While he was ambassador to the United States, he negotiated commercial treaties . . . and loans . . . to increase the fortunes of the Four Big Families.[16]
>
> When victory descended upon the entire nation he left Peking and left China to become a 'White Chinese', foolishly following the example of the 'White Russians'. Today, having received the education of the Communist Party, I am no longer awed by that historical 'Big Mountain'. I have the courage to recognize his real nature and to overthrow him. I boldly use the scales of historical materialism to weigh his worth to the people. From the standpoint of class analysis, I clearly see him as a faithful minister of the reactionary class and an enemy of the people. . . .[17]

When the campaign was stepped up in the latter part of 1951, the Communists decided on a national concerted attack on Hu Shih. It began in Peking University, where Hu Shih had many ardent followers among his colleagues and students. In organized accusation meetings participants reviewed and analysed Hu's 'reactionary' record and found him to be a faithful servant of the reactionary rulers and foreign imperialists. Friends and colleagues of many years testified how they had fallen under his evil influence and had advocated liberalism, reformism, and class-aloofness, all of which amounted to an acceptance of China's reactionary rulers and a sceptical attitude toward the Communist-led revolution of the people.

What happened at Peking University shows clearly how the Communists use a personal target as a means of thought reform. The former friends and colleagues of Hu Shih had to hold repeated 'discussions' before they arrived at the 'correct' conclusions. The authorities considered the first two discussions unsatisfactory because the participants failed to point out the specific mistakes of Hu Shih and connect his offences with their own shortcomings. The intellectuals were convened for another 'discussion' and the topic of the discussion was 'What kind of a man is Hu Shih?' It was reported that the participants made progress but still lacked thoroughness in self-examination. Finally, marked progress was recorded when prominent members of the university faculty made pointed criticisms of Hu Shih and themselves.[18] For example, T'ang Yung-t'ung, a philosophy professor and acting president of the University in the early days of the Communist regime, testified that, under Hu Shih's influence, he had lacked the class viewpoint and had on one occasion attended a dinner given by Chiang Kai-shek, thus failing to make a clear distinction between friend and enemy.[19]

The Hu Shih campaign was not confined to Peking University, for intellectuals in other universities and in other cities were asked to join in. Those who had been close to Hu saw the necessity of clearing themselves in the eyes of the authorities. One well-known educator met with official disapproval because of what was considered a merely superficial criticism of Hu Shih, and this person had to rewrite his criticism of Hu Shih three different times before it was accepted.[20]

5. LIANG SHU-MING

Another personalized target in the thought reform of 1951 was Liang Shu-ming. Unlike Wu Hsün, who was no longer living, or Hu Shih, who was residing in the United States, Liang was in China and trying to adjust himself to the new regime. Before the Communist conquest, he was known as a liberal, even a leftist, who was critical of the Nationalist Government, but under the new regime he was considered not thorough enough in his ideological transformation; and since he was bold enough to express his independent views he became a target of attack.

Liang, born in Kwangsi in 1893, became nationally famous more than thirty years ago as a philosopher and writer. His comparative studies of Oriental and Western civilizations aroused great interest among China's modern intellectuals. Later, he devoted himself to the cause of rural reconstruction and to the establishment of 'model' rural centres. Before World War II, he was the head of the Rural Reconstruction Research Institute in Shantung. His interest in rural problems brought him to Yenan in 1938, when he discussed such problems with Mao Tse-tung. In Chungking during the war, he was at one time a member of the People's Political Council, which was established by the Nationalist Government as an expression of a desire to relax in some degree the one-party control of the Kuomintang. His keen desire for national unity and for co-operation between the Kuomintang and the Communists brought him into conflict with government policies, and he left for Hong Kong in 1941, where he was instrumental in forming a group which later became the Democratic League, a coalition of minority political parties standing between the Kuomintang and the Communist Party.

While the Communist armies were marching to victory in 1948–1949, Liang was living in retirement in Szechwan, devoting himself to education and writing. When there was still hope of peaceful negotiations in the critical months of early 1949, he in an open letter to Li Tsung-jen, then acting president of the Nationalist Government, urged concessions for the sake of peace. At the same time he published a 'Message to the Chinese Communist Party' to caution the Communists against over-dependence on military power.

In 1949, he was made a delegate to the People's Political Consultative Conference which formally proclaimed the birth of the People's Republic of China. He did not attend the conference but went to Peking later. The fact that he took part in the land reform in Szechwan is an indication of his intention to adjust himself to the new conditions.

Nevertheless, Liang was not an opportunist with no scruples. He had for many years been a man of independent views and he found it hard to abandon completely what he had developed after many years of patient research and careful deliberation. His troubles began with the publication of an article in October 1951 under the title: 'What changes I have undergone in the past two years'.[21] Liang said that he had learned much since 'liberation' and had come to appreciate the achievements of the Communist Party. He had revised his views on the class struggle, an ideological

concept which had constituted a major point of disagreement between himself and the Communist Party. But, added the intrepid
philosopher, 'though I have nodded my head on certain questions,
there are other questions on which I cannot nod my head, and thus
I have not abandoned my original views'.

The article then went on to discuss the questions on which its
author found his old views still unchanged. These, unfortunately
for Liang, were questions of great ideological importance to the
Communists. The Chinese Communists have always maintained
that old Chinese society was a feudal society and that the primary
tasks of the Communist revolution are to overthrow feudalism at
home and imperialism from abroad. Liang, however, stubbornly
held to the view found in his earlier writings, that China ceased to
be a feudal society after the Ch'in and Han dynasties and that the
Chinese feudal class disintegrated with the collapse of the feudal
system of the Chou dynasty some two thousand years ago. 'On
this question' said Liang, 'my views have not changed'.

He questioned the Communist interpretation of history. The
'history of the development of society' is an important topic in the
political creed of Communist China. The Communists believe that
the development of society is governed by laws which apply to
any society, but Liang maintained that Chinese society had
characteristics which made it different from Western society, and
consequently China could not follow the course of historical
development outlined by Marxism-Leninism.

Liang went even further. He disagreed with the Communist
treatment of the class problem. He maintained that one of the
special characteristics of Chinese society was the absence of class
distinctions and that those who did not recognize this did not
really understand China. 'Even today', he said in the same article,
'I maintain that my [old] views are still correct'. The Chinese
people, he insisted, were not class-conscious and the class standpoint—a key concept in Marxism-Leninism—was alien to the
Chinese way of thinking.

Liang's article contained other points of disagreement with the
Communist viewpoint. While he tried at different points to tone
down his disagreement and to express his new appreciation of the
class standpoint and the Marxist interpretation of social development, it was unquestionable that he had serious reservations in his
mind and he was far from accepting the new ideology which the

thought-reform movement sought to popularize. Although his article concluded with his acceptance of the leadership of the Communist Party, it had repeated his former misgivings and the reasons for his previous rejection of the Communist line.

Liang's article was followed by many articles by well-known intellectuals of China condemning his views and charging him with the lack of 'study' and 'self-criticism'. For a while, attacking Liang became an important task in the thought reform and many an insecure person was led to write or speak in criticism of this reckless challenger of the truths of Marxism-Leninism. A few months later, Liang wrote another article in reply to his critics.[22] Instead of bowing to the pressure, he insisted on his views and dismissed the charges of his critics as a waste of time and printing space. As in the case of Hu Shih, this episode was not the end of the campaign, and the attack on Liang was resumed at a later date.

6. CH'EN HO-CH'IN

There were other personalized targets in 1951. Mention may be made of two in the field of educational thought who were used in the reform of educational workers. One was Ch'en Ho-ch'in, a graduate of Teachers College, Columbia University, who for many years was a well-known professor of education and a widely-read writer on childhood education. He was made a target of attack because he consistently stood for the 'reactionary educational theories' of John Dewey and of American imperialism. Educators joined in criticizing his educational ideas and in demanding the elimination of 'Dewey's insidious influence' on educational thinking in China. Ch'en was compelled to admit his errors and to express his new understanding of the class nature of man and the political significance of all educational work.

7. CH'IN MU

The other target was Ch'in Mu, editor of an educational journal in Canton. He was accused of publishing articles setting forth unprogressive educational ideas at variance with the concepts of Marxism-Leninism. He was opposed for his 'petty bourgeois ideas' contrary to 'the interests of the people'. This released a flood of criticism against this target and educational and cultural workers were convened in 'discussion meetings' to examine the Ch'in Mu's ideas.

8. SUMMARY

It may be useful at this point to summarize the Communist use of personalized targets in the thought reform of intellectuals. In the first place, personalized targets make thought reform concrete and specific. Study of Marxism-Leninism may remain in the realm of generalities and abstractions, but the 'analysis' of specific short-comings of individuals reduces the generalities to concrete attitudes and actions.

Secondly, the personalized targets are used as 'types', or examples of ideological mistakes commonly committed by intellectuals. The important part of the attack on personalized targets is self-examination. Participants in the 'discussions' are supposed to look within themselves and ask in what concrete ways they share the errors symbolized in the target of attack. The target is the mirror, so to speak, in which the participants are to see themselves vividly. One group of participants in the discussion of Ch'in Mu summed up their experience thus: 'Ch'in Mu's problems are not his own. They are the problems of the petty bourgeoisie. When we criticize Ch'in Mu, we are at the same time criticizing ourselves'.[23]

Thirdly, the attacks on the personalized targets call for the need of a clean break with the past. Wu Hsün, Mei Yi-ch'i, Chang Po-ling and Hu Shih represent traditions which are an integral part of the intellectual make-up of the people whose thought the Communists have set out to reform. The targets are symbols of the past; to denounce them is to get ready for the future.

Finally, while thought reform is basically an individual affair, the Communists want to exploit group psychology by 'mass movement'. Concerted attack on a common target constitutes mass action and is likely to engender the emotions of ideological zealots. The mass emotions and mass pressure help mould the thinking and emotions of the individuals. This is one of the chief values of the 'mass movements'. Concerted attack on a personalized target amounts to a mass movement or campaign on a small scale.

CHAPTER VII

THE THREE-ANTI AND FIVE-ANTI CAMPAIGNS

THE Chinese Communists give credit for the consolidation of their power since 1949 to a few major developments, among which are the land reform, the Resist-America Aid-Korea campaign, the 'three-anti' and 'five-anti' campaigns, and the ideological reform of the intellectuals.[1] The three-anti campaign was started late in 1951 and was merged with the five-anti campaign which gained momentum in the spring of 1952. Both campaigns involved the intellectuals; both were carried into the schools and colleges to push further the reform of the educational workers.

1. THE THREE-ANTI CAMPAIGN

The original object of the three-anti campaign seemed to be economic. The government directive[2] officially launching the campaign declared that to increase production and practise economy were the important tasks of the moment, but 'corruption and waste are the big enemies of production and economy' and 'bureaucratism is the breeding ground of corruption and waste'. To combat these enemies the directive called for a national 'anti-corruption, anti-waste, and anti-bureaucratism struggle' and asked all citizens to help expose cases of violation so that the offenders might be duly punished and the 'three evils' might be stamped out.

The 'struggle' became another 'mass movement' in which the 'progressive elements' took the lead and the not-so-progressive had to participate in order to show their devotion to the people's cause. While people of all walks of life were 'mobilized' to join a 'mass investigation campaign', persons in positions where any of the three evils might have flourished were asked to examine their own records and to confess their wrongdoings. Offences, either confessed or exposed, ranged from personal luxuries to unnecessary public expenses and embezzlement of public funds. Accusations and confessions filled the air; 'public trials' and swift punishment in the form of dismissal or fines or imprisonment or even summary execution were given wide publicity; and all 'patriotic citizens' were urged to take up 'tiger hunting', i.e. to expose specific cases of corruption, waste, and bureaucratism. To be a member of a 'tiger-hunting team' was considered a mark of progressiveness.[3]

What began as an economic campaign, however, was soon expanded into a major phase of the Communist class struggle. Corruption, waste, and bureaucratism were found to be prevalent in government and Party. The Communist Party itself, which boasted of its freedom from corruption, found in its very ranks many who indulged in bribery, misuse of public funds, extravagant luxuries, and other acts of malpractice. Happily the Communists hit upon an explanation that not only saved their 'face' but also fitted well into their ideology of class warfare. The explanation was direct and simple: good Party members had fallen under the influence of 'bourgeois ideology' and had been led astray by the cunning bourgeoisie with its schemes against the moral integrity of hitherto morally stalwart revolutionaries. To get at this root of the evils, it was necessary to center the attack on the bourgeoisie and their ideology in the five-anti campaign.

2. THE FIVE-ANTI CAMPAIGN

The specific 'evils' to combat were bribery, tax evasion, fraud, theft of state assets, and leakage of state economic secrets. These, charged the Communists, were the 'sugar-coated bullets' the bourgeoisie used to attack the moral fibre of government and Party personnel and thus destroy the people's democracy. Agents of the bourgeoisie, they claimed, had infiltrated the ranks of the labour unions as well as government and Party personnel to bribe and corrupt them. The entire nation was asked to launch a vast 'counter-offensive to repel the ferocious attacks of the bourgeoisie'.

The five-anti campaign was an even bigger mass movement than the three-anti. It was a broadside attack on the city bourgeoisie. The 'five evils' were so broad in scope that one or several of the evils could be pinned on any merchant, industrialist, or business man the Communists wished to persecute. This campaign turned out to be the urban counterpart of the land reform. While the land reform sought to eliminate the landlords as a class, the 'five-anti' broke the back of the city bourgeoisie and its influence in Chinese society. Those were months of extreme terror for the city bourgeoisie; they were marked by harrowing accusations, public trials, forced confessions, confiscatory fines, even summary executions.

Wives were encouraged to report on their husbands and children to expose the 'reactionary' activities of their parents. The pressures exerted were so great that many were driven to suicide.[4]

In this long stride toward a complete control of the nation's economy by the state, the Communists noted with satisfaction that the five-anti campaign had paved the way for the first five-year plan and the subsequent 'socialist transformation' of private enterprises into state enterprises.[5]

3. IMPACT ON INTELLECTUALS

The intellectuals in institutions of higher learning were among the chief objects of the reform. Many had shown little enthusiasm for the 'reform of higher education' undertaken by the Communists. Some objected to the merging of institutions, others opposed measures which reduced the engineering course from four to three years, or which introduced wholesale Soviet methods, materials and theories. The two campaigns affected the intellectuals in two specific ways. First, they were asked to scrutinize their work to see to what extent the 'evils' were present and in what ways they had themselves contributed to the spread of the evils; secondly, they were enlisted in an intensified war against 'bourgeois ideology'. From the attacks on individual merchants and industrialists the five-anti campaign moved on to a 'systematic struggle' against 'bourgeois ideology'. The intellectuals were again reminded of their bourgeois background with its 'bourgeois ideology'; their duty, therefore, was to cleanse themselves of the bourgeois ideas that still remained in their thinking.

Each phase of this continuous process of thought reform was co-ordinated with the larger political and economic tasks of the hour. The over-all aim was to impress the intellectuals with the inescapability of the class struggle and its close relation to thought reform. As part of the discredited bourgeois class they must turn their backs irrevocably on any thought pattern or attitude reminiscent of their unworthy past. The guiding hand of the Party had to be accepted; to do so was progressive, to hold any reservations or to lack enthusiasm for the new order was evidence of 'bourgeois ideology'.

According to a report in *Kuang-ming jih-pao*, waste, corruption, and bureaucratism in higher institutions had caused heavy losses to the country and seriously hampered educational work in the New

China.[6] In ten institutions in the Peking area alone, damage and loss due to waste were estimated to exceed fifty billion *yüan*, the equivalent of the estimated cost of thirty-four jet fighters. These losses, according to the report, were due to the existence and prevalence of 'bourgeois ideology' and bourgeois practices, e.g. particularism, as manifested in various departments fighting for larger shares of the budget than they actually needed, with the result of holding large quantities of unused equipment and sometimes unused funds. In an exhibit held in Peking in early 1952 to expose waste, it appeared that the Peking College of Engineering, obsessed with the idea of gaining a reputation as the top engineering school in the country, had wasted four hundred million *yüan* to buy five new sets of apparatus simply 'because Tsinghua University had six sets'. Tsinghua University, on the other hand, had eighty bottles of a chemical for organic analysis, which, at its normal rate of use, would last 4,000 years.[7]

4. 'BOURGEOIS IDEOLOGY'

Exhibits, discussions, accusations, self-examination, and public confessions were the methods used in the campaign in the schools and colleges. Students were organized to expose their teachers and to force confessions from them. Some scholars had to revise their self-criticism and their confessions time and again before they were left alone. A professor of philosophy, formerly much under fire by the Nationalist Government for his leftist views, had to appear in three successive public meetings to confess his mistakes.[8] The Communists then gleefully noted that 'teachers have become profoundly educated following the exposure of mistakes they never imagined existed'.[9]

In time, the specific charges of waste, corruption and bureaucratism in educational institutions led to broad charges of 'bourgeois ideology' in general. In other words, the campaign was another aspect of the thought reform of the intellectuals. In an article under the title, 'The three-anti movement in institutions of higher education should be co-ordinated with the ideological reform movement',[10] president Li Ta of Hunan University said: 'The three-anti campaign in the institutions of higher learning is not only a class struggle in political and economic fields, but also an ideological struggle. It aims not only at crushing the attacks of the bourgeois class, but also at eliminating the bourgeois mentality'.

Getting down to specific points Li Ta listed the following concrete
expressions of 'bourgeois mentality' common among the intellectuals in the higher institutions:

i. Pride and conceit. Looking down on labouring masses. *ii*.
Objectivism. Holding one's self aloof from politics and from class
distinctions. *iii*. Hireling's viewpoint. Working only for pay. *iv*.
The sense of being a guest. No devotion to the institution. *v*.
Technical viewpoint. Technical skill is enough; no need to study
politics. *vi*. Isolation of theory from practice. Teaching divorced
from China's practical needs. *vii*. Irresponsibility. Much overlap-
ping and duplication of teaching material. *viii*. Departmentalism.
Departmental competition results in hoarding quantities of equipment which rot unused. *ix*. School ties. Formation of cliques.
x. Pro-American outlook. Even after the Resist-America Aid-
Korea campaign 'on the surface they have reduced their pro-
American outlook, but they are still incapable of fostering a hatred
for America'. *xi*. Rejection of fundamental reform. Resisting the
Communist attempt to reform the schools and universities. *xii*.
Neglect of students' political study. Failure to encourage students
to study Marxism-Leninism.[11]

The 'bourgeois mentality', said Li, was common among the
university students as well as among the faculties. The following
errors among students were traced to 'the bourgeois mentality, the
petty bourgeois mentality, and the feudal landlord mentality':

i. Preoccupation with technique. Neglect of ideological and
political study. *ii*. Desire for qualification. Primary interest in
graduating and getting a job. *iii*. Exploitation of the people.
Applying for scholarships when they are not needed; demanding
that the university provide free text-books and stationery. *iv*. Waste
of public property. *v*. Lack of discipline. No interest in collective
life and group discussions. *vi*. Hedonism. Indulgence in pleasure.
vii. Ulterior motives. Sabotaging the educational programme and
secretly opposing the People's Government.

The Communists lump all non-Marxist philosophies together
without distinction between pragmatism, idealism, liberalism, and
other non-Marxist ideas. Sometimes these ideas are indiscriminately
referred to as idealism, and at other times they are given the general
label 'bourgeois ideology'. If teachers are inefficient in their
teaching or slow in accepting the Communist 'reform' ideas, if the
products of education fail to meet the practical needs of the people's
democracy, if there is waste or lack of co-ordination in educational

work, the root of the trouble is always found to be 'bourgeois ideology' and the cure-all is its liquidation accompanied by a big dose of Marxism-Leninism. The effect of the two campaigns was to break further resistance of the intellectuals, to drag them from their ideological moorings, and to anchor them more firmly to the new state. It was a campaign against all ideas or attitudes not favourable to the new regime.

One of the specific targets of the campaign against 'bourgeois ideology' was individualism. In the pursuit of 'selfish' personal interests the scholars were accused of neglecting public welfare and ignoring the 'masses' when in their academic studies they did not concern themselves with politics and confined themselves to their specialization and departmental programmes. Their 'bourgeois ideology' blocked the progress of education and made impossible the necessary reforms.

The scholars were told to discard their preoccupation with academic pursuits which advanced their own personal ambitions; that it was wrong to be too much concerned with raising one's 'scholarly status' or one's reputation as a 'top scholar' in a particular field.[12] They should even desist from efforts to bring fame to their own department or their own university; they must accept the government plans for the consolidation of departments and for the reorganization or merging of certain institutions of higher learning.

5. AMERICANISM

The 'pro-American mentality' in institutions of higher learning was the most severely criticized. When professors in Tsinghua University hesitated to accept the government plan to change the university into a technical college for fear that this may result in a deterioration of academic standards, the Communists pointed out that these 'standards' were really 'American standards' and that their preference for a 'university' was a result of their pernicious 'worship-America mentality'. Though Tsinghua[13] had long been a national university, a report in 1952 on the 'anti-bourgeois ideological struggle' in that university stated that 'a serious worship-America mentality still exists in Tsinghua'.[14] One scientist was severely censured for participation in a research project sponsored by the U.S. Army, and for his desire to become a scholar of 'international fame'. As a result of the campaign he confessed: 'I sold out myself; I sold out my nation; I thought that

I was achieving fame and status; gleefully and unashamedly I thought that my expert knowledge could get me to places'.[15] Another professor was castigated because he had sent an article for publication to an American journal. Others were reproved for having encouraged students to cherish ambitions of personal success and fame. To flaunt academic degrees, to advise a student to take up a field of study because it offered good opportunities of advancement, to teach according to 'international standards'— all these were attacked as expressions of 'bourgeois ideology' or 'American bourgeois ideology'. Yielding to the pressure, one scholar after another loudly repudiated his American connections. A mathematics professor said: 'While in the past I used to consider the six years I spent studying in the United States as my golden age, I now see this as the darkest and most dangerous period. When in America I became virtually steeped in a tub of poison, and my very pores were permeated with the venom to enable me to return and in turn to contaminate the youth of China'.[16]

Another university where 'pro-American mentality' was considered especially serious was Yenching University, one of China's Christian universities before it was taken over by the Communist government. In March 1952, an exhibit was held at Yenching University to show 'irrefutable' evidences of American cultural aggression.[17] The reports and statistics on display at the exhibit were supposed to show that Yenching had been the 'headquarters' of American cultural aggression and that the 'worship-America mentality' was still prevalent among its faculty. A year after the take-over by the government, the curricula had remained basically unchanged, and the department of political science was still placing orders for reactionary books written by 'war criminals' such as John Foster Dulles and Winston Churchill.[18]

According to the statistical reports displayed at the exhibit, of the nineteen graduates from the research division of the department of sociology from 1932 to 1947, all but one were either working for the 'Kuomintang bandit gang' or for Americans. Of the 93 graduates of the chemistry department from 1933 to 1947, seventeen were in the United States, eleven in Taiwan, two in Hong Kong and one in Indonesia. The department of journalism had in twenty years graduated 103 students, of whom 101 were working for the reactionaries. Of interest in the exhibit were the theses of graduating students. They were either anti-Soviet and anti-Communist in tone or they sought to 'eulogize the American imperialists from all possible angles', or 'to expound bourgeois ideologies'.

Furthermore, Yenching was accused of being an intelligence agency for the American imperialists. It was said that the department of economics had received yearly subsidies from America specifically for the collection of economic data. These 'facts' were presented at the exhibit to support the demand that a most determined effort must now be made to rid Yenching and other educational institutions of the deep-rooted American influence. The reform must be to clean out once and for all that 'admire-America, worship-America mentality' in educational work.

Pro-Americanism was not restricted to one or two institutions; it was found to be very prevalent among university faculties. A report on the 'anti-bourgeois ideological struggle in Tientsin' stated that many teachers in institutions of higher learning were addicted to the 'American way of life'. They used American goods, subscribed to American magazines, even followed American styles of interior decoration.[19] They talked 'democracy' and 'freedom' but they were unaware of class distinctions and uninterested in the class struggle. They rated American science and American culture above Soviet science and culture.

To summarize, the three-anti and five-anti campaigns, as far as the intellectuals were concerned, were an 'ideological struggle'.[20] It was a war against all ideas and attitudes not wholly acceptable to the New Regime. The Communist stand on ideological questions and on major policies of the state is not always consistent. Shifts and sudden turnabouts are often made in the light of expediency. While the general goals are constant, the methods of achieving them are subject to constant review and modification in the light of 'objective conditions' or the 'concrete situation'. Methods considered as orthodox today may be condemned as rightist or leftist tomorrow; what is today opposed as conservatism or 'bourgeois ideology' may tomorrow be the realistic view adopted by the powers that be. In the long run thought reform means the softening up of all resistance and making the intellectuals the submissive servants of a dictatorial state.

CHAPTER VIII

THE CONFESSIONS

IN the earlier programmes of 'study' and political indoctrination the Communists set much store, as we have seen in Ch. III, on the written personal testimony of the ideological change that each person had come to in his 'study conclusions'. In this they were applying to the public a means of thought control long used within the Party. In the thought reform of 1951–52, the 'thought conclusions' became more elaborate, with great emphasis on the confession of past errors and failings. The confessions of numerous leading intellectuals were given wide publicity in the press. While each confession was supposed to be intimately related to the confessor's personal experience and ideological struggle, yet it had to be written in such a manner as to satisfy the general pattern set by the authorities for all confessions.

The term 'confession' describes the various forms of personal testimonies which the intellectuals were asked to submit as evidence of their reform progress. Many are confessions in the strict sense of the word; some are 'thought conclusions' or testimonies of what has been learned in the process of 'study', while others may be called 'criticism and self-criticism' documents. For the sake of convenience all are here referred to as confessions.

1. THE GENERAL PATTERN

An important part of every confession is autobiographical; to be satisfactory it must be 'complete', have no gaps, and leave nothing of the past concealed. It must not be a mere chronicle of events, it must reveal the individual's personal reactions to his past and to each important episode of his life. Many an autobiography was rejected because of omissions or insufficiently clear-cut reactions of the individual to some phases of his past.

Practically every confession of the intellectuals had to begin with his birth and to give in no uncertain terms the class status of his family. Since most intellectuals had come from families of rich peasants or landlords or the bourgeoisie, they were born with this original sin. To the class-conscious Communists, outside the proletarian family none can escape the influence of non-proletarian ideologies. In their confessions the intellectuals were to realize that they had started life under an ideological handicap and their thought reform could not be considered completed until they were brought to see in what specific manner and concrete ways the 'ideology of the exploiting classes' was reflected in their past ambitions and plans.

The emphasis on 'class origin' is also related to the importance the Communists attach to 'differentiation between friend and enemy', meaning, of course, class friends and class enemies. To the Communists, a major fault of the intellectuals is their inability to make class distinctions and to appreciate the importance of the class struggle. Political consciousness to the Communists is synonymous with class consciousness; conversely, to be unaware of class distinctions or to stand aloof from the class struggle indicates political backwardness and 'bourgeois ideology'. In examining his class background, the intellectual has to show how his new awakening has enabled him to see the 'poisonous effects' of bourgeois society and to realize the necessity of learning 'the viewpoint of the working class'.

The ideological errors considered most common among Chinese intellectuals are the admiration of the United States, a suspicious and even hostile attitude toward the Soviet Union, individualism (as opposed to collectivism), identification with the exploiting classes (as opposed to the working class under the leadership of the Communist Party), the pursuit of scholarship from the idealistic and capitalistic viewpoint, failure to relate professional work to politics, etc. In making his confession, it was not enough for the individual to say that he had committed these errors; he must demonstrate specifically when and how the 'erroneous ideologies' were reflected in his work.

Finally, every confession must contain a definite pledge to make a clean break from the unsavoury past, with a determined effort to 'study' Marxism-Leninism and the ideology of the proletariat revolution. It must promise a new start in life, a fresh resolution to take part in the 'people's revolution' under the guidance of the Communist Party.

2. WHY THE CONFESSIONS?

The confessions serve many purposes in the thought reform of the intellectuals. First of all, they give tangible evidence of ideological conversion and provide a basis for determining what further 'remoulding' remains to be done. The first confession is often considered unsatisfactory but has the value of revealing the 'gaps' in one's self-examination; these become the specific targets of further remoulding, whose effectiveness is examined in subsequent confessions. Without written conclusions it would be hard to check the progress of the thought reform.

Next the 'arrogance' of the intellectuals had to be shattered. Conscious of their historical role in Chinese society, the Chinese intellectuals tend to look upon the Communists as their cultural inferiors, and this attitude makes it difficult for them to accept the 'leadership' of the Communist Party. So they must be put through a process of self-abasement and abnegation; they must come to realize their inadequacies and to feel ashamed instead of taking pride in their past.

Thirdly, the psychology of the human desire to appear to be consistent in the eyes of fellow men is exploited. When a person makes an oral statement, he finds it relatively easy to forget what he has said, but when he records his reactions in black and white he has made a commitment not so easily set aside. When, further-more, his confession or personal testimony is published in news-papers and given wide publicity, he finds it even harder to retreat from a position which he has declared in public. Even were the first confession made with one's tongue in one's cheek, repeated confessions tend to make the commitment more binding on the individual.

Fourthly, the confession makes the process of thought reform an intimate personal affair. It is no longer feasible to talk in generalities. It is not enough to condemn bourgeois ideology in abstract terms or the past failings of intellectuals in general. Every person must dig up his own past and expose his own personal failings, mentioning specific times and places. He is no more an onlooker in the ideological struggle, for he must wage the struggle with himself.

Finally, the public confessions are used to create a climate of public sentiment. The confessions of the well-known intellectuals are used to drum up other intellectuals to follow the same path of ideological conversion. The wide publicity given to the confessions of 1951–52 gave the impression that numerous intellectuals had embraced the new ideology of the proletarian revolution and had placed themselves in the service of the leaders of the proletarian revolution—the Communist Party.

3. PRO-AMERICANISM

To find out what specific errors the intellectuals had to confess, the author examined about a hundred confessions and personal testimonies written by Chinese intellectuals during the thought reform of 1951–1952.[1] The errors most commonly mentioned represented the major targets of the thought reform. Pro-Americanism was given more attention than any other form of 'incorrect thought' which the Communists set out to eradicate. Among the confessions examined, more than seventy per cent deplored the corrupting and decadent effects of Americanism in their past life.

The Communists have centred their fire on pro-Americanism not only because they are ideologically opposed to capitalism and the United States today has become the symbol of capitalism, but also because few Chinese intellectuals in recent decades have been free from American influence. A large number of China's top-rank intellectuals have been educated in American universities or in American-supported colleges in China. American influence has been a major factor in the development of modern Chinese education and American ideas have in one way or another crept into the mental make-up of a large portion of China's intelligentzia. So the Communists concluded that before the intellectuals could be converted to Marxism-Leninism, they must be purged of the 'capitalist class mentality' which resulted from their 'admire-America' and 'worship-America' habit. They must be brought to view the American way as bad and detestable and to feel ashamed of their connections with the United States.

Many examples may be cited, but a few typical samples will suffice. The following came from the pen of a prominent physicist who was educated at the California Institute of Technology:

> During the four years of my first sojourn in the United States I saw only the skyscrapers, automobiles and the licentious and shamelessly free-spending life of the exploiting classes, but I did not see the tragic exploitation of the toiling masses by the monopolistic capitalists. . . . I did read in the newspapers about the oppression and lynching of negroes but I did not understand that it had been the consistent and oppressive policy of the imperialists to create dissension and hatred among national groups. I mistook the persecution of negroes to be the work of a small group of white rowdies, opposed by the 'good' whites. Therefore I erroneously thought that American 'democracy' was good and the people had freedom of speech. Were not the American newspapers free to print stories criticizing the President of the United States? At that time, I did not realize that the American President and the so-called government officials were slaves of the monopolistic capitalists, and the bickerings reported in the newspapers were merely the ravings of one ruling clique against another. In a word, when in 1929 I returned to China to teach at Tsinghua University, my whole body had been saturated with the pernicious germs of the bourgeoisie. . . .

I went to America again in 1943, hoping to become an 'international scholar' and thus fully exposed my ugly selfishness. During the time of our hard struggle against Japanese aggression, I was willing to cast my lot with the imperialists and take part in the military research work supported by the American imperialists and designed to murder the peace-loving people of the world. . . .

My second trip to the United States in 1943 was the most shameful chapter of my life. I went in the name of a scientific worker from a democratic country engaged in opposing fascism, but actually, in early 1945, during my stay in America, the glorious victories of the Soviet Union in Eastern Europe had already spelled the ultimate doom for Fascist Germany. . . .

Before joining the research, I was required to answer two insulting questions. One was: Are you a Communist? The other was: Are you willing to bear arms for the U.S. government? I was willing to supply the answers the American imperialists wanted, and thus betrayed my nation and myself. . . . I became an instrument of American imperialism and yet felt it was my 'honour'. . . .[2]

Many an American-educated scholar wrote in the same vein. The fact that so many confessions referred to the same specific points gives ground for believing that the confessors were following a prescribed pattern rather than expressing their own ideas. Here is another example.

In the past I looked at American science and technology on the surface only and did not carefully analyse the power that controlled them. . . . Because I blindly admired American science and technology, I unconsciously acquired an admire-America attitude . . . I failed to see the line of demarcation between the enemy and myself.

In the course of the Resist-America Aid-Korea campaign, my emotions were greatly stirred. The beastly and blood-thirsty exploitation of American imperialism aroused my deep hatred. . . .

From 1942 till the surrender of Japan, I worked for three and a half years on military projects including research on atomic bombs and radar. . . . I had thought that such research would be of value to the allies in their war against German and Japanese fascism. Therefore, I praised even more than before the achievements of American science and on occasions I even felt greatly honoured to have a part in these achievements. But, how significant a role did the atomic bomb and radar play in the war? . . . The American imperialists killed innocent Japanese civilians with the atomic bomb on the eve of the Soviet attack against Japan in fulfilment of an agreement. . . . This proves that although the invention of the atomic bomb and radar devices is an achievement in science and technological advance it becomes a menace when placed in the hands of the reactionary classes.[3]

Another scholar who made pro-Americanism the major theme of his confession was a professor of biology at Wuhan University. He confessed that he had reflected his blind admiration of America in all phases of his work. He had used American laboratory equipment and followed American methods of teaching. He had taught Darwinism instead of the theories of Michurin. He had used English labels for his botany specimens and had committed 'the extreme error' of exchanging specimens with American scholars.[4] He also confessed the mistake of having accepted financial aid from Harvard University and of collecting specimens for the U.S. Department of Agriculture. 'I failed to realize that botanical resources were a matter of great value to the imperialists in their exploitation of colonial and semi-colonial countries. I not only did not feel ashamed of serving the cause of imperialism; I was even proud of it'. After a lengthy confession of his past errors the biologist concluded, 'Only by applying Marxism-Leninism—the thought of Mao Tse-tung and the theories of Michurin—is it possible to have a Chinese botanical science dedicated to service for the people'.

The concluding statement just quoted may help explain why so much attention was given to the pro-Americanism of the scientists. The scholars in the social sciences and the humanities had been the first to be condemned for their bourgeois scholarship and the first to yield to the demand that they discard the capitalist theories in favour of Marxist learning. But the scientists had thought they might be exempt from this onslaught on scholarship; they had thought that the Communists, recognizing the importance of science to industrialization and national reconstruction, might not inject politics into scientific learning. But the Communists were in 1951-1952 determined to wipe out all capitalist influences in education and culture and they demanded that scholars in all fields must learn from the Soviet Union. It was precisely because the Communists attached so much importance to science that they wanted to make sure that scientists should be purged of all anti-proletarian ideologies.

Confessions of pro-Americanism by non-scientists are too numerous to mention. The more extensive a person's American connections, the greater was the pressure for him to prove his new awakening by exposing 'the true nature of American imperialism'. Those who had received American scholarships or academic honours from American universities felt all the more keenly the need of expressing their newly awakened sense of shame over what had previously been mistaken for honours. That this renunciation of what one had cherished for years was not easy can be seen in the confession of a professor of geography who told how he returned to China in 1950 after having lived for four years in the poisonous atmosphere of American capitalist society. He arrived in China in the midst of the Resist-America Aid-Korea campaign. He described his initial reaction as follows:

> Soon, volunteers were going to Korea to join the war and the Resist-America Aid-Korea campaign was launched throughout the country. I again

was seized by a fear-America mentality. I had seen the powerful navy, air force, the big guns and tanks of the American imperialists, but I did not understand the fundamental reason for the invincibility of the people's army. As a result, I felt uneasy. Since the New China had been established for only a short time, why didn't she engage in construction instead of going to war? Were the volunteers certain of victory? Why didn't the Communist Party take a 'middle road'? Though I participated in demonstrations and shouted slogans, in my heart I could not resist America, I could not hate and despise America. My mental agony reached the highest degree.[5]

4. ATTITUDE TOWARD THE SOVIET UNION

A corollary of pro-Americanism is a suspicious and hostile attitude toward the Soviet Union. The Communists found that many intellectuals were guilty of this and such 'reactionary ideas' were a serious obstacle to the development of the socialist outlook. So in the thought reform of intellectuals an effort was made to see if any change had taken place in their attitude toward the Soviet Union; and the intellectuals, in the writing of confessions, found it wise to refer specifically to this subject. An administrative officer of the University of Nanking confessed as follows:

> Because of my pro-America, admire-America, and fear-America attitude and because I accepted ridiculous American opinions, I was hostile to the Soviet Union. Furthermore I did not differentiate clearly between Czarist Russia and the Soviet Union and I thought of the Soviet Union as 'Red imperialism'. I was misled by American propaganda . . . and believed that 'there is economic equality but no political freedom in the Soviet Union'. My 'understanding' of the Soviet Union came from the American-made movie *The Iron Curtain* and from the propaganda publication of American imperialism titled *I Found Freedom* [sic]. After I was educated by the tremendous progress in China's production and construction of the last three years with the assistance of the Soviet Big Brothers . . . I came to realize that I had failed to differentiate between friend and enemy.[6]

Another college professor confessed that for thirty years he had been plagued by pro-Americanism and suspicion of the Soviet Union, committing the serious error of not recognizing friend and enemy. He was in America when the Korean war broke out; misled by American propaganda, 'I wrongly believed that the Soviet Union instigated the attack on South Korea by North Korea, and the United States had no choice but to fight back'.[7]

It is sometimes possible to detect mental reservations in the confessions. When an intellectual elaborated on reasons for his past 'erroneous thought' was he stealthily defending himself while engaged in outward self-denunciation? When he said that shouting slogans against America caused him 'mental agony',[8] was he sneaking into his confession a veiled protest against the pressure to which he was subjected? In the confession from which we have just quoted, the professor explained his anti-Soviet past as follows:

'I could not forget the historical facts of the exploitation of China by imperial Russia . . . and, at the time of the Bolshevik revolution, when I saw the numerous homeless White Russians roaming abroad, I detested the cruelty of the Soviet Union'.[9]

The professor also testified that he had not found it easy to change his established pattern of thinking. In the Resist-America Aid-Korea campaign, he said, 'I shouted the resist-America, hate-America, and despise-America slogans, but inwardly I found that I could not resist, I could not hate, and I could not despise . . . I was merely following the crowd'. Had the professor smuggled into his confession a statement designed to satisfy his 'inward' self? Be it as it may, he had to conclude in the way desired by the authorities. He concluded: 'I now understand that anti-Americanism and pro-Sovietism are two sides of the same thing. Since I now hate American imperialism, I unconsciously have come to know the Soviet Union as worthy of love, respect and admiration'.[10]

5. INDIVIDUALISM

The Communists want a collective society; they preach collective living. The individual must submit to the group, and obey the 'organization'. Consequently a specific target of the thought reform is the individualism of the intellectuals, as expressed in their personal ambitions, in seeking fame and personal gain, in the desire for individual freedom, in various forms of 'selfishness', etc.

A professor of Chinese literature confessed that the central motive of his professional career had been his personal benefit and the welfare of his family. He described his 'mistakes' as follows:

> I was deeply in love with my wife and we never parted in twenty years of married life. . . . The more children I had, the more I loved them. . . . I used to say to my wife, 'We live for our children'. My whole life was dominated by individualism.[11]

Other scholars confessed that individualism had led them to pay too much attention to salaries, to write for publication either to gain fame or for monetary reward, and to refuse additional responsibilities in their preoccupation with tasks that would bring monetary gain. One said he had opposed 'political study' for fear that it would interfere with his personal plans. Many confessed that they had aspired to 'international fame'. Still others confessed that they had pursued their personal interests in research and teaching to the neglect of the needs of the 'people'.

The implication of these confessions was that the intellectuals must give up their individualism and place themselves without reservation at the service of the Party and the state. Personal needs and personal interests should be subordinate to the needs of the state and the 'people'. Just as students in China today are assigned to study certain subjects and at certain schools to meet the personnel quotas of the state, and the graduates of secondary and higher schools sent to posts regardless of personal desires, so too the Communists expect the intellectuals and scholars to discard their individualism and take up the tasks the Party and state want them to perform. For effective state planning presupposes state control of all human as well as material resources.

6. CLASS AND POLITICS

Among the prevalent 'mistakes' of the intellectuals was their aloofness from politics and from class differences. So a specific aim of the thought reform was to make them see the mistake of the 'supra-politics' and 'supra-class' mentality. 'Pure professionalism' or a 'purely technical viewpoint' was condemned as failure to see the political significance of all work and the need of all people to engage in political 'study' and political tasks. It is not enough to be competent in one's field.

In confessing his 'purely professional viewpoint', a scientist and university dean told how he had preached 'the reactionary ideology of saving China by science' thus neglecting the importance of politics.[12] During the war he had opposed student strikes and student demonstrations, and maintained that students had better concentrate on their studies. He was thus leading the students into the same shameful neglect of politics that had characterized his own work. 'Because I had been heavily saturated with the poisonous supra-politics and supra-class ideology of the bourgeoisie', he said, 'I took the preposterous position that all that intellectuals needed was technical competence and they could be aloof from politics'.[13] He further confessed that when in 1949 his daughter wanted to join the Communist work teams to go to South China, he had stopped her on the pretext that she was not well. Again he was acting from his 'supra-politics' mentality.

Reference has been made to the emphasis laid on 'class origin' in the autobiographies. This emphasis is supposed to help overcome the 'supra-class mentality'. The dean of an engineering college said: 'I was reared in the exploiting class and nurtured in bourgeois education. Consequently for many years I was disdainful of the broad masses of labouring people. . . . I knew nothing about the theories and politics of the Communist Party'.[14] Another scholar testified: 'I was born, in 1895, of an impoverished landlord family in a city. I lost my mother at the age of ten . . . I resolved to study hard in order to attain fame and fulfil the hopes of my mother'.[15] From the pen of the dean of a medical school: 'I was brought up in a landlord-merchant family. Since childhood my parents had hoped that I would become a scholar and bring glory to the ancestors. . . . My mind was filled with feudalistic and exploitative ideas'.[16] And a secondary school teacher said that his past life had been perverted by a double dose of bourgeois influence, because he was not only brought up in the family of a 'big landlord', but he married the daughter of a landlord 'and after that my life became even more corrupt'.[17]

7. BOURGEOIS IDEOLOGY

Among other phases of bourgeois ideology which came to be condemned in the thought reform were reformism, liberalism, conciliationism, and bourgeois sentimentalism. In the Communist lexicon reformism means the false hope that society can be gradually improved by reform instead of being changed by revolution; it is the trick by which the exploiting class prevents the revolt of the masses. Consequently to advocate reformism is to serve the exploiting class.

Liberalism means not only a warped view of personal freedom but also unwillingness to accept the discipline of the group. Conciliationism means a tendency to compromise and to placate the enemy. It is opposed to the resolute courage and determination of the class warrior. Bourgeois sentimentalism refers to what the Communists call 'hypocritic bourgeois virtues' of kindness and humaneness which condemn the class war as cruel and ruthless and make a person flinch before the hard realities of class warfare. All of these must be overcome in the process of the thought reform.

Besides these specific shortcomings, the intellectuals were asked to examine their professional activities and to state in their confessions how they had reflected various forms of bourgeois ideology in their work. A professor of philosophy confessed that he had taught metaphysics completely isolated from the realities of society.[18] An architect confessed the folly of adhering to the Greek and Roman forms he had learned as student and attempting to apply 'idealistic architectural concepts' to the designing of workers' dormitories.[19] A professor of journalism said he had made the mistake of teaching the journalistic principles of the American capitalists and had openly expressed before his students his admiration of the American 'freedom of the press' which he now recognized as false and hypocritical.[20] A professor of economics confessed that he had for more than ten years taught the economics of the capitalists without understanding its reactionary character and eventual doom; he had thus served as the 'unpaid spokesman of the monopolistic capitalists'.[21]

The most common confession of the writers and artists was that they had 'isolated themselves from the masses' and had violated Mao Tse-tung's injunction that literature and art should be produced for the workers, peasants and soldiers. A director-producer admitted that his films had not sufficiently portrayed the class struggle or described the exploitation of the labouring class by the ruling cliques. He had been known as a leftist playwright but now he saw that his work had not been thorough. Said he: 'I told myself that I ought to use the motion picture as a weapon for the broad masses (but actually for only the city people, the students, and the intelligentzia), that I ought to reflect the class viewpoint and portray the class struggle in my productions . . . but I could not depart from my petty bourgeois patterns of thinking and feeling. Influenced by bourgeois ideology and feudal ideology, I could only apply the world-view, the life-outlook, and the art concepts of the petty bourgeoisie to my productions'.[22]

8. WHY DID THEY CONFESS?

It is not possible to make any sweeping generalizations regarding the motives of China's intellectuals under the Communist regime. Some beyond doubt held leftist views and were already inclined toward Marxism before the Communist victory. For them the new adjustments were perhaps not too difficult—in the beginning at least.

Then there must have been a small number of opportunists who cherished political ambitions and were eager to join the bandwagon, shouting the slogans with the greatest gusto and gladly leading in the various activities and campaigns ranging from the mass rallies and demonstrations to criticism and self-criticism in small groups. They and the leftist intellectuals have served as 'activists' among their friends and fellow intellectuals, and in official posts in the 'democratic united front' of Communists and non-Communists. It is quite possible, and not unlikely, that the years since 1949 have brought disillusionment to these two groups of intellectuals but they are so far committed that to retreat, even if they should wish to, would not be easy.

A considerable number of intellectuals are patriots eager to see the regeneration of their nation; they threw in their lot with the Communist regime because they saw in it the best chance of achieving what they had hoped for. Many had cast their lot with the Kuomintang in the late twenties and early thirties for the same reason. They would have preferred to remain politically independent, many of them found the Communist methods repellent, but to see China strong and modernized under a stable unified government the chaff was worth the corn.

For the majority of the intellectuals, to co-operate with the new rulers is not a matter of choice, but of necessity. To live in China they must accept the conditions which they cannot change. They join the mass campaigns and participate in thought reform as the only way of making their peace with a situation which may stay for quite a while. To some it must be very hard to resolve their inner conflicts and find some measure of inner peace. In doing so, a number may bring themselves to see the logic of the Marxist mode of thinking and to agree that the proletarian-socialist revolution is the only 'way out' for China. But for many others outward conformity does not necessarily mean full-hearted acceptance.

To what extent the intellectuals went through the form of ideological conversion—signing confessions, denouncing the past, and singing the praises of Chairman Mao[23]—without genuine acceptance of Communist indoctrination, it is impossible to say. Many intellectuals appear to have signed the confessions with mental reservations to temporize with those in power today. That so many confessions were considered 'lacking in thoroughness' and had to be 'improved' again and again may be taken as evidence of this. In elaborating on his past mistakes and explaining in childish detail how he had resisted 'study' and how he had opposed criticism and self-criticism as degrading, the intellectual seems to be trying to preserve a small part of his 'self' from the totalitarian rulers.

Belief that many intellectuals signed the confessions without complete surrender of their inner selves is strengthened by the developments of 1957 which will be discussed in the final chapters. If intellectuals, who from 1950 to 1956 seemed to have followed the Communist line without reservation, made such pointed criticisms of the Communist regime when given an opportunity, they could not have thrown overboard their past heritage and their established patterns of thinking as completely as their confessions would make out. On the contrary, after the bold criticisms of 1957, we have much reason to suspect that while doing everything necessary to placate the Communists and to relieve the pressure brought to bear by the thought reform and the ideological remoulding, many intellectuals were biding their time. Despite the attempt of the thought reform to probe the inner depths of their mind, they managed to keep inviolate the secret recesses of their being from which later welled the rebellion against the oppressors.

It would be a mistake to think of the thought reform of the intellectuals as similar to the brainwashing of prisoners. The confessions of prisoners or political offenders have been exacted by physical as well as mental torture. No physical torture was ever used in the thought reform of the intellectuals. We have reason to believe that the confessions neither broke the spirit nor warped the mind of the intellectuals as they did in the case of many prisoners.[24] On the contrary the evidence is that many intellectuals retained their mental alertness and their sense of moral values.

CHAPTER IX

OPERATIONAL PRINCIPLES OF THOUGHT REFORM

THE Chinese term for thought reform, *ssu-hsiang kai-tsao,* literally means the remaking or the reconstructing of thought. As 'thought' in Communist vocabulary is practically synonymous with ideology, 'thought reform' and 'ideological remoulding' are also almost synonymous. Its negative aspect has been colloquially called 'brainwashing', the cleansing the mind of non-Marxist thoughts and ideas. Thought reform is more than thought control, more than the suppression of 'erroneous ideas'. It has for a positive aim the remoulding of thought to produce new patterns of thinking.

The discussion of different phases of thought reform up to this point has already brought out such methods as group discussion, criticism and self-criticism, writing 'thought conclusions', etc. It is proposed at this juncture to summarize these methods and to list some of the principles guiding the programme of thought reform.

1. THOUGHT REFORM A 'STRUGGLE'

'Struggle' is a key concept in Communist ideology. The Marxist holds that all existences are 'complexes of opposing elements or opposing forces', and that conflicts or contradictions between the opposing elements are inevitable and produce changes. Therefore conflict and change are inherent in all existences. Conflict means struggle which, therefore, is a normal function of existence. Moreover, progress comes through struggle; to avoid struggle is to stop progress.[1]

Struggle is not a smooth and peaceful process; but often fierce and bitter, and at times violent. The 'reformists' of bourgeois society suffer from the delusion that progress can be brought about by 'peaceful reform'. The Marxist is a 'revolutionary', not a reformist; he fears not violent struggle. As Mao Tse-tung said in 1927: 'The revolution is not a dinner-party, it is not essay-writing, it is not painting a picture or making embroidery; it cannot be anything so refined, so calm and unhurried, so mild and courteous, so gentle and magnanimous. The revolution is a violent uprising, the overthrow of a class by another class by violent means'.[2]

In the land reform that swept across China, the Communists severely attacked any proposal to carry it out by peaceful means. The reform must be a bitter struggle, marked by violence and bloodshed. Some landlords had to be killed, otherwise there could be no thorough reform. Chou En-lai explained: 'No exploiting class voluntarily makes its exit from the stage of history, and the Chinese landlord class, which has a history of several thousand years, is no exception'.[3] In other words, the landlord class could be dislodged only by force, and bloodshed was unavoidable.

Thought reform is also a struggle. Reactionary thought does not easily die out, feudalistic ideologies do not just fade away; they must be uprooted and the process is often violent and painful. Ai Ssu-ch'i elucidates:

> Thought reform must be carried out through thought struggle. Anyone who is willing to learn . . . must be prepared for a strenuous struggle between his new and old ideologies. The old things in this world cannot be expected to die of themselves, they fall only under the struggle and the blows of the new. Old ideas cannot be overcome peacefully and nonchalantly. For the intellectuals who are habitually disdainful of the labouring masses, when they are now asked to befriend the workers and peasants, they are bound to go through a period of unhappiness. It would be difficult for them to change without the criticism and encouragement of people close to them and without an ideological inner-struggle of their own. Therefore, the study of Marxism-Leninism should be considered as revolutionary work in the realm of thought and a battle assignment in the realm of thought. In order to complete this revolutionary task and fulfil this [ideological] war, the skilful use of the most important weapons—criticism and self-criticism—is of impelling necessity.[4]

2. THE IDEOLOGICAL TARGETS OF ATTACK VARY

Although the broad objectives remain constant in all reform campaigns—namely, the liquidation of non-Marxist and anti-Marxist ideas and the dissolution of anti-Communist attitudes—certain ideological shortcomings have been given more prominence at a particular time or in the reform of a particular group. For example, the failure to portray the class struggle was a major charge in the reform of writers and artists, attachment to bourgeois concepts of law and justice was attacked in the reform of the lawyers and judges, idealism and anti-materialism loomed large in the reform of philosophers, and so on. One writer elaborated as follows:

> The [thought reform] movement is undertaken so as to meet the needs of people from different classes, occupations, cultural levels and so forth. The expectations for workers in natural science, engineers, doctors, technicians, therefore, are necessarily different from the courses prescribed for students of economics, political science and other social sciences.
> It is natural that the social scientists should make a profound study of Mao Tse-tung's thought and the philosophy of Marxism-Leninism. The objectives

asked of the bankers, merchants and manufacturers are obviously very
different from those asked of government workers. For instance, the immediate reaction desired from the businessmen is that they should abandon
their habitual ideas of speculation, illegitimate hoarding, manipulation of the
market, etc.[5]

3. THOUGHT REFORM MUST BE SELF-REFORM

The Communists make a fetish of voluntarism. Whether it is
enlisting for the Korean War, subscribing to state bonds or
joining the agricultural co-operatives, while pressure is exerted by
propaganda and 'persuasion', the Communists still want the
individuals to yield 'voluntarily' at the last moment. There is no
doubt that 'persuasion' often becomes mandatory in nature, but
the Communist method is to avoid direct, undisguised coercion
whenever possible. Though force or compulsion is always around
the corner, to be exerted when necessary, the preference is to resort
to different forms of persuasion, at times semi-coercive or covertly
coercive, until resistance is overcome and the victim 'chooses' to
submit. His submission can then be hailed as 'voluntary' action.
This kind of pressure is more subtle than direct, undisguised
coercion; it is less likely to arouse a violent reaction; and, furthermore, it enables the Communists to boast that they use 'democratic'
instead of dictatorial methods on the people. Mao Tse-tung was
obviously thinking along these lines when he said: 'Buddhist idols
must be thrown away by the peasants themselves; ancestral tablets
must be smashed by the peasants themselves; shrines for virtuous
women and memorial arches glorifying chastity and filial piety
must be destroyed by the peasants themselves'.[6]

The Communists leave no doubt that intellectuals must undergo
reform, but insist that the reform must be voluntary, that re-
education must be self-education. The individual must wage a
relentless struggle against his own past and set patterns of thought.
He must virtually destroy himself for a new self to be born. The
ideological conversion comes after the individual has been brought
to see how unworthy his past and how necessary a new life, with a
new outlook and a new 'standpoint'.

If action can be compelled, a person's inner thoughts cannot.
To be sure, the stage should be—and is—set in such a way that
thought deviations are subjected to prompt and sharp criticism
as soon as they are detected, but the Communists realize that the
transformation takes time and the final change from old to new
must be made by the subject himself. This is especially true of

intellectuals who are not easily shaken from their established mode of thinking. Ideological remoulding is neither accomplished overnight, nor is completed once for all. Hence the frequent rectification campaigns.

4. 'POSITIVE ELEMENTS' SET THE PACE

The most effective indirect compulsion comes from group pressure. While the original source of pressure is the Communist agitator who works behind the scenes, the immediate pressure comes from the group of which the individual is supposed to be a member. The group is the medium through which the Communist Party or the state controls the people; though the control is sure and firm, it is nevertheless indirect; and the Party can claim that the individual submits to the majority of his own group and the procedure is 'democratic'.

The groups range from the small discussion groups for political 'study' to such 'voluntary people's organizations' as the women's organizations, the trade unions, the teachers' federation, the writers' union, and so on. Within each group, a select number of 'positive elements' (also called 'progressive elements' or 'activists') are chosen as leaders who call upon their fellow members to rally to a worthy cause. These 'positive elements' may be genuinely inclined to Communism, or they may be opportunists on the bandwagon. Under the suggestions or the instructions of the Communists and their cadres, they set examples of ideological conversion or 'revolutionary action' and endeavour to create an atmosphere in which lukewarm or indifferent members feel the heat to move with the group. They are often the most articulate members of the group and are actually the voice of the Party or the state, but since they are not Party members or state officials but speak as members of their group, they help to maintain the myth of 'voluntarism' and minimize the feeling of direct Party or state control.

Thus the Three-self Movement was spearheaded by 'progressive Christians' who had adopted 'the standpoint of the people' and accepted the new regime of the People's Republic of China; and the reform of the university professors was led by 'democratic elements' from among them, who had been quick to accept the basic postulates of the New Democracy and of Marxism-Leninism. The role of these 'positive elements' in thought reform is described in the following report:

In developing our work [thought reform of professors] we must depend upon the positive elements, unite with the intermediate elements and win over the backward elements. This is because the positive elements have a steady and adequate class standpoint, and are able to analyse problems and assist others; through these people we can carry out the correct policies and Party line to the masses. In order to understand and handle correctly the ideological situation, we must depend on the positive elements for information and for reports of their investigations and to see to it that the spirit of the reform reaches each and every individual. . . .

We cannot depend on the intermediate elements as positive elements because, although they are willing to reform, their viewpoints are unstable. . . . At the present time, most of the teaching and administrative personnel are willing to become progressive and only very few are backward. At times, they are ideologically similar to the intermediate elements. We can still win over and reform the backward elements.[7]

5. THOUGHT REFORM
MUST BE CONCRETE AND SPECIFIC

To talk in generalities is not enough; to declare that one is turning a new leaf in life and to confess that one has been wrong in the past is not enough. One must confess specific offences and give concrete examples of one's reactionary ideology in the past. Personalized targets, as shown in Chapter VI, make thought reform concrete and specific. The attack on the personalized targets is directed against the specific offences of the condemned persons. In the same way, 'models' or 'heroes' are set up as personalized examples of virtue—both in thought reform and in the emulation drives in farming and industry. The good and bad characteristics must be made tangible and visible in personalized targets.

6. THE GROUP PRESSURE ON THE INDIVIDUAL

The mass meetings and the big rallies arouse the emotions and set the stage, but the real job of 'soul searching', of 'examining' one's own background and one's own thought is done in small groups, in which 'positive elements' 'help' each individual to see his past errors, to muster 'courage' to confess before his comrades, and to declare his determination to mend his ways. In this process of 'free' discussion in small groups, day in and day out, the individuals are caught off their guard and are led to reveal their inner thoughts. It is extremely difficult not to do so in the long sessions which continue until everyone comes to speak his mind. The Communists do not accept neutrality or indifference, and refusal to speak is considered as a hostile act. If there is no 'freedom of silence' in Communist China there is a *compulsory* 'freedom of speech' from which none are exempted.

The 'small group' usually consists of no more than ten or fifteen persons, and is further subdivided into 'mutual aid study groups' of three or four persons each. It may be engaged in the study of Marxist theories or in the discussion of current events or in the examination of individual 'thought conclusions' growing out of 'study'. In each and every instance, every member is given his turn to talk. The group analyses the thought of each person and 'exposes' his errors. This, it is said, is the 'democratic way'. Moreover, it is an expression of 'collective living', and to refuse to participate is to commit the offence of 'alienating one's self from the group'.

This is, in essence, the technique of criticism and self-criticism. The group criticizes the individual and helps him to criticize himself. Members criticize one another and they criticize themselves. In the name of mutual aid, they take up the task of mutual surveillance. Since some Party member or cadre is likely to be present in the group or drop in and, since everyone knows that all that happens within the group is fully reported to the authorities, anyone who opens his mouth at all has no alternative but to practise criticism and self-criticism in the approved manner. He criticizes his own past background, he relates in detail his past enslavement by bourgeois and imperialist ideology, and he is full of praise for the New Democracy and the Chinese Communist Party. Many adopt this 'line' at the beginning to keep themselves out of trouble; as time passes, by repeating the same stereotyped statements 'progressive ideas' take hold slowly under the hypnotic spell of brainwashing. Not a few experience an ideological conversion, for the duration of the 'study' period at least.

The leader of every 'mutual aid study group' makes regular reports on the 'progress of the thought struggle' of each member to the 'small group' to which the subgroup belongs. The 'small group' in turn reports through its leader to the 'central study group' for each institution or area. On appropriate occasions, the 'small groups' join in large mass meetings either to hear important speeches or reports or to participate in more formal 'discussions'.

The 'thought conclusions' which everyone submits as tangible evidence of his 'thought change', after they have been discussed and analysed in the small groups, are carefully scrutinized by the higher authorities. It is not uncommon for a person to rewrite his 'thought conclusion' six or seven times: he has not gone far enough in the denunciation of his past; sometimes, he has not yet 'completely' told the story of his failings and now must fill the gaps discovered; at other times he lacks thoroughness in criticism and self-criticism. Many cry and suffer sleepless nights before they reach satisfactory 'thought conclusions'.[8]

7. REFORM AND REVOLUTIONARY ACTION

Reference has been made to the Communist emphasis on the 'unity of thought and action' and the Communist disdain of book knowledge or what they consider to be theory unrelated to action. They maintain that change in thought must be tested and re-enforced in action, and vice versa. Thought reform, therefore, is not merely an intellectual process. The intellectuals are 'mobilized' to take up actual tasks in the revolutionary struggle, from participation in mass movements to menial projects such as scrubbing floors, washing windows, laying pavements, etc. In these tasks, so the theorists claim, the intellectuals come to appreciate the dignity of labour and to learn to work in teams and to experience the satisfaction of 'collective living'. They cease to be onlookers; they learn to discard their 'objectivity'; they become direct participants in the class struggle.

Teachers and students have been enlisted for different forms of 'service to the people' such as writing letters for soldiers in the hospital or conducting 'current affairs discussions' among peasants or workers. The government issues at different times lists of 'central tasks' which are considered most important for a given period, e.g. a week, or a month, or even longer. Examples of 'central tasks' are the celebration of the Russian October Revolution, intensified propaganda against American imperialism in Formosa, the elimination of flies, rats and such pests, the reduction of illiteracy, planting trees, patriotic parades, selling bonds, etc. The interference of such 'central tasks' with regular school work becomes so serious at times that the Communist leaders have had to curtail the political activities required of students and teachers.

Participation in labour tasks is important in another way. The Communists glorify labour and the working class. In their view, a majority of intellectuals lack experience in labour, which now becomes an important phase of the reform of intellectuals. Large numbers of intellectuals have been 'mobilized' to work on construction projects such as the Huai River in 1950–51. As early as 1949, the *Common Programme of the People's Republic of China* stipulated (Article 7) that reactionary elements 'shall be compelled to reform themselves through labour so as to become new men'. In extreme cases, intellectuals have been sentenced to long-term labour in mines, detention camps and prisons.[9]

8. REALIZATION OF INADEQUACY

It is evident that some reform measures are calculated to humiliate the intellectuals, whose education and cultural background the Communists condemn as bourgeois and feudalistic. They drum it into the ears of the intellectuals that unless they 'remake' themselves they will not be of any use to the new society. They insist that the intellectuals step down from their ivory tower and become a part of the 'masses', that they acquire the new proletarian culture from the working class.

If the confessions shatter the self-esteem of the intellectuals, it is a necessary step in their ideological conversion. If it hurts their pride to 'study' and work under the guidance of cadres with far less education, it is a part of their 'old baggage' to be discarded anyway. If it goes against the grain to talk in groups about their past without concealment and in plain direct language, they learn thereby to overcome their 'bourgeois sentimentalism and sensitivity'. They are required to humble themselves, even to vilify themselves and their family background, to denounce their past outlook and intellectual heritage, and to take up labour tasks and revolutionary activities which they had considered beneath their professional dignity. In so doing they prove that they are ready to start out as 'new men'.

9. DISCARDING INDIVIDUALISM

As long as intellectuals retain their individualism they will be independent in thought and behaviour. Individualism is therefore a central target of attack. The new way of life is the collective life. The methods of thought reform utilize group pressure. To the group the individual bares his thoughts in self-criticism and confessions. He must tell all without any reservation. He must not have any secrets.[10] Inasmuch as the 'group' is always directed by capable manipulators and the acme of group life or collective life is the Party or the state, the replacement of individualism by collectivism means in the last analysis the total surrender of the individual to the Party and the state. Once this has been accomplished, thought reform will have been complete.

CHAPTER X

THE 1955 CAMPAIGN

BY 1954 the Chinese Communists had sufficiently consolidated their power on the mainland to step up their programme of socialism. The first five-year plan was in its second year, and its success depended on increasing the state control of the economy of the land and on the dominance of state-owned enterprises over private enterprises. From the ideological point of view, the five-year plan was a major move in the direction of socialism. While in 1949 the Communists were loudly trumpeting their policy of protecting private capitalism and giving the capitalists their rightful and necessary share in the construction of a new China, the emphasis in 1954 was on a steady march toward socialism and a dwindling role for private enterprise.

The change of policy is clearly reflected in the differences between the *Common Programme* of 1949 and the *Constitution* of 1954. The concept of the New Democracy, which was of central importance in the Common Programme, merely got a passing mention in the Constitution, the keynote of which was 'the attainment of a socialist society', with the emphasis on 'the socialist transformation of agriculture, handicrafts, and capitalist industry and commerce'.[1] On July 31, 1955, Mao Tse-tung made his famous speech to order a stepped-up campaign for agricultural co-operatives. He declared: 'Throughout the Chinese countryside a new upsurge in the socialist mass movement is in sight. . . . Soon it will sweep the whole country'.[2] In a short time the whole country was talking about this 'upsurge of the socialist tide' and the Communists called for the final liquidation of capitalism and stern measures to prevent its possible rebirth either in the countryside or in the cities.

The implications for the thought-reform movement were clear. All vestiges of 'bourgeois ideology' must now be wiped out, and all obstacles in the way of the 'socialist construction' of the country removed. The Party and the state were now ready to lead the country in its steady advance toward socialism and they would brook no interference from any source. 'Socialist construction' and the 'socialist transformation' of all private enterprises demanded centralized control of the entire economy by the state and the further consolidation of political power. The purge of two top-rank

Communists, Kao Kang and Jao Shu-shih, early in 1955, was related to this consolidation of power. Orders were sent to all Party organizations to take up a thorough job of overhauling and house-cleaning so as to strengthen themselves for this all-important task of guiding the country's advance to socialism.

1. 'DREAM OF THE RED CHAMBER'

The call for the removal of all obstacles to socialism meant a renewed campaign against 'bourgeois ideology'. The methods used in 1955 were not unlike those related in Chapter VI. Personalized targets came into prominence once more. In place of the motion picture of the historical figure of Wu Hsün, a tempest raged now over the interpretation of a well-known Chinese novel written in the 18th century, *Hung Lou Meng* or the *Dream of the Red Chamber*. Since the novel was among the most popular in China and was widely read by men and women, young and old, of all walks of life, it was deemed useful for an object lesson to the literate population.[3]

The central figure in the controversy was Professor Yü P'ing-po, who was long a recognized authority on the *Dream of the Red Chamber*. He had written numerous books and monographs, all of which interpreted the novel as 'mystical, non-committal and naturalistic',[4] and not primarily a criticism of contemporary society.[5] In 1953 one of his earlier books was re-issued with minor revisions.[5] For a while, it was enthusiastically received by the reading public and was favourably accepted by other writers. This initial popularity was not unlike that which greeted the motion picture of Wu Hsün before the Communists struck.

In September and October 1954, there appeared two blistering reviews of Professor Yü's book by two young students of Chinese literature, Li Hsi-fan and Lan Ling. The major review article was published in *Wen-yi-pao* (Journal of Literature and Art) and *Kuang-ming jih-pao*, followed by a supplementary article in the former. *Wen-yi-pao* had at first rejected the original review but later reproduced it after it had been published in a Shantung University periodical. In publishing the article, both *Wen-yi-pao* and *Kuang-ming jih-pao* prefaced it with derogatory remarks to the effect that the authors were two young men whose opinions were obviously immature.[6] The authors challenged Yü's description of the nature of the novel and insisted that the *Dream of the Red Chamber* is a great work of realism, a vivid reflection of the society of 18th century China.

Li and Lan also criticized Yü's method of research. First, it was alleged that he 'attaches undue importance to textual criticism' by making it an end in itself. Secondly, he believed that 'there is no objective standard in literary criticism'. According to the young reviewers, literary criticism is an ideological weapon. In a class society, they argued, the attitude of any class toward literature depends first of all on whether or not it is beneficial to that class and whether or not it serves the political and economic interests of that class.[7] Furthermore, they said, Yü's interpretation of the novel apart from its social and historical background was an outgrowth of his 'art for art's sake' approach. By studying the novel purely as a matter of personal interest, they continued, Yü had entangled himself in isolated incidents and details and had thus failed to recognize the social tragedy portrayed by the novel.[8]

The opinions of the two reviewers were endorsed by articles in *Jen-min jih-pao*, mouthpiece of the Chinese Communist Party Central Committee. Their criticisms were hailed as 'the first valuable shot fired against the ideology and methodology of the bourgeoisie in thirty years'.[9] Thus began the campaign against 'bourgeois idealism' in literature which spread to every part of mainland China. The *Wen-yi-pao* was severely reprimanded for its editorial note which slighted Li Hsi-fan and Lan Ling as immature writers. This journal was the official organ of the China Federation of Literature and Art, edited by a group of non-Communist left-wing writers headed by Feng Hsüeh-feng. In a scathing article, *Jen-min jih-pao* accused it of taking an arrogant attitude towards young writers and of abetting the growth of bourgeois idealism.[10] Following the lead of *Jen-min jih-pao*, a joint conference, held in Peking, of the presidium of the Federation and the presidium of the Chinese Writers Union, resolved on December 8, 1954 to reorganize the *Wen-yi-pao* editorial staff; the new editors were directed to correct the past mistakes of the journal.[11]

Meanwhile, the first organized 'discussion' of Yü's interpretation of the *Dream of the Red Chamber* had been called by the Classical Literature Department of the Chinese Writers Union in Peking on October 24, 1954. Forty-nine writers and artists attended and scores of newsmen and other onlookers were also present at the meeting, which lasted seven hours. Nineteen speeches were delivered to criticize Yü's idealistic viewpoint and method of research. The presidium of the China Federation of Literature and Art and the presidium of the Union also held eight joint meetings from October 31 to December 8, 1954 to discuss Yü's approach and method in his study of the novel. The Communist press published numerous articles written by persons who participated in the meetings criticizing Yü P'ing-po. Another mass campaign against a personalized target had been launched.

The attack on Yü for his subjective and idealistic viewpoint went beyond him to condemn a better-known advocate of anti-proletarian ideology. Yü was described as a follower of Hu Shih. As one writer admitted, 'although Marxism has gained a dominant position in our intellectual life since liberation, Hu Shih's influence in the study of classical literature has remained undiminished; herein lies the seriousness of the problem'.[12]

Yü later 'confessed'. In a preliminary statement, he said: 'I started from the standpoint of personal interest and failed to grasp fully the political and ideological nature of the novel. I failed to stand on historical materialism. . . . I am grateful for the various articles criticizing me'.[13] Subsequently, he made a fuller self-criticism, of his past errors in interpreting classical literature from the bourgeois point of view and expressing his desire to 'humbly correct' his methodology.[14] By the end of 1954, the storm that raged over Yü P'ing-po and the *Dream of the Red Chamber* had blown over, and the Communists moved on to another target in the campaign.

2. RENEWED ATTACK ON HU SHIH

Since Yü's errors were traced back to Hu Shih, the attack against Hu Shih was renewed. As one writer pointed out, 'Hu's political ideology perished with old China, but his academic ideas and his pragmatism still exert considerable influence upon our intellectuals'.[15] Another added:

> The influence of Hu Shih's reactionary political, cultural and social views is manifest in our social and historical research work. His ideas lead people to discern only individual phenomena in history and society. . . .
> Hu Shih's influence has not been completely removed. . . . We must continue and persist to struggle against the imperialistic and thoroughly reactionary idealism which the imperialists are using to enslave the people of the world. . . . Hu Shih's ideology is a type of bourgeois-imperialistic ideology which in the past has sought to obstruct the Chinese people's democratic revolution and now it may again obstruct the work of socialism. Therefore to repudiate the ideology of the Hu Shih clique is still necessary.[16]

Leading the attack against Hu Shih was the joint presidium of the two literary organizations mentioned above. It was pointed out at the meetings that to criticize 'bourgeois idealism' in the study of the novel 'we must further develop all-out criticisms of the reactionary ideology of Hu Shih'.[17] Following the lead of the literary organizations, the Chinese Academy of Sciences and the Chinese Writers Union resolved jointly to convene discussion meetings to criticize Hu's political, philosophical, and historical views. From the end of December 1954 to February 1955, fifteen such meetings were held, six of which were devoted to the 'discussion' of Hu's philosophy, one to his political views, one to his *History of Chinese Philosophy*, and seven to his interpretation of the *Dream of the Red Chamber*.[18]

Subsequently, a great number of articles on Hu Shih's 'bourgeois ideology' appeared in the Chinese Communist newspapers and periodicals. *Jen-min jih-pao* in the month of January 1955 alone carried no less than ten special articles attacking Hu Shih. Later, a collection of anti-Hu Shih articles was republished in three volumes.

The campaign against Hu Shih's ideas soon spread to the universities and local literary organizations throughout the country. The Language Department of Peking University organized three discussion groups to examine Hu's works on literature. Early in 1955 the propaganda department of the Communist Party organization in Kiangsu province called a conference of representatives of all institutions of higher learning and research agencies to form a provincial organization for the critical examination of Hu's ideology. The critical study would continue for a year or a year and a half, and all newspapers and periodicals in the area were to step up their propaganda against idealism.[19]

The major criticisms of Hu Shih's ideas may be briefly summarized. One writer put him in the same class with John Dewey and Bertrand Russell as an idealist and anti-Marxist. A professor of philosophy and former colleague of Hu Shih published the following criticism:

> What Hu Shih expounded was the reactionary bourgeois idealism of imperialism, especially the reactionary pragmatism of John Dewey and William James. Therefore, to remove the prevailing malignancy caused by Hu Shih's ideology from our academic world is of major significance to the task of opposing the idealist ideology that serves modern imperialism.[20]

Another critic concentrated on Hu Shih's 'political intrigue':

> Hu Shih is a camouflaged scholar, a political intriguer, and a traitor. The influence of Hu Shih's reactionary ideology has not been eliminated, not only because prejudices of bourgeois individualism, supra-class viewpoints isolating scholarship from politics, and other idealistic viewpoints still exist among many of our scholars, but also because in the past thirty years, the

spread of Hu Shih's reactionary ideas has been intimately connected with reactionary political activities. Hu Shih is an extremely cunning and deceitful intriguer, and the spread of his reactionary ideas has been aided by his faction of academic czars. After liberation, Marxism-Leninism has grown on an unparalleled scale among our broad masses . . . but it cannot be said that bourgeois idealism is non-existent, and it cannot be said that the influence of the most pernicious faction of idealism—Hu Shih's—has been eliminated. In real life, Hu Shih's reactionary ideology is still menacing the people, and detrimental to the present task of socialist construction. Therefore, to expose Hu Shih's reactionary ideology and to purge his insidious influence from academic ranks and from society is of great realistic significance. All those who have consciously or unconsciously followed Hu Shih in the past should face the facts, should see clearly the true picture of Hu Shih, and should actively and boldly take part in the thought struggle against Hu Shih, and by dint of this struggle reform themselves and become genuine builders of socialism. Communists and Marxists, too, should learn a lesson from this struggle. We should regard the propaganda of materialism and anti-idealism among the masses as a regular battle assignment, and work incessantly to strengthen the leadership of Marxism-Leninism in the realm of thought, so as to insure the successful completion of our socialist revolution and socialist transformation.[21]

Hu Shih's baneful influence on literature was condemned because he denied the class character of literature,[22] and had led youth astray by his 'reformism', his 'formalism', and his 'individualism',[23] all of which are unforgivable ideological deviations in Communist China. He was called a 'cultural compradore imbued with the feudal ideology'.[24] His pragmatism was attacked as an unmitigated evil because 'pragmatism is anti-Marxist'.[25] But the campaign against Hu Shih subsided when a new and sensational target appeared on the horizon of the ideological war.

3. THE CASE OF HU FENG

Hu Feng, the new target, was a person whom the Communists had admitted into their inner circles. He had been a writer and editor of magazines since the early 1920's. During the Sino-Japanese war he was a member of the Left-Wing Writers' League, a Communist front organization. In 1952 he became professor at the Central Literary Research Institute and was an active member of the China Federation of Literature and Art.[26] For some time, however, there had been a feud between Hu Feng and Chou Yang, who had been vice-minister of Cultural Affairs of the Chinese Communist Government and a dominant figure in the formulation of literary policies.[27] He had on several occasions been in league with some lesser writers in an attempt to displace Chou.[28] During one of the early meetings of the presidium of the China Federation of Literature and Art in which the role of *Wen-yi-pao* in the *Hung Lou Meng* controversy was discussed, Hu Feng criticized both that journal and *Jen-min jih-pao* for supressing younger

talents, adding that the mistake of the journal was the mistake of
the entire literary front. Chou immediately seized this opportunity
to launch a severe attack on Hu, accusing him of *i.* denying the
value of Chinese classical literature, *ii.* opposing Marxism in the
disguise of anti-scholasticism, *iii.* incorrectly emphasizing what he
called 'subjective fighting spirit', and *iv.* assuming a nihilistic
attitude towards China's literary heritage.[29]

It is interesting to note that Hu Feng's views had annoyed the
authorities even before the outburst of this phase of thought
reform. He had been bold enough to challenge the official policy
on literature and had gone so far as to propose to the propaganda
department of the Central Committee of the Communist Party
that all official literary organs be replaced by a small number of
publications free from Party control and that compulsory political
'study' for writers be abolished.[30] The theoretical part of Hu
Feng's proposal argued that good writers did not need to have the
Marxist world outlook, did not have to labour among the workers,
peasants and soldiers (as demanded by Mao Tse-tung at Yenan
in 1942) and did not have to serve a political purpose.[31] He maintained that creative work is the culmination of the blending of the
'spirit' with reality, and he pointed to Balzac as an example of
how even a writer with a reactionary world outlook could produce
highly penetrating and analytical works if he was faithful to his
art and to reality.

After the initial attack against Hu Feng, writers vied with
one another in assaulting him. Numerous articles appeared in the
Communist press exposing his anti-Party intrigues. Whole pages
of *Jen-min jih-pao* were devoted to letters to the editor accusing
Hu of deviationist tendencies.[32] Mao Tun, one of the better known
writers, asserted that Hu Feng's theory was bourgeois idealism
under the cloak of Marxism, that his activities were designed to
form factions and cliques.[33] The fact that Hu Feng had for years
been accepted as a Marxist writer made his 'deviationism' more
obnoxious. Mao Tun said that Hu Feng's attitude was more
deceptive and more harmful than the ideas of Hu Shih because
'he uses the Marxist terminology'.

The publication of charges against Hu Feng brought to light the
existence of a deep rift within the ranks of Communist and left-
wing writers. The published record showed that as far back as the
war years in Chungking and even earlier Hu Feng was already
violently opposed to the official policy regarding literature and

writers, and had been criticized by Mao Tun and Kuo Mo-jo.[34] He was resentful of Party control. He spoke bitterly of 'five swords hanging over the heads of writers'; one of these swords was the demand that writers must have the 'world revolution viewpoint', and must undergo thought reform.

To gather evidence against him, *Jen-min jih-pao* issued a call for Hu Feng's friends and associates to submit personal letters which they had received from him through the years so that anti-Party and anti-Marxist ideas might be brought to light. It published excerpts from thirty-four letters on May 13, 1955, more excerpts from sixty-eight letters on May 24, and another collection of excerpts from sixty-seven letters on June 10. These showed that Hu Feng had little respect for the official Party spokesmen or for the cowardly writers who meekly accepted the dictation of Party bosses. He called the Party bosses by such contemptuous terms as 'the Mandarin Jackets',[35] 'these lord-masters', and 'the bigwigs'; sometimes he simply used 'they' or 'them'. In one letter he compared himself to an animal in a cage whose roars elicited no response at all from the spectators. In another, he told how he found it difficult to temporize with the Party bosses. He repeatedly urged his friends to keep up their fighting spirit and to resist the political pressure that threatened to kill the creative spirit of literary workers.

Rebellious as he was, Hu Feng found himself helpless against the might and fury of the Party organization. Unable to withstand the onslaught of an organized purge and mindful of the fate of such top-rank Communists as Kao Kang and Jao Shu-shih, he capitulated and finally wrote a self-confession. This was entitled 'My Self-Criticism', and began with the following words:

> In the course of the current campaign against bourgeois ideology, I began to realize my grave error. The root of my error is to mistake the revolutionary character and viewpoint of the petty bourgeoisie for those of the working class. . . . This error [led me to] neglect the viewpoint of the working class . . . in defiance of Marxism and in violation of Chairman Mao's policy on literature and art. In working style and in attitude, I for a long time rejected thought reform. . . . I lacked the spirit of self-criticism, separated myself from the masses, and scorned collective organization.[36]

Hu went on to confess that he had quoted the words of Mao Tse-tung but distorted their meaning and that he had stubbornly clung to his petty bourgeois viewpoint. Now, he declared, his eyes had been opened and he realized that all workers in literature and art must undergo thought reform and must learn to serve the people by the study of Marxism and by actual participation in the class struggle. He concluded with a pledge to reform himself under the direction of the Party and with the aid of continued criticisms by his comrades.

The directors of the purge were, however, unwilling to forgive him. They were determined both to take this chance to get rid of a foe who had been troubling them for years and to use Hu Feng as the vehicle for a needed purge in literary circles. Although his confession was written in January 1955, *Jen-min jih-pao* did not publish it till four months later. When it finally came out in the May 13 issue of the paper, it was accompanied by a long article by a former associate of Hu Feng who quoted from the thirty-four private letters to prove that Hu Feng's anti-Marxist and anti-Party activities extended over a period of twelve years. The confession itself was preceded by an editorial note explaining that the paper had purposely held up the publication of the confession in order that the readers might be able to read at the same time the irrefutable evidence contained in the article based on Hu Feng's own letters. The editor emphatically declared that the confession was unacceptable and that the attacks must continue.

Radio Peking announced on May 26, 1955 that Hu Feng had been relieved as editor of *Jen-min wen-yi* (People's Literature and Art) and as delegate to the National People's Congress.[37] He was also expelled from the Chinese Writers Union. A later report accused him of being a member of a counter-revolutionary clique which used literature and art as camouflage for criminal deeds.[38] He was also called an agent of the imperialists. In the earlier days of terrorism, a man accused of such crimes would have been given a death sentence; but in 1955 the Communists were not eager to use the drastic measures of 1951–52 which had given the new regime such a bad name, and Hu Feng was sentenced to indefinite imprisonment.

4. HU FENG ELEMENTS

The campaign against Hu Feng did not cease with the arrest of Hu Feng. After the publication of the first batch of Hu's private letters by *Jen-min jih-pao*, the campaign was extended to a nation-wide scale. The so-called Hu Feng elements or 'the counter-revolutionary clique' of Hu Feng, meaning his friends and associates all over the country, were exposed. *Jen-min jih-pao* reported that it received 11,800 letters from all over the country between May 13 and July 9, 1955, demanding appropriate action against

Hu Feng and his clique.[39] Throughout June and July, the paper devoted whole pages to these accusatory articles and letters. In the ensuing two months the campaign against Hu Feng elements followed in manner similar to previous thought reform campaigns. In Peking, it was reported, more than 200,000 people attended thousands of meetings when the second batch of Hu Feng's letters was released. After the third release of his letters, all municipal government agencies, people's organizations, the twenty-seven institutions of higher learning, and professional groups 'unanimously' demanded that the Hu Feng elements be given due punishment.[40]

In July 1955, the college students in Peking who should have been graduated in June were ordered to stay on to participate in the growing 'movement' to purge Hu Feng elements, when endless meetings were held with Communist cadres reporting on the activities of Hu Feng and clique. In 'small group' discussions followed by 'individual self-examinations', participants had to expose any 'Hu Feng tendency' they might have themselves.[41]

Among the better known 'Hu Feng elements' to be purged was Liu Hsüeh-wei, onetime head of the Literature and Art bureau of the propaganda department of the East China branch of the Communist Party. He was denounced as a follower of Hu Feng and a promoter of anti-Party activities.[42] Another was A Lung, who taught literature at Nankai University in Tientsin and other schools. He was accused of being a 'reactionary former military officer' who had infiltrated into the Communist Party through the 'Hu Feng dominated' Tientsin Federation of Literature.[43]

The Communists also started a drive against Hu Feng elements in industry, in agricultural co-operatives, and in schools and colleges. It was charged that the Hu Feng gang had not only penetrated the ranks of the Party and carried on counter-revolutionary activities within the Party organization, but was also responsible for sabotage work in the co-operatives and in the land-reform programme. A university professor, Chu Ku-huai, one of the alleged followers of Hu Feng, was accused of sabotaging the land reform in his native district in Eastern Kwangtung and of helping his family remove property to Hong Kong shortly after 'liberation' for fear of expropriation by the Communists.[44]

Thus, an individual case was again made the beginning of a general campaign to eliminate all suspected opposition, for an extensive purge of 'counter-revolutionaries' and 'class enemies'.

Institutions of higher learning were urged to clean out the Hu Feng elements in their midst; intellectuals who tried to remain aloof from politics were considered to be influenced by Hu Feng's anti-revolutionary ideology.[45] Elementary schools were ordered to ban the use of a song contained in a commonly used primary school reader because it had been written by a 'Hu Feng element'.[46]

In the Hu Feng case the Communists show the importance they attach to literature and art. Their control had not been effective as expected. Though all writers and artists seemed to be following the Party line, undercurrents of dissatisfaction and resentment existed which only then came to the surface. Hu's private letters, from which incriminating excerpts were published, date as far back as 1943, and show that the Party leadership in literary matters had been challenged by a group within the Party. The differences were not merely due to personal rivalry for power; they rose from fundamentally opposed views on the Party control of literature and art.

The objective of the anti-Hu Feng campaign to eliminate all intellectual opposition is clearly stated in two government reports of a few months later.[47] The one by Tung Pi-wu, president of the Supreme People's Court, on the liquidation of counter-revolutionaries, says:

> As we know, from 1951 to 1953 we waged a great campaign for the suppression of counter-revolutionaries. By that campaign we made a clean sweep of large groups of exposed counter-revolutionaries and dealt a crushing blow to enemies at home and abroad who conspired to undermine the democratic cause of our people. . . .
> In order to smash the activities of the remaining counter-revolutionaries and to ensure the smooth progress of the socialist revolution in our country, we began in the summer of 1955 to expose the criminal activities of the Hu Feng gang of counter-revolutionaries and then launched a nation-wide struggle to liquidate all hidden counter-revolutionaries.

The other report was by Kuo Mo-jo. Speaking of the continuous efforts to remould the intellectuals, he said:

> Large numbers of intellectuals took part in the land reform, the campaign for the supression of counter-revolutionaries, the Resist-America Aid-Korea campaign, and the gigantic 'three-anti' and 'five-anti' struggles. They observed the construction work in the factories and in the rural areas. They visited the Soviet Union and took part in different kinds of international activities. Thus they had the opportunity to accept the progressive ideology through the media of practice and observation in social life. At the same time, by means of studying Marxism-Leninism in a big way, by the systematic criticism of bourgeois idealism, and by exposing the Hu Feng counter-revolutionary clique, the intellectuals were able to recognize more clearly the difference between our outlook and that of the enemy, and to heighten their political consciousness.   (*JMJP*, Feb. 1, 1957)

5. RENEWED ATTACK ON LIANG SHU-MING

The attack against Hu Shih was followed by a fresh attack on Liang Shu-ming.[48] The first shot in the campaign was fired by philosopher Feng Yu-lan. In the *Jen-min jih-pao* on May 11, 1955, Feng cited passages from Liang's books to prove that his ideas had been consistently anti-Marxist and anti-Communist. Liang had written in 1921 *Tung hsi wen-hua chi ch'i che-hsüeh*[a] (The Culture and Philosophy of East and West) which analysed Chinese society and its basic problems. Among his later writings were *Chung-kuo min-tsu tzu-chiu yün-tung chih tsui-hou chüeh-wu*[b] (Final Conviction Concerning the Self-Salvation of the Chinese Nation), *Hsiang-ts'un chien-she li-lun*[c] (Theory of Rural Reconstruction) and *Chung-kuo wen-hua yao-yi*[d] (Essentials of Chinese Culture). According to Feng, Liang's writings showed the influence of the idealistic world-view of Buddhism and constituted a typical example of feudalistic ideology. More specifically, Feng charged that Liang had failed to appreciate the importance of class antagonism and the class struggle; by his espousal of the 'mean' and of conciliation as a way of life, he was serving the feudal rulers in their policy to stupefy the people and deprive them of the will to struggle against their oppressors. Moreover, Liang had stated in one of his writings that neither European democracy nor Soviet Communism was practicable for China, thus exposing his opposition to the proletarian revolution.

Feng Yu-lan further cited Liang's views on rural reform. Liang had once said that a better rural programme than that of the Communists was necessary. This showed, said Feng, that Liang set out to challenge Communist leadership over the peasantry with the clear purpose to replace the 'anti-landlord revolutionary peasant movement under Communist leadership' with a reactionary peasant movement supporting the landlord class. By advocating that the intelligentzia should go into the villages and become one with the peasantry, Liang was proposing the leadership of the intelligentzia and opposing Communist leadership.

Another critic well known in the West was Wu Ching-ch'ao, a prominent sociologist. His charges were in the main similar to those made by Feng—failure to recognize the importance of the

[a] 東西文化及其哲學.
[b] 中國民族自救運動之最後覺悟.
[c] 鄉村建設理論.
[d] 中國文化要義.

class struggle in Chinese society, opposition to Soviet Communism, the advocacy of a rural movement to compete with the programme of the Chinese Communist Party, and serving the interests of the landlords and the imperialists. All reactionary ideologies, said Wu, sprang from idealism, to which Liang Shu-ming's thought was no exception.[49]

An article in *Jen-min jih-pao*, August 10, 1955, attacked Liang's anti-industrialization views. The basis of the accusation was his *Theory of Rural Reconstruction*, the burden of which was that the economic reconstruction of China must begin with rural reconstruction. According to the article, although Liang said a few years back that his thinking had undergone modification since liberation and although he could no longer advocate openly his rural movement, there had actually been no basic change in his reactionary viewpoint. On recent occasions Liang had said that the peasants had suffered far too much and that it would be better to slow down the industrialization programme.[50] This charge was especially serious as at that time the Communists were frantically pushing ahead their first five-year plan.

Following these articles the Academy of Sciences and other organizations called meetings to discuss Liang Shu-ming, who was present at some of the earlier meetings. All reiterated the charges against Liang's ideas and pledged to continue the struggle.[51] From August to December 1955, numerous articles appeared in *Jen-min jih-pao* and other Communist publications on the same theme. For example:

> The reactionary nature of Liang was manifested in every stage of the revolution. . . . He was opposed to science and democracy during the May Fourth Movement. In the 1920's, he allied himself with the reactionary warlord Han Fu-ch'ü [onetime governor of Shantung, where Liang centred his rural reconstruction work] and led many young people . . . to win and reform the peasants and 'forestall the Red bandits'.[52]
> Liang Shu-ming's attacks have always been directed at Communism and Marxism and the people. Even after liberation, he was insincere in his thought reform. . . . His ideas are a combination of Buddhism, Confucianism, and Bergsonian philosophy . . . all of which are anti-Marxist.[53]

Liang Shu-ming made no attempt to defend himself at this time. Towards the end of 1955, he was sent to Kansu by Mao Tse-tung to inspect agriculture. According to Liang himself, Mao asked him four times between 1950 and 1952 to take observation trips but he had refused and in 1952 he had again declined an invitation to investigate agricultural co-operatives. Early in February 1956, after a fifty-day stay in Kansu, Liang made a 'confession' at the Second

Session of the National Committee of the People's Political Consultative Conference in Peking. A summary of his remarks follows:

i. After reading the many articles criticizing me, I realized my mistakes, but within me I still had an urge to resist.

ii. All my ideas and deeds in the past few years were wrong. (a) On the class question, I gave undue emphasis to the Chinese peculiarities; I rejected the class concept and hindered the revolution. (b) In the past I judged people by my own ideas; not to stand with the people is anti-people. (c) My reactionary past is detestable; my life in the years after liberation has been for me a process of learning.[54]

Whether this was an acceptable confession is not certain. The renewed attack on him served a useful purpose in the thought reform campaign. Whether he will again be made a target of ideological attack remains to be seen.

CHAPTER XI

THE UPSURGE OF THE SOCIALIST TIDE

THE 'upsurge of socialist tide' increased the pressure on the peasants to join co-operatives and collectives and on private business people to convert their enterprises into state-owned or at least state-directed enterprises. At the same time a positive appeal was made to all of them to undertake the 'socialist construction' of the country, to fulfil or 'over-fulfil' the first five-year plan (1953–1957), and to get ready for the second five-year plan (1958–1962).

Any plan of development for a country as vast as China requires a huge force of trained personnel: engineers, technicians, industrial and agricultural specialists, administrators and managerial personnel, teachers, doctors, scientists, cultural workers (writers and artists), *ad infinitum*. It calls for the service of all the available intellectuals in China, and many more. The Communists could not talk about this nation-wide 'socialist construction' without making plans for enlisting the service of China's intellectuals, and they had to take a fresh look at the problem. They had to face realistically the fact that many intellectuals were still unwilling to identify themselves completely with the new regime, notwithstanding six years of intensive 'ideological remoulding'. New ways of inducing the intellectuals to give their whole-hearted service had to be thought of, and new methods of thought reform devised that might prove more effective than those of the past.

The Communists were fully conscious of the existence of a widespread restlessness, a sense of frustration, and a deep-seated dissatisfaction among the intellectuals. They were realistic enough to see that unless the conditions were changed and some of the causes of dissatisfaction and restlessness removed, a large part of the plans for 'socialist construction' would remain on paper only.

1. THE PLIGHT OF THE INTELLECTUALS

The intellectuals had good reasons to feel unhappy. They no longer enjoyed the honour and prestige which had always been accorded them in China's long history. Not only had they ceased to be the favoured and highly respected class in Chinese society, but they were told that they were out-of-step with the times and had to be 'remoulded' to become acceptable by the new society.

The events since 1949 had had devastating effects on the self-respect and mental calm of the intellectuals. They were under ceaseless pressure to 'study' and to 'reform'. In their confessions they had to bow low and to renounce what they had cherished. They were made to understand that they were not only politically 'backward' and ideologically uninformed, but that even in their scholarly pursuits they had been on the wrong path. 'Foolishly' they had worshipped capitalist science and capitalist scholarship; they now had to take a new direction and to learn from the Soviet Union, study Soviet theories and use Soviet teaching materials. Many had to give up the fruits of lifetime study and research and to make a desperate attempt to acquire the vocabulary of the Soviet scholars.[1]

Some idea of the Sovietization of Chinese education may be obtained from the report that in the reorganization of higher education in 1951; of the courses offered at the University of Harbin 82·2% had almost completely adopted Soviet text-books and teaching materials and another 5% of the courses had partially adopted Soviet teaching materials. The only classes not using Soviet materials were Chinese language, Chinese history, the history of the Chinese revolution, and the policies and laws of the new regime.[2]

Soviet material was included not only in the studies of Marxism-Leninism, but in such general courses as international relations, finance, statistics, economics, bookkeeping and accounting, world history, etc. In Peking University, it was reported in 1953 that of the 230 courses offered, half had adopted Soviet materials or used them for reference purposes.[3] According to an observer in Hong Kong, ninety per cent of the faculty in this university had learned Russian in order to read Russian books.[4] Since few Chinese scholars until recently were at all familiar with Soviet education, to adapt themselves to the new system must have caused them great strain and worry.

That this Sovietization in education was of grave concern to China's intellectuals may be seen from a statement made by Ma Yin-ch'u, president of Peking University, who had gone further than most intellectuals in the acceptance of the Communist policy. Concealing his criticism in mild language, he said: 'That we must learn from the Soviet Union is, of course, an unalterable principle, but

does this mean that we have to make an exact copy of the model?' [5]
The teachers of the Chinese People's University, where the faculty
is supposed to be free from past traditions of bourgeois society,
have also voiced criticism of the pressure to 'learn from the Soviet
Union'. A report on the opening of the university contains the
following:

> Some teachers were learning from the Soviet experts on the one hand and
> teaching the students at the same time. In the most pressing period, they used
> to take what they learned from the Soviet experts one day, to lecture to the
> students the next day. Consequently . . . the mechanical adoption of Soviet
> teaching materials, methods and curricular organization became inevitable. . .[6]

How this narrow Sovietization resulted in the mechanical
conformity to political requirements and in the degradation of
academic learning was described by a well-known social scientist
as follows:

> In the early stage of educational reform, teachers went through a period of
> great tension. Because it was necessary to learn from the Soviet Union, they
> had to prepare new teaching materials. Furthermore, as a result of the thought-
> reform movement, they had to discard what they had studied, but they had
> not been able to establish a new system to take the place of the old. The task
> of rushing to produce Russian or translated syllabi kept them extremely
> busy. . . .
> Books from England and America merely took up room on the bookcases;
> they were sold as scrap paper. There was no time to study Russian, and so the
> teachers had to be satisfied with the small translated editions they could buy.
> When they wrote articles or lectured in class, all that they needed to do was
> to cite passages from the words of the approved authorities, and to pick out a
> few British or American scholars to criticize and revile. This was not difficult
> to do, and it was exactly what many scholars did.[7]

2. THE DOMINEERING CADRES

Of all the aggravating frustrations, the hardest must have been
the necessity of accepting the supervision and 'leadership' of
cadres whom the Communists trusted as progressive persons 'rich
in revolutionary experience' and well indoctrinated in the dogmas
of Marxism-Leninism, but who, in their academic achievements,
could not even qualify as students in the colleges and universities
where they held sway. These symbols of the authority of the Party
and the state not only browbeat the intellectuals in their thought
reform and political indoctrination but even told them how they
should carry on their professional activities.

The Party functionaries interfered with the research activities of
scientists. A plant pathologist engaged in research on the cause of a
plant disease was subject to long harassment because his findings
did not agree with the preconceived ideas of the officials of the
local agricultural office of the government. Not only were his

findings rejected as unsound, but he was censured for adherence to 'bourgeois theories and methods' of research. He was criticized in public meetings and his pleas for an impartial investigation of the problem went unheeded. It was not till a new policy of relaxation appeared in 1956 (see Ch. XVI) that this scientist was able to voice his grievance and finally got the government to send an investigation team of scientists who completely vindicated his views.[8] In a scientific conference in 1951, this scientist also reported, he read a paper based on his research findings, but as soon as he cited American sources, he was asked to stop without finishing his lecture. On the other hand, the report of a young Party member who based his discussion on Lysenko received official approbation.[9] Here are two quotations, which, though subdued in tone, provide clear evidence of the frustrations of the intellectuals under cadre 'leadership'. An engineer wrote as follows:

> It cannot be denied that some Party comrades still have inadequate understanding of the policy of the Party toward intellectuals. They do not understand clearly the role of the intellectuals in national construction. Some Party cadres in leadership positions do not trust technical personnel. . . . There are new Party cadres who do not understand the Party policy; they treat the high technical personnel with a wrong attitude, thus hurting their feelings.[10]

A similar complaint was voiced by a language professor.

> I feel that some of the comrades, especially those of younger age, do not have the right attitude toward intellectuals . . . Probably because they are too young, they do not know the condition of the intellectuals before liberation, and they have impractical demands and expectations of the intellectuals.[11]

Numerous instances could be cited to show what the intellectuals had to endure. Kuo Mo-jo admitted in an interview with a Bulgarian editor visiting in Peking that playwrights and painters had been put out of work because what they produced could not measure up to the requirements of the politicos, and that the studies of a scientist which would have brought much benefit to agriculture were suppressed because they did not agree with the theories of Lysenko.[12] Until 1956, Kuo frankly acknowledged, it was not permissible for anyone to criticize the theories of Lysenko.

The straight-jacket in which scholars found themselves confined was described by a professor of economics as follows:

> Since liberation, the responsible representatives of Party and state in the universities have come to evaluate the lectures given by a professor not in terms of his 'creativity' or his ability for independent scholarly research, but according to his willingness to submit to 'discipline'. 'Discipline' means that the professor lectures in class exactly according to the outline or lecture notes previously approved by the 'leadership'; he is not allowed to use any lecture material not previously approved. . . .
>
> At present, what keeps us professors most busy are the meetings and the writing of lecture notes. Especially time-consuming is the search for

'authority'. Every word and every bit of content must be based on 'authority'. The best authority is of course the words of Marx, Lenin or of some prominent official of the Party or government.[13]

He went on to say that the persons who considered themselves most authoritative on 'authority' were the young graduates from the Chinese People's University and the Institute of Marxism-Leninism. Having been schooled in Marxism-Leninism, they felt they had much to teach the older scholars. In case of any question, their standard reply, spoken with finality, was 'This is what is stated in my class notes in the Chinese People's University'.

A common complaint of the intellectuals was that they were so burdened with political tasks that they had little time and energy for their professional duties. We have already noted (Ch. IV and IX) that the Communists demand that intellectuals should take part in 'revolutionary activities' so that their thought reform may be integrated with 'revolutionary action'. This demand placed an excessive burden, especially on the teachers. Besides the inescapable duties in connection with parades, demonstrations and various mass campaigns, teachers were asked to share the office work of government agencies. In one locality, teachers had to help the local 'people's government' in compiling data, preparing reports, etc. Teachers spent their evenings in attending to such office chores, and on one occasion some teachers were summoned from their sleep at night to work on statistical tables for a government office.[14] In another district, teachers were drafted to help in grain collection work and it was necessary to suspend school for two weeks. Teachers who questioned such practices were accused of 'disobedience to the organization' and 'alienation from the masses'. The ridiculous extremes which the domineering cadres allowed themselves to go to, are well summarized in the following paragraph from an editorial of the *Teachers' Journal* in Peking:

> Some of the letters to the editor reaching us recently reported that discrimination against intellectuals still exists in some areas. This is evidenced by the unreasonable treatment of primary school teachers. Some cadres, particularly those on the district and village level, are disdainful of the labour of primary school teachers, treating them in an impetuous and unreasonable manner, sometimes embarassing and ridiculing them, even labelling them with anti-Communist epithets, defaming their personal character and jeopardizing their personal liberty. In some localities cadres of government agencies treat primary school teachers as their personal servants, bossing them around and using them at will.[15]

A specific case of this abuse of power came to light in 1956. A cadre in charge of education and culture in a district in Shantung province unreasonably chastised and persecuted the principal and dean of discipline of an elementary school who, in the eyes of their colleagues, had committed no wrong. In the name of a meeting for the purpose of 'study', the cadre convened the teachers to discuss cases of 'violation of law' and 'opposition to the government'. Much to the surprise of the teachers, he directed the charges against the principal and the dean and ordered them to be placed in custody. He had brought to the meeting a number of 'positive elements' to help create an atmosphere favourable to ruthless persecution, and for two successive days, including evening sessions, he kept up the vilification of his two victims and demanded their confessions. When the group was slow in responding, he threatened to broaden the scope of the purge and declared that since seven out of eight teachers in the school had come from the families of 'rich peasants, landlords, or counter-revolutionaries', no one could be considered free from backward and reactionary ideologies.[16]

Shut up in a cold room, the accused were driven to sign confessions. Each confessed, 'I have consistently opposed the leadership and I have hurt the unity of the group'. Other teachers were under pressure to make confessions. One who had had many years' experience in teaching said: 'I wanted to do well the work of my own class; in doing this, I committed the error of particularism'. At the close of the period, all teachers present were asked to sign a joint accusation of the principal and the dean. Those who were slow in signing were severely reprimanded. So great was the tension that more than twenty out of the fifty-odd teachers present became ill and it was reported that several teachers were afraid to speak at all for a number of days.

The accused appealed to higher authorities, and had the support of their colleagues, but their appeal got them a reprimand as another instance of 'opposition to leadership'. When after four months of delay a perfunctory investigation was made, the investigator merely upheld the action of the imperious cadre. If it had not been for the open criticism made possible by the new policy of 1956, this case would not have been known to the public. Undoubtedly, this was no isolated incident of what teachers suffered from overbearing cadres.

3. RE-EXAMINATION OF THE PROBLEM

Two factors co-operated to make necessary a re-examination of the problem of intellectuals: an urgent need for their service and the dissatisfaction of the intellectuals with the new order of things. By the end of 1955 the situation had become serious enough to call for a fresh reconsideration of policy. As a first step, word was sent to the 'democratic parties'[17] to start forum discussions on the problem of intellectuals. They were charged with two specific tasks: *i*. to find out how the intellectuals were faring, how they felt about their work, their livelihood, etc., and *ii*. how their thought reform might be raised to a higher level in the cause of 'socialist construction'.

Accordingly, the theme for the discussions sponsored by the various 'democratic parties'[18] was the 'unity and reform of the intellectuals'. A round table discussion was held by key members of the Democratic League on December 2, 1955. The central idea was that inasmuch as 'socialist construction' had given the intellectuals a new opportunity for service, the 'democratic parties' should make comprehensive investigations of the problems confronting intellectuals in order to find out 'what progress in thought reform had been made since liberation, how thought reform could be furthered and improved on, what arrangements the state should make for the intellectuals and their livelihood, and how leadership should be provided for scholarly research'.[19] It was decided that local branch organizations of the League throughout the country should carry out such investigations by means of personal interviews, informal discussions and round table conferences, and establish close contacts with individual intellectuals.

The Chiu-san Society also held discussions on the 'unity and reform of the intellectuals' in November and December 1955. It was pointed out that since the country had advanced to a new stage of socialism the intellectuals ought to take further steps in thought reform. The society decided to make thorough investigations of the conditions of work of the intellectuals and to formulate a preliminary plan of future work in order 'to assist the Communist Party and the government . . . thus fulfilling the functions of a democratic party'.[20]

Similar conferences and investigations were held by other 'democratic parties'. As in everything else, the identical pattern followed by the various parties and the same terminology used by all groups leave no doubt that the initiative for such activities came from the Communist Party.

4. THE PARTY SPEAKS

As usual, the Communist Party deferred official action until a favourable climate had been prepared for it. After the 'democratic parties' had spread the word that a fresh look was being given to 'the question of intellectuals', the Central Committee of the Communist Party called a special conference to discuss the matter. A total of 1,279 delegates from Party organizations all over the country gathered in Peking on January 14 to 20, 1956, to discuss 'the question of intellectuals'. To usher in this new phase of the Communist effort to win over and reform the intellectuals, Chou En-lai spoke. So important is his speech that we must discuss it at some length.[21]

The purpose of the conference, said Chou, was 'to strengthen the Party's leadership of intellectuals, and of scientific and cultural work as a whole'. It was a part of the effort of the Central Committee to combat 'rightist conservative ideas'. The question of intellectuals had become especially important because socialist construction could not move ahead without the intellectuals. 'We must rely . . . on the fraternal alliance of workers, peasants and intellectuals. . . . To find a correct solution for the question of intellectuals, to mobilize them more effectively and make fuller use of their abilities . . . has therefore become essential'.

As a result of the Party 'policy of uniting, educating and remoulding the intellectuals', Chou observed, 'a fundamental change has taken place among Chinese intellectuals in the past six years'. He reported that among China's higher intellectuals[22] engaged in scientific research, education, engineering, public health, cultural work, and the arts, about forty per cent now actively supported the Party and the government and 'forty per cent or so' formed an 'intermediate section' who also gave their support 'and generally complete the tasks assigned to them, but are not active politically'. 'Of the rest, over ten per cent are backward intellectuals who lack political consciousness and ideological oppose socialism, while less than ten per cent are counter-revolutionaries or other bad elements'.

If the statistics are anywhere near accurate, the Communists were indeed confronted with a grave situation, when less than one half of the intellectuals could be counted on for enthusiastic support, and even they did not fully measure up to the Communist expectations. According to Chou: 'A great many progressive intellectuals still display a greater or lesser degree of bourgeois idealism and individualism in their outlook and behaviour. This is even more true, of course, of the middle group'. In other words, the Communists had not succeeded in changing the intellectual's thought patterns after six years of indoctrination.

The Party leaders had to recognize the inadequacy of their policy; Chou admitted the existence of 'certain irrational features in our present employment and treatment of intellectuals'. These 'shortcomings' must be overcome so that the Party leadership over the intellectuals be strengthened. One shortcoming was that of putting intellectuals in wrong positions where they could not make their most useful contributions, as for instance, assigning research scientists to do administrative work in offices or schools. 'We must take firm measures to correct this bureaucratism, sectarianism and departmentalism in the treatment of intellectuals'. Another was the failure to show them appropriate confidence. Party members and Youth League members, said Chou, not only did not respect the non-Party intellectuals but considered them as outsiders with the result that 'mutual understanding is lacking' and 'a certain remoteness easily arises between us'.

The premier promised an improvement of working and living conditions: better housing conditions, more reference books and equipment, higher salaries, more rewards and incentives. Taking cognizance of the prevalent complaint of the intellectuals that too much of their time was consumed in meetings and political activities, he reported that the Central Committee had ruled that they should have 'at least five-sixths of the working day (40 hours a week) available for their work', with the rest of the time to be given to political 'study', meetings and various activities.

5. MORE IDEOLOGICAL REMOULDING

On the paramount problem of remoulding of intellectuals, Chou declared: 'The question of intellectuals, cannot be considered in isolation from the class struggle'. 'The remoulding of the intellectuals is a reflection of the class struggle'. Intellectuals must become 'Red experts' devoted to the cause of socialism, but unfortunately quite a few of them were still opposed to socialism today. . . . Chou described them as follows:

Failing to differentiate between friend and foe, between the Communist Party and the Kuomintang, between the Chinese people and imperialism, they are dissatisfied with the policies and measures of the Party and the People's Government and hanker after capitalism or even feudalism. They are hostile to the Soviet Union and unwilling to learn from her. They refuse

to study Marxism-Leninism, and sneer at it. Despising labour, the labouring
people and government workers who come from families of working people,
they refuse to mix with workers and peasants or government cadres of worker
or peasant origin. Unwilling to see the growth of new forces, they consider
progressives as opportunists, and often stir up trouble and hostility between
intellectuals and the Party as well as among intellectuals themselves. They
have enormous conceit, thinking themselves Number One in the world, and
refusing to accept anyone's leadership or criticism. Denying the interests of
the people or of society as a whole, they view everything only from their
personal interests. What is to their personal advantage they accept, what is
not to their personal advantage they oppose. Of course, there are very few
intellectuals today who have all these faults; but not a small number have one
fault or another. Even some of the middle group often hold some of the wrong
views mentioned above, let alone the backward intellectuals.[23]

The goals of remoulding were clearly stated by the premier.
The counter-revolutionaries among the intelligentzia must be
'completely weeded out'. It was hoped that by the end of the
second five-year plan (1962) the progressive group would have
been increased (from the present forty per cent) to seventy-five
per cent and the backward elements would have been reduced to
five per cent. Furthermore, more and more intellectuals should be
drawn into the Communist Party so that 'by 1962 one third of the
total number of higher intellectuals will be Party members'.

Finally, Chou En-lai called for an overall plan for the development of science and technology and for research 'not only in the
natural sciences but in social sciences as well'. He ordered 'all
cultural and educational organizations [to] draw up long-term plans
for 1956–1967 and take the most effective steps to realize them'.

CHAPTER XII

THE ROLE OF THE 'DEMOCRATIC PARTIES'

UNDER a Communist regime it is not safe to voice dissatisfaction or to register complaint unless the authorities let it be known that they, too, are dissatisfied and are ready to introduce some change. But it often happens that the authorities, having themselves decided to bring it about, encourage individuals and groups to express their criticisms and create thus a climate favourable to the change and make it appear as the response to public opinion or the 'will of the people'.

The intellectuals had hitherto suffered in silence and, in general, had refrained from voicing their discontent. But when the Party passed word to the 'democratic parties', at the end of 1955, that it was ready to listen to their woes, many intellectuals seized the opportunity to speak. Fei Hsiao-t'ung said that Chou En-lai's speech in January 1956 had cheered many scholars who felt depressed and lonely, and many had expressed the hope that the new policy in education might mean their 're-liberation'.[1] This implied that the 'liberation' of 1949 had brought shackles and not freedom.

Articles by intellectuals began to appear in the Communist press. In unmistakable terms they spoke of the difficulties arising from the inept interference of cadres or from Party directions made by persons quite unfamiliar with actual problems of education and culture. These criticisms brought to light cases not previously known—about the ridiculous applications of collectivism in universities;[2] about the confusion in schools and universities arising from the numerous political activities imposed on them; about the mechanical conformity to directives on the part of scholars, resulting in the suppression of all creativity; facts about the decline of academic standards, about a deep sense of frustration on the part of intellectuals outside as well as inside the universities, and so forth.

The emotional release brought by such open criticisms was perhaps the first concrete benefit that came to the intellectuals as a result of the modification of Communist policy. But there were other benefits, too. The Communists did not stop with the sweet words of Chou En-lai; they evidently did realize some of their own mistakes which they were set to correct.

1. LIVING AND WORKING CONDITIONS

Concrete measures were adopted to improve the living and working conditions of the intellectuals.Party organizations throughout the country were ordered to take the lead in providing them with better living quarters and better facilities for carrying out their professional activities. In Shanghai, where there were concentrated more than 10,000 higher intellectuals, the local Party organization drew up a two-year plan 'to bring out the latent strength of the intellectuals by improving the relationship between the Party and the intellectuals and by ameliorating the living and working conditions of the intellectuals'.[3] It designated 500 housing units in that city for their use. A few months later 127 more units were made available.[4] In Peking, similar action was taken by the individual universities themselves. The University of Peking and the Peking Normal University reduced the floor space for administrative purposes thereby making available 300 square metres for the living quarters of university personnel.[5]

Effort was made to place intellectuals who had not been able to find employment. For those already employed, higher salaries were ordered. Chou En-lai in his speech had attacked the concept of equalitarianism which frowned upon wide differences in wages. He recommended 'suitable adjustments in the salaries of intellectuals on the principle of remuneration according to work, so that their earnings are commensurate with their contribution to the state'. Since then, the salaries of intellectuals have been measurably raised, and those who make special contributions have been rewarded with additional allowances.[6] The increases have benefited not only the higher intellectuals, but also the elementary school teachers. It was reported that in the wage adjustments of 1956, the salaries of elementary school teachers increased by 32·88%, which was 10% more than the increase for the employees of industries and government agencies.[7]

A major complaint of the intellectuals was about time wasted by too many meetings and by the irrational distribution of the workload. In a meeting of engineers called by the Shenyang Administrative Bureau of the Ministry of the Coal Industry in July 1956, it was revealed that the key personnel of the industries in the Mukden area generally had to work 12 to 13 hours daily and one chief engineer had to work a 24-hour shift once a month and a night shift every week in addition to his regular 12 to 13 hours.[8] When on top of the heavy load were added political tasks, the burden on the intellectuals was indeed severe. Efforts were made to correct such conditions.

To insure that teaching personnel would have five-sixths of their weekly working time for professional activities, various schools in the country reduced the social and administrative chores of the faculty. This was gradually accomplished by assigning more people to share such tasks as making speeches for the school or the government and by the provision of more assistants to relieve the pressure on the professors.[9] Students were asked not to bother the professors outside the designated office hours.[10]

2. NEW PRIVILEGES

Library and research facilities were improved and expanded to aid intellectuals in their research. In July 1956 the Ministry of Cultural Affairs called a conference of library workers in Peking to discuss ways of improving library service, which was described by the conference as a mighty weapon 'in our assault on science'.[11] From December 5 to 14, 1956, another conference of library workers was sponsored by the Ministry of Higher Education. Following these conferences, many libraries in the country revised their regulations to improve their service. Extra reading rooms were added. Universities in Shanghai reported an increase of library budget by fifty to one hundred per cent.[12] Funds were set aside for the purchase of books from abroad, and catalogues of foreign publishing firms were made available to the professors. An old and hitherto little-used library in Shanghai was refurbished and reorganized into a scientific and technological library. The library was said to have a collection of more than 60,000 books and 1,800 periodicals from forty-six countries and in nineteen languages. A microfilming service was set up in the interest of scientists in other parts of the country.[13] Among other examples, Tsinghua University opened a new reading room for the faculty and stocked it with encyclopaedias in Japanese, German, English, French and Russian. The Shanghai Library of the Chinese Academy of Sciences planned to subscribe to 200 periodicals and order 3,000 books from abroad for the use of research scholars.[14]

Funds were made available for the expansion of scientific equipment and laboratory facilities. Much new equipment was ordered from abroad. The Communists were determined that China's scientists must keep abreast of the world's latest advances in science. Besides better research facilities and a less crushing load of professional and political activities, intellectuals were offered other privileges and services, including improved medical service for them and their families. Tsinghua University issued to its faculty special courtesy cards which entitled them to prompt service without delay, in the university clinic as well as in the dining room and the co-operative store. In other institutions of higher learning, faculty members were given similar privileges. The Chinese Medical College not only expanded the living quarters of its faculty but also provided additional furniture and bathrooms.[15] In January 1956, the Peking Bus Company scheduled a regular bus service on week-ends between Peking and the universities outside the city for the benefit of the professors.[16] Special buses for faculty personnel were also provided by institutions of higher learning in Chungking in co-operation with the government.[17] The University of Nanking established on the campus a 'Teachers' Home' where the faculty could relax in quietness and in pleasant surroundings, and where refreshments could be obtained at reasonable cost.[18]

In line with the new policy of making fuller use of the intellectuals, the Chinese Academy of Sciences, the Ministry of Higher Education, the Ministry of Education, the State Commission of Technology, and the newly established Experts Bureau of the State Council joined hands in a co-operative effort to provide employment for the yet unemployed intellectuals—by no means a small number. In Peking alone there were 2,321 cases known in May 1956, of whom 1,482 were university graduates. By the end of July 1956, 317 of these had been given jobs.[19] The *Jen-min jih-pao* editorial of August 12, 1956, on the employment of intellectuals said that one of the reasons for unemployment was that institutions and government offices too often had been unwilling to have anything to do with intellectuals whose political past and social background might be open to question. This, said the editorial, must be corrected if their talents were to be utilized. That they were unemployed not of their own choice is attested by the fact that on August 27, the first day for the registration of unemployed intellectuals in Peking more than 800 turned up to apply for suitable work.[20]

3. THE 'DEMOCRATIC PARTIES'

One of changes announced by Chou En-lai was the Party decision to admit to the Party a larger number of intellectuals. The class-conscious Communists have always emphasized that theirs is a class organization, the 'organized vanguard of the working class'. In view of the weakness and undeveloped state of the working class in China, the Communists found it necessary to cultivate the peasants as the 'indispensable ally' of the workers and to build up the worker-peasant alliance as the foundation of the 'people democracy'. Most of the cadres carrying out the actual tasks of the revolution were of 'worker-peasant origin', with peasants in the majority. Although provision was made for admitting into the Party 'progressive elements' from other classes, the Communists were never eager to have too many of them. From figures released by the Party in September 1956, out of the total Party membership of 10,734,384 persons, those of working-class origin constituted 14%, of peasant origin constituted 69·1% and intellectuals made up 11·7%.[21]

The Party's decision may have been forced on it by the realization that 'socialist construction' could not possibly proceed without the intellectuals. Or, it may have been inspired by a new confidence of Party leaders who felt that after six years of thought reform at least a portion of the forty per cent of 'progressive' intellectuals could be considered safe for Party membership. Moreover, the Communists wanted to forge a 'fraternal alliance of workers, peasants, and intellectuals'[22] for which a new drive was needed to induct trustworthy intellectuals into the Party.

The 'democratic parties' were entrusted with the task of organizing the intellectuals and keeping them under close watch. The regime in China has permitted the existence of eight 'political parties' besides the Communist Party. They are called 'democratic parties' partly because the existence of several political parties is claimed to be a mark of democracy, and partly because all of these minority parties subscribe to the Communist concept of 'democracy' and the Communist programme for the Chinese revolution. One of their leaders recently explained that the 'democratic parties' of China are by no means comparable to the 'opposition parties' of the capitalist countries, because their primary function is to assist the Communist Party, not to oppose it.[23] The central task of these parties today, he said, is 'to further consolidate the dictatorship of the proletariat and facilitate the advance to socialism; and we know it is impossible to realize the dictatorship of the proletariat and build socialism without the leadership of the Communist Party'.[24] There are no independent political platforms for these parties. They all accept what is proposed by the Communist Party.

Theoretically these parties recruit their members from the bourgeoisie and the petty bourgeoisie while the Communist Party remains as a proletarian Party. Actually each party is assigned a section of the population to 'mobilize' or 'educate' for service to the state under the leadership of the Communist Party. They of are briefly introduced below, with the names of officers in 1957.

i. The *Kuomintang Revolutionary Committee*. This group was organized in January 1948, by former members of the Kuomintang gathered in Hong Kong who were all opposed to Chiang Kai-shek. Its chairman and one of the original organizers is Li Chi-shen, who was one of the vice-chairmen of the People's Republic from 1949 to 1954. The late 'Christian general' Feng Yü-hsiang was a member of this group.

ii. The *China Democratic League* is an alliance of small political parties organized in 1941. The more conservative groups later left the League, abandoning it to the more or less leftist elements. Its chairman is Shen Chün-ju, another vice-chairman of the Standing Committee of the National People's Congress. Lo Lung-chi, minister of Timber Industry, and Shih Liang, minister of Justice, are vice-chairmen.

iii. The *China Democratic National Construction Association*. Organized in 1945, this group consists mainly of industrialists, business men and intellectuals engaged in industry and commerce. It has played a major role in the 'socialist remoulding' of the capitalists and in persuading them to put their enterprises under state control. Its chairman is Huang Yen-p'ei, a vice-chairman of the Standing Committee of the National People's Congress. Chang Nai-ch'i, minister of Food, and Li Chu-ch'en, minister of Food Industry (not including grain), are vice-chairmen.

iv. The *China Association for Promoting Democracy* draws its members from educational and cultural workers. Its chairman is Ma Hsü-lun, one time minister of Education. Its vice-chairmen are Chou Chien-jen, vice-minister of Higher Education, and Lin Han-ta, vice-minister of Education.

v. The *Chinese Peasants' and Workers' Democratic Party* was originally known as 'the Third Party' and was organized in protest against Chiang Kai-shek's anti-Communist purge of 1927 which ended the Kuomintang-Communist co-operation. Its chairman is Chang Po-chün, minister of Communications.

vi. Chih-kung-tang. The name of the group has a long history; it began with overseas Chinese who supported the revolution of Dr Sun Yat-sen against the Manchus. The present group in China came into being in 1947 and its mission is to appeal to Chinese abroad on behalf of the Communists. Its chairman is Ch'en Chi-yu, a member of the Standing Committee of the Chinese People's Political Consultative Conference.

vii. Chiu-san Society. Organized in 1945, this group recruits its members from intellectuals in scientific and technical fields. Its chairman is Hsü Te-heng, a member of the Standing Committee of the Chinese People's Political Consultative Conference; its vice-chairman is Liang Hsi, minister of Forestry.

viii. Taiwan Democratic Self-Government League. This very small group of persons from Taiwan agitates for the return of Taiwan to the motherland. Its chairman is Hsieh Hsüeh-hung.

The 'democratic parties' serve a very useful purpose to keep the intellectuals in line and relieve the Communist Party of too much direct pressure on the intellectuals. As the intellectuals are deeply immersed in 'bourgeois ideology' they are not acceptable to that exclusive Communist club—The Party. To leave them without any political affiliation would make control difficult. By assigning the intellectuals to the 'democratic parties' and placing these parties under the supervision of the United Front Department of the Central Committee of the Communist Party control would be easier to control them.

From the standpoint of the intellectuals the 'democratic parties' also serve a convenient purpose. Those who could not swallow *in toto* the Communist ideology and had no desire to become Communists, by joining one of the 'democratic parties', would not appear in the eyes of the Communists to be over-independent or wanting in 'political consciousness'. In joining an approved party, they could keep some mental reservations about Communism, while living among people with common interests and more or less the same cultural background, secretly sharing their misgivings and frustrations, however repressed. It is a compromise solution between becoming a Communist, for which they were not yet ready, and staying unaffiliated and open to the charge of 'isolation from the masses'.

The 'democratic parties' are also supposed to serve as 'feeders' or 'testing ground' for future Communists in the same manner in which the Youth organizations prepare 'progressive elements' and 'activists' for future membership in the Communist Party. The parties are instructed to watch the record of their members in thought reform and in 'revolutionary activities'. Those who have shown enthusiasm are given a closer look to see whether they can possibly advance further up the ideological scale and eventually become worthy of consideration as candidates for the Communist Party.

4. MORE INTELLECTUALS TO ENTER THE PARTY

In November, 1955, nation-wide publicity was given to the induction of two intellectuals into the Party. One was 65-year old Liu Hsien-chou, an engineer of high reputation and the vice-president of Tsinghua University. The other was 66-year old Ou-yang Yü-ch'ien, a well-known playwright and president of the Chinese College of Drama. Both, it was declared, had benefited so much from 'the education of the Party' that they had finally reached an ideological level high enough for Party membership.[25]

The personal testimony of Liu Hsien-chou sheds an interesting light on how an intellectual gave satisfactory evidence of his ideological conversion. He told how he benefited from the thought reform of 1952 and how he was shocked and broke into tears when he heard the news of Stalin's death on March 5, 1953.[26] He deeply mourned the 'irreparable' loss of 'Stalin, the great teacher of mankind' and 'the leader who had at heart the welfare of entire mankind'. Nevertheless, he continued, there were still old habits and old thoughts which he had not got rid of, and he could not yet qualify for Party membership. By more 'study', however, he succeeded in raising his political consciousness, until on March 6, 1954, the first anniversary of Stalin's death, when he was seized again with the emotions of the previous year, and he decided that the time had come for him to apply to the Party for membership. He was formally initiated on a most auspicious day, the '38th anniversary of the great socialist October Revolution'.

The desire to bring intellectuals into the Party gained momentum in the spring of 1956. An editorial of the *Jen-min jih-pao* of March 21, 1956, titled 'Do well our membership drive among intellectuals' declared that the strengthening of Party leadership in the education

of intellectuals should go hand in hand with the drive for membership among them. Although some intellectuals still had serious
shortcomings in thought and in 'working style'[27] and others from
the 'complicated background' of landlord or capitalist families or
of past political affiliation could not for the moment qualify for
membership, the editorial urged that the Party should be patient
with them, try to educate and help them in overcoming their faults
so that they might one day measure up to the standards of Party
membership. These high standards must still be maintained,
warned the editorial, and that is why the work of 'cultivating,
educating and investigating' is of crucial importance.

In January and February 1956, 110 intellectuals in Shanghai
were admitted into the Party. They consisted of 'experts, scholars,
writers, artists and engineers who had made great contributions in
teaching, scientific research, engineering technique, and cultural
and artistic pursuits'.[28] The membership drive was especially
active in the universities. Much publicity was given to the fact that
professors, deans, presidents and vice-presidents had led the way.
Successful drives were reported from all parts of the country. In
the first three months of 1956, 114 intellectuals in Sian joined the
Party, 228 professors in Changchun, 198 professors, engineers,
physicians, and scientists in Nanking, and so on.[29] From the faculty
and staff of Futan University in Shanghai came 84 new Party
members in February alone.[30] In the first half of 1956, 300 higher
intellectuals joined the Party in Peking and Shanghai[31] and the
total for the country was reported to be 2,592.[32]

Among those who joined the Party in the spring of 1956 was
Yang Chung-chien, a palaeozoologist who was the head of a department of the Academy of Sciences. His article 'I want to live up to
the glorious title of Communist Party member' tells an interesting
story which may reflect the experience of some of the others.
Although he had opposed Communism, he said, he had been a
person of no political consciousness who chose to pursue science
for its own sake, and it took quite an 'inner struggle' for him to
decide to apply for membership in the Communist Party.[33] His
conversion began with the thought reform, which made clear to
him the great superiority of socialism over capitalism. He did not
apply for membership, however, because he was still weighted
down by the bourgeois ideology and the idealism which he had
carried over from the old society; knowing his own shortcomings
and the very high standards held up by the Party, he was afraid he

would never qualify. It was Premier Chou's January speech that gave him new courage and new determination, which was later re-enforced by reports of many intellectuals deciding to become Party members. He asked himself 'Why should I be satisfied with being a progressive intellectual instead of striving to become a Red expert?' He was grateful to the Party for its 'concern and education' and for accepting his application. 'I look upon my day of admission into the Party', he said, 'as the beginning of a new page in the history of my life'.

5. THE INTELLECTUAL QUOTA

The large-scale admission of intellectuals into the Party was not without its problems. As in all other matters in the Communist state, the directive from above was given to the local functionaries and cadres to carry out and these political workers were often carried away by their simple-minded enthusiasm. Whenever there was a drive, the lower echelons of Party workers always strained to 'fulfil or over-fulfil the quotas' to avoid reprimand for inaction. Their main concern was to report success in terms of statistics. This happened also in the drive for Party membership among intellectuals.

An amusing instance was reported in a letter to the editor published by *Jen-min jih-pao* on May 29, 1956. It said that on March 11 the Party branch of a factory in the city of Hengyang received a message from the Party organization of the city instructing the branch to get ready for the administration of the membership oath to two engineers of factory in a formal ceremony to be held on March 14. The local branch was caught by surprise; they had not investigated either candidate and one of the two had not even applied for admission to the Party. This was reported to the city Party organization, but the latter insisted that the two engineers must be inducted on March 14. The secretary of the local branch had no alternative but to persuade the man who had not yet applied to make an application at once and to submit an autobiography according to the usual procedure. On the afternoon of March 13, a meeting of the local branch was convened to pass on the application. In view of the order from the city organization, the application was granted without much discussion. According to the letter, this was not a lone case of careless admission of intellectuals without due investigation. When publishing it, the editor of *JMJP* again gave warning that the membership drive among intellectuals should not result in lowering the standards for admission and that no one should be accepted for membership until the Party organization had fully investigated and educated the prospective candidate over a long period of time.[34]

Reports of this nature, however, make one wonder how many of the intellectuals joined the Communist Party as a result of the drive without ideological conversion and how many had been herded into mass initiation for the statistical record.

6. INTELLECTUALS ABROAD

The drive for enlisting the services of intellectuals was extended to the Chinese intellectuals residing abroad. Their families and relatives in China were asked to write to persuade them to return to the fatherland and take part in the 'glorious tasks of national construction'. A special effort was made to effect the return of Chinese students, especially scientists and engineers, who were residing in the United States after finishing their studies. The demand for the 'release' of Chinese intellectuals 'detained' in the United States played a prominent role in the negotiations between the U.S.A. and Chinese Communist representatives which opened in Geneva in the summer of 1955. At the same time, families of Chinese intellectuals 'detained' in America were encouraged to write open letters demanding that the U.S. government 'return' to them their loved ones.

In an appeal to Chinese intellectuals abroad to return home, Kuo Mo-jo spoke as follows:

> There are nearly 10,000 Chinese scientists and students working or studying in the United States, Britain, France, Japan and other countries whom we regard as precious to us. Most of them have mastered specialized knowledge of quite a high level. In the past six years or more, over a thousand have returned and are all making a contribution in scientific research, industry, agriculture, education, culture and other fields. The country and the people have high regard for them and our motherland has an enthusiastic welcome waiting for the nearly 10,000 others and look forward to their early return. We would like them to be able to use their specialized knowledge and technique in the work of construction which is rapidly growing on an increasing scale.[35]

Intellectuals from abroad were offered attractive terms of service: high salaries (in terms of current wage standards in China), housing, medical and holiday privileges, high positions, and improved research facilities. Intellectuals in Hong Kong and Macao were assured that they would receive on the mainland the same amount of money they were getting abroad; they were even promised the privilege of keeping their families in Macao and Hong Kong if they so desired.[36] The government in Kwangtung province established a special Employment Committee to solicit and process applications from intellectuals in Macao, Hong Kong, and Southeast Asian countries.[37] At the same time Chinese intellectuals abroad were encouraged to come on a visit; they were promised no difficulty would be made in granting exit permits if they should decide to get out again.

7. THE TWELVE-YEAR PLAN

Before coming to the next phase of the new Communist policy, mention should be made of the twelve-year plan for the promotion of education, culture and research. Chou En-lai had in his speech ordered all educational and cultural organizations to make such plans. In a special session of the Supreme State Conference held in January 1956 to discuss a twelve-year plan of agricultural development, Mao Tse-tung also emphasized this when he said: 'Our people must have a long-range plan aiming to rectify, within a few decades, our backwardness in economic, cultural and scientific development, in order to reach quickly the highest level attained by other nations of the world'.[38]

Accordingly, scholars, professors, scientists and other intellectuals began to formulate twelve-year plans. Under the stimulus of the Scientific Planning Committee (set up by the State Council and headed by vice-premier Ch'en Yi) and—of course—the guidance of Soviet scientists, almost a thousand scientists were reported to have taken part in making plans. These were assembled to form a 'draft outline of a long-range plan for the development of science in 1956–1967', which was submitted to the Scientific Planning Committee for consideration and revision.[39] The plan dealt with the most urgent areas of study and research, the expansion of equipment and other material facilities, the training of promising young students in order to produce a large crop of modern scientists, etc.

Out of 57 projects proposed by the scientists, the Scientific Planning Committee selected twelve for special consideration. These include the peaceful use of atomic energy, new techniques in radio engineering and electronics, jet propulsion, prospecting for petroleum and other urgently needed resources, construction works along the Yellow and Yangtze Rivers, and the 'chemicalization, mechanization and electrification of agriculture'.[40]

Conferences were held throughout 1956 to discuss the twelve-year plan. The sciences were given major emphasis, but the social sciences and humanities were not left out. The Scientific Planning Committee called on scholars in these fields to contribute their ideas for a 'draft of the 1956–1957 plan for philosophy and social sciences'. To a conference to discuss this were invited university professors and research scholars in philosophy, economics, law, international relations, history, archaeology, education, linguistics, literature, art, library science, etc.[41] Among the specific tasks selected as of particular importance were the application of Marxism-Leninism to the socialist construction and practical problems of China, research on Chinese history, the struggle against bourgeois ideology and idealism, etc. Scholars were asked to publish research papers and text-books to aid study and research in these fields. For example, a group of historians were asked to co-operate in writing a history of Chinese literature in nine volumes and to try to complete the work by October 1957.[42] To guide the scholars in their writing, the editorial committee in charge of the project laid down certain principles, among which were the need for an accurate portrayal of the contradictions and struggles in the development of literature, and adequate inclusion of the literary achievements of 'fraternal states'.[43]

Other projects, large and small, were co-ordinated under an overall plan of a 'grand march toward science', *hsiang k'o-hsüeh chin-chün*.[44] By February 1957, it was reported that the faculties in twenty-two institutions of higher learning had submitted more than 3,000 individual projects. In Nanking University, 80% of the professors, 67% of the lecturers and 50% of the assistants had joined this 'grand march'.[45] The government appropriated large sums of money for scientific research. In a report to the National People's Congress on June 27, 1957, Chou En-lai said: 'An atomic reactor of the heavy water type with a power put of 7,000 kilowatts and a cyclotron producing alpha particles with 25 million electronic volts energy is being rapidly built in our country with Soviet help'.[46]

The Communists are making a genuine effort to raise the level of cultural and scientific achievements in China. Their dream of 'socialist construction' would come to naught without marked and speedy progress in science and culture. The success of this vast programme hinges on the enthusiastic support of the intellectuals.

CHAPTER XIII

'LET A HUNDRED SCHOOLS CONTEND'

THE most sensational slogan which grew out of the new Communist policy toward intellectuals in 1956 was: 'Let a hundred flowers blossom together; let a hundred schools (of thought) contend together' *(pai-hua ch'i-fang, pai-chia cheng-ming^a)*. For six years no one in China had been allowed to talk about any other school of thought besides Marxism-Leninism, except in vitriolic words of condemnation. This policy of suppression would now be replaced by one of 'free and open discussion'. The term 'hundred schools of thought' in the past described the 'classical age of China', from about the sixth century to the third century B.C., when scholars were free to think and to propose plans for social, economic and political betterment; and there was a mushroom growth of different schools which got to be known later as Taoism, Confucianism, Mohism and Legalism. 'Hundred' is merely the Chinese way of saying numerous. This is the period of China's intellectual history Chinese scholars have always been proud of. That the 'hundred schools' could freely 'contend to be heard' seemed to promise a return to freedom of thought and tolerance dear to the Chinese intellectual.

Mao Tse-tung is credited with the first use of the slogan in his address to the Supreme State Conference on May 2, 1956, but the text of Mao's address has not been published. The purpose of the new policy was partially revealed by Ch'ien Chün-jui, former vice-minister of Education and then deputy director of the second office of the State Council. In speaking at the Advanced Producers' Representatives Conference on May 9, 1956, on the need of raising the level of cultural and scientific achievements in China, he said:

> To raise the level of our science and technology, we must, in matters of scholarship, thoroughly carry out the policy of free discussion and 'letting a hundred schools contend'. We not only must learn the advanced scientific techniques of the Soviet Union and the people's democracies, but we must also learn the advanced scientific techniques of the capitalist countries, especially those of the United States, Britain and France. If there is any scientific or technical knowledge that can be applied to our socialist construction, we must make a business of studying it, no matter what country it comes from. Of course, the Soviet Union is our Big Brother and we must first of all learn from the Soviet Union. This must be firm and not open to question.[1]

---

^a 百花齊放, 百家爭鳴。

1. NEW FREEDOM

The intellectuals had by this time learned to be cautious in accepting Communist slogans, and neither the report of Mao's speech nor Ch'ien Chün-jui's speech drew any pronounced reactions. Evidently to impress upon the intellectuals that some relaxation of the rigid control on thought and scholarship was intended, Kuo Mo-jo, president of the Academy of Sciences, called a meeting of leading intellectuals in Peking on May 26, 1956 and asked Lu Ting-yi, director of the Propaganda Department of the Central Committee of the Chinese Communist Party, to make a full statement on the new policy. 'The meeting was attended by scientists, social scientists, physicians, writers and artists, among whom were members of the Communist Party as well as friends of the democratic parties and those who do not belong to any political party.[2]

The title of Lu's address was 'Let a hundred flowers blossom, let a hundred schools contend'. After tracing its origin to Mao's speech at the Supreme State Conference, Lu explained that the basic reason for the new policy was to promote the 'luxuriant development of literature, art and science'. To allow a hundred flowers to blossom and a hundred schools to contend meant 'freedom of independent thinking, freedom of debate, freedom of creative work, freedom to criticize, to express and maintain one's own views' in literature, art and scientific research. This broad statement, however, he qualified with a lengthy explanation that the new policy differed from that of China's classical age and from the freedom of the capitalist countries. In the age of the 'hundred schools' in the sixth to the third centuries B.C. he said, 'conditions were very different from those of today. Society was then in turmoil and the various schools of thought contended with one another spontaneously and with no conscious and unified leadership. Moreover, the thinkers of the earlier age had not grasped the importance of the class struggle'. He justified the attack on Hu Feng in the realm of literature and Hu Shih in the field of philosophy, and reiterated the Communist dictum that 'literature, art and science are, after all, weapons in the class struggle'. The class struggle was present even in scientific work, because although science itself had no class character, yet scientists had their political viewpoint. When scientists of former days blindly worshipped the United States or maintained that they had no political interest and pursued science for its own sake, they needed criticism and 'this criticism is a reflection of the class struggle'.

Lu warned that the freedom advocated by the capitalist countries could have no place in China today. Freedom in the capitalist countries was limited to a minority; the labouring people had no freedom. In the United States the Rosenbergs were put to death for advocating world peace. 'We, on the other hand, do not permit freedom to the counter-revolutionary elements; we must exercise dictatorship over them. But we have democracy and freedom for the people. This is a political demarcation line; we must draw a clear political line between friend and foe'.

The freedom for 'contending schools' was, therefore, a freedom for the 'people'[3] to be exercised 'within the ranks of the people themselves'. Even for the people, the amount of freedom to be granted had to be commensurate with the success of keeping things under government control. 'In the degree that the people's political power is consolidated, the freedom of the people will be increased'. The new freedom did not apply to all matters; it applied only to certain points of difference within the people themselves. There could exist no difference of opinion, said Lu, in the love of father-land and the support of socialism; on these major issues all people should be in agreement and there could be no debate. But ideo-logical differences between materialism and idealism did exist; these contradictions reflected the contradictions between classes in society which had not yet become classless, and they might be openly discussed in an 'ideological struggle'. As dialectical materi-alists, Lu said, the Communists were of course opposed to idealism and there could be no doubt on that point. They made a clear distinction between an ideological struggle among the people and the struggle against counter-revolutionaries; only to the former was the new policy or 'contending schools' to be allowed.

In announcing the new policy of 'contending schools' the Communists had not for a moment relinquished the ideological supremacy of Marxism-Leninism, nor did they concede the survival of idealism and non-Marxist ideologies. Instead of relax-ing their 'ideological struggle' they were proposing a new method of struggle; they were forced to this by a realization that the old methods of thought reform had not been successful. As Lu candidly admitted, the counter-revolutionary elements could be suppressed and wiped out but 'ideological questions cannot be settled by ad-ministrative orders. . . . Only through open debate can materialism overcome idealism step by step'. This was the essence of the new 'freedom' of blossoming and contending; people with non-Marxist ideas were to be encouraged to come out into the open so that their views might be 'discussed' and their errors shown, to the end that Marxism-Leninism would triumph over all other ideologies.

Lu made it clear that the new 'freedom' was a new phase of the continuing 'ideological struggle' and no reversal of policy. The 'freedom' to blossom and contend was only possible, he said, because the country had won a 'decisive victory in socialist transformation', because internal enemies have been subdued, and because thought reform had already produced 'a fundamental change in the political outlook of the intellectuals'. He lauded the recent campaigns against Hu Feng, Hu Shih and Liang Shu-ming, for they had paved the ground for the new 'freedom'. If there were still places where such reactionary ideas had not been completely eliminated, the campaign against them must continue and 'must not stop halfway'.

To permit the 'hundred flowers' and 'hundred schools', said the propaganda chief, was 'a policy to strengthen unity'. He distinguished between two kinds of unity; the unity that comes from mechanical obedience and the unity based on conscious and voluntary agreement; the latter was wanted, and the 'freedom' now offered was a means of attaining it. He asked the intellectuals to study once more Mao's previous pronouncements on ideological remoulding: that literature and art must 'praise the workers, peasants and soldiers'; they must 'raise the new society and the positive people' just as they must 'criticize the old society and the hostile people'. Within the limits of these guiding principles, there was much leeway and 'freedom' in the choice of subject matter. His long address concluded with specific instructions:

> We must learn from the Soviet Union, from the people's democracies, and from the peoples of all countries. To learn from the Soviet . . . this is a correct watchword. We have learned a little, but much remains to be learned. The Soviet Union is the first socialist state of the world, the leader of the world camp of peace and democracy. It has the highest state of industrial development. . . . In many important branches of science it has caught up with and surpassed the most advanced capitalist countries. . . . Not to learn from the Soviet Union would be fundamentally wrong.
>
> But . . . our method of learning must not be mechanical imitation in a doctrinaire manner. We must integrate what we learn with the actual conditions of our country. . . .
>
> People in other countries will continue to live and make progress. . . . We must critically study all their good points. . . .

We must also learn from our enemies—not their reactionary systems, but what is worthwhile in their methods of management and their scientific techniques. The purpose of our learning is to speed up our socialist construction. . . .

Party members must learn from people outside the Party. . . . Many intellectuals . . . are not Party members . . . Party members must learn from them.

2. SUBSEQUENT POLICY DISCUSSIONS

The intellectuals were asked to express their reactions to Lu's speech in forum discussions or in articles for publication in newspapers and periodicals. The forum discussions were sponsored by the Scientific Planning Committee of the State Council, by the Academy of Sciences, and by the 'democratic parties'. Since the new policy most directly concerned the members of the 'democratic parties', the Democratic League and the Chiu-san Society were particularly active in stimulating discussions of the scope and practical significance of the new policy.

Generally speaking, there were two sides to the new policy. One side emphasized the new freedom granted to intellectuals in their scholarly pursuits and in ideological discussions. The other side laid stress on the qualifying aspects of the 'hundred schools' policy: socialism and the supremacy of the Party and state were not matters for 'contending' and the ideological struggle was to continue. The new freedom was not granted to counter-revolutionary elements, and no counter-revolutionary would be permitted to operate under the pretext of 'contending'.

The intellectuals were mixed in their reactions. In the numerous discussions held in 1956, all praised the new policy but many asked probing questions to find out its scope and practical significance. Some spoke with real enthusiasm, some with guarded caution, and others were eager to take advantage of the new flexibility to advance their scholarly pursuits in ways not hitherto possible.

The questions raised reflected their concern with the actual application of 'contending' to their work. Did everybody have the right to contend? Did one have to belong to a 'school' in order to 'contend'? Was Marxism-Leninism now to be considered as one of the contending schools, or was it *the* school above all contending schools? Were the 'free discussions' permitted to crititicize all schools, including Marxism-Leninism, or should their purpose be to expose the inadequacies of all other schools in order to set forth 'rationally and voluntarily' the superiority and 'absolute truth' of Marxism-Leninism?

How much criticism would be permitted? Were there other forbidden subjects besides socialism and the leadership of the Communist Party? Where did one draw a line of demarcation between the permissible criticisms of a 'contender' and the reactionary thoughts of a counter-revolutionary? What assurance was there that in participating in 'free discussion' a person was not exposing himself to the charge of holding counter-revolutionary ideas?

Differing views were expressed. For example, in regard to idealism, some maintained that since Marxism-Leninism had been accepted as the ideological basis of the new society, none should be permitted to present the idealist's point of view. Others, however, argued that to deprive the idealists of the right to speak would be to deny the right to 'contend'; furthermore, there would be no chance of showing the superiority of Marxism-Leninism without comparing it with idealism, so the discussion of idealism should be encouraged in order to strengthen the ideological convictions of Marxists.

It is interesting to note that in these questions, the leaders of the 'democratic parties' and the non-Communist government officials tended to be more cautious and to put more emphasis on the qualifying factors than the official Communist spokesmen. In the direction of liberalization they may have feared to advocate something not intended by the Communists; they considered it safer to emphasize the importance to safeguard the Marxist-Leninist supremacy. Kuo Mo-jo, for example, maintained that even in the contending of diverse schools, scholars 'must master Marxism-Leninism as a tried weapon in the quest for truth'. 'Since the aim of all our academic work is to find better ways of building a socialist society, we need to study Marxism-Leninism and learn better ways of applying it to conditions in China'.[4] The contending schools represented a form of 'socialist emulation'. It was not enough for the schools to contend, he said; the important thing was for them to contend 'properly'. He stressed the 'struggle' aspect of contending. 'We must criticize any ideology opposed to socialist construction—this is what we mean by struggle'.[5] Kuo also compared the contending schools to the various instruments of an orchestra. He said:

> The motif of 'letting a hundred schools contend' is socialist construction and eventual advance to communism.
> We have to build our orchestra around this motif, and play symphonies of unprecedented grandeur. Let ten thousand instruments play singly or in

unison, but they all must play according to the music. We want to 'contend' but we must not do so in confusion.

For this reason, to learn Marxism-Leninism and to learn from the advanced experience of the Soviet Union is still the keypoint of our work. . . . While we let all schools 'contend', we still have to carry out our tasks according to plans and this is no contradiction. When all instruments play the same music, there is emulation; when they play different music, there is even more emulation.

We not only 'contend'; we must contend properly and contend in such a way as to advance socialist construction. If you contend in confusion or beat the instruments any way you want to, then other people will simply cover their ears or even ask you to leave the concert hall.[6]

Lo Lung-chi, the Democratic League leader who a year later was to overstep the boundary line and to be denounced as a 'Rightist' to be muzzled, took pains to stand on the safe side in the early days of the discussion. Although he praised the new policy, saying that it should dispel the misgivings of the intellectuals and enable the state to make fuller use of their abilities, he repeated Lu's statement that the contending should be done by 'the people within their own ranks' and not disrupt the unity of the people. The contenders, he said, should be guided by 'common aims, common goals and a common future'.[7] Contending should be based on 'mutual aid and co-operation'. He also used the simile of the instruments of an orchestra.

The *Kuang-ming jih-pao*, which claimed to speak for the 'democratic parties', reflected this cautious attitude in an editorial on May 23, 1956. 'It is clear', it said, 'that there is no room here for idealism to contest materialism. It is necessary to hold firmly to the viewpoint of dialectical materialism'. Free discussions in matters of scholarship, it continued, should still hold 'Marxism-Leninism as the guiding ideology'.

While the non-Communists in responsible positions found it wise to dwell on the qualifying conditions of contending, the official Communist spokesmen, aware of the scepticism of the intellectuals, tended to stress the liberalizing aspects of the new policy to allay their fears and dispel their doubts, and to convince them that the new policy really meant greater freedom than before. The *Jen-min jih-pao* devoted a front-page editorial to discuss the 'doubts and misgivings' of the many scholars.[8] The right to contend, the authoritative voice of the Party said, should put no restrictions on the contender or demand that he represent a 'school' of thought, or that the contending voices should 'harmonize' like the instruments of an orchestra or follow the baton of the conductor, or even that they should contend 'properly'.

Since to contend is not the same thing as singing in chorus, there are bound to be discordant notes. All the various schools of thought must compose their own pieces of music, not play the music required by any one conductor. As long as the music one plays is not counter-revolutionary in tune, one is free to contend. . . . Those who represent a school, as well as those who do not, the 'bigwigs' and the 'small potatoes'—indeed anyone who has studied things seriously and whose views are well grounded and well reasoned, may contend. They are welcome if they contend well; if not, it really doesn't matter.[9]

On the question whether the policy of contending schools should apply to the classroom, the intellectuals were not agreed among themselves. Some argued that the discussion of diverse schools of thought should be permitted only for mature scholars engaged in research, while others maintained that teaching would be seriously hampered if students were not made aware of the existence of diverse schools.[10] The president of the Northeast College of Geology categorically stated that college teachers should lecture according to the course outlines approved by the government and they had no business to talk about other things in the classroom.[11] Again, the *Jen-min jih-pao* stood on the liberal side. 'It is permissible', it said, 'to include different opinions in lectures . . . to help students develop the aptitude for independent thinking'.[12]

In taking a seemingly liberal position, the *Jen-min jih-pao* was merely trying to carry out the Party policy of winning over the intellectuals, of encouraging and reassuring them. Even then, it did not quite forget the qualifying aspects of the policy. While it advocated that 'people still have the right to express their views even though they do not choose to apply the method of dialectical materialism, or come to conclusions which are at variance with Marxism', the *JMJP* hastened to add that this contending should never result in ideological confusion: 'Our academic controversy is based on political unity. . . . There is no question that Marxism is the leader of thought in the academic and cultural world. This is a settled question, a matter of fact. Marxism is always the compass the Party uses in guiding our work both in academic studies and culture'.[13]

The intellectuals, of course, hoped that the liberal aspects of the policy would outweigh the restrictive qualifications. Since none cared to challenge directly an official spokesman of the Party, they directed their criticisms to persons like Kuo Mo-jo and Lo Lung-chi. They argued that the simile of orchestral music was misleading. The president of Szechwan University said, 'Harmony is important in symphonic music, but it is impossible in any real contending of diverse schools'.[14] A historian said: 'After reading

Kuo Mo-jo's statement, none would dare attempt any contending'. Apart from those who were extremely cautious by nature or those who wanted to be on the right side politically, the intellectuals in general were against too many limitations on the freedom to contend.

3. SOME PRACTICAL CONSEQUENCES

The Party had realized that progress in 'socialist construction' required a broader approach than the past regimentation. With the death of Stalin, changes within the Soviet Union had hastened the process. Lysenko had been dethroned. Soviet leaders were now talking of the need to study capitalist science. But it was significant that the main public speech on the 'hundred flowers' and 'contending schools' was made by the propaganda head of the Party and not by the minister of Education or some other government official.

The new policy did make some significant changes in the life of the intellectuals. Coercion was abandoned in favour of persuasion. If idealism was still opposed and condemned, its followers were not treated as harshly as before.

The narrow blinkers of learning from the Soviet Union were widened by the recognition that there is even something to be had from the capitalist countries. This broader scope of study and research was especially noticeable in the sciences. But even social scientists, philosophers, playwrights, artists and other non-scientist intellectuals were able to breathe somewhat more freely, and voiced their long suppressed grievances and discontent. They openly criticized the mechanical copying of Soviet models and the blind acceptance of Soviet theories. They pointed out the detrimental effects of regimentation on education and culture. They condemned the loss of initiative and creativity on the part of teachers and students alike, when the teachers read mechanically from approved notes and students thoughtlessly copied the very notes of the teachers to the last punctuation mark.[15]

The year 1956 was one of considerable intellectual activity in China. There were more open criticisms than at any time since 1949. In forum discussions, participants ventured to express independent views instead of repeating the party line and the officially approved cliches as they had done for six weary years. The twelve-year plan in education and culture had encouraged more proposals and more publications. New literary magazines made their appearance. With better living and working conditions, and with the promise of a greater flexibility in their professional activities, the intellectuals of China were more encouraged than they had been for years. A professor of philosophy spoke of 'a healthy intellectual ferment' as a result of the new policy. He reported: 'Publishing houses, besides publishing large numbers of Marxist-Leninist classics, are putting out a stream of books on science and philosophy (including the classics of Western philosophy) both ancient and modern, foreign and Chinese, written from many viewpoints. Peking University is providing new courses on the philosophy of Kant, Hegel and Bertrand Russell . . . the economic theories of Keynes, etc.'[16]

In the field of drama, the effects of the new policy were described by a playwright as follows:

Before the announcement of the policy of permitting a hundred flowers to blossom, the repertoire of some dramatic troupes had been reduced to three plays. [Since the new policy] more than 10,000 traditional plays were unearthed in Fukien province and around 500 were given public performance. . . . Literary workers acclaim this as the final liberation since Liberation.[17] In Szechwan province there also appeared many plays which no one dared bring out into the open until the new policy.[18]

CHAPTER XIV

MAO TSE-TUNG SPEAKS

1. ON CONTRADICTION

ON February 27, 1957, Mao Tse-tung made an important address at a meeting of the Supreme State Conference. Its full text was not made public for some months, but quotations and excerpts appeared in the Communist press and publications. It was known that he had spoken on the general topic of contradictions in Chinese society during the period of transition to socialism. Until the full text was released and subsequent events made clearer the intent of the address, what he said was held to be much newer and more startling than it actually was. Some thought that Communist China had inaugurated a new era of freedom and tolerance which would mean a Chinese brand of Communism more humane and more reasonable than the Soviet. Others saw a new exposition of Marxist theory which constituted a strong bid for ideological leadership in the Communist world. Those who hoped for signs of 'Chinese Titoism' believed that at long last Mao Tse-tung had come openly to a parting of ways with the Kremlin. This belief was especially strong among the Poles, who wished to get the ideological backing of the Chinese in their advocacy of 'national Communism'. They interpreted the 'hundred flowers' policy 'as an approval for Poland's effort to achieve independence from the Soviet Union'.[1] They saw in Mao's ideas on contradictions 'an important revision of Marxist ideology'[2] which could 'rock the Communist block to its foundations'.[3]

In fact, the speech was not a startlingly new development. 'Contradiction' and 'struggle' are key concepts of Marxism, as we have already said (page 72). Twenty years earlier, in 1937, Mao had made a systematic exposition of the concept of contradiction. In February 1957 he was merely repeating himself and applying the old formula to later conditions. He proposed the formula 'criticism—unity—criticism' as a means of resolving contradictions, and this became a prominent slogan in the rectification campaign which followed by his speech.

Observers not familiar with Chinese Communist history referred to the formula as if it contained a new element. But in his speech Mao plainly stated that the method had been in use by the

Party since 1927, that the phrasing of the formula came in the 1942 'rectification campaign' and that 'during the Anti-Japanese war this method was used much more purposely'.[4] It may therefore be instructive to quote a few key passages from his 1937 treatise *On Contradiction*.[5] In the opening two sentences comes the basic idea of 'criticism—unity—criticism'.

> The law of contradictions in things, that is, the law of the unity of opposites, is the most basic law in materialist dialectics. Lenin said: 'In its proper meaning, dialectics is the study of the contradiction within the very essence of things'.

Quoting Engels and Lenin on the 'universality of contradiction', Mao said, 'There is nothing that does not contain contradiction; without contradiction there would be no world' (p. 12). The Communist Party could not be free of contraditions, either. 'If in the Party there were neither contradictions nor ideological struggles to solve them, the Party's life would come to an end' (p. 14). Progress, in the Marxist view, came through the process of struggle, of solving contradictions. There was unity in contradiction, theorized Mao, because, as Lenin had taught, 'opposites can transform themselves into each other and become identical', and identity meant unity.

> Contradiction and struggle are universal, absolute, but the methods for solving contradictions, that is, the forms of struggle, differ according to the nature of the contradictions. Some contradictions are characterized by open antagonism, some are not (p. 67).

He went on to say that ideological contradictions within the Party are non-antagonistic in nature, but they may develop to become antagonistic.

> The history of the Communist Party of the Soviet Union shows us that the contradiction between the correct ideology of Lenin and Stalin and the erroneous ideologies of Trotsky, Bukharin and others, was in the beginning not yet manifested in an antagonistic form, but subsequently developed into antagonism. . . . At present the contradiction between the correct ideology and the erroneous ideologies in our Party is not manifested in an antagonistic form, and, if comrades who have committed mistakes can correct them, it will not develop into antagonism. . . But if those people who have committed mistakes persist in them and increase the gravity of their mistakes, then it is possible that such contradictions will develop into antagonism (p. 68).

His essay *On Contradiction* ends with another quotation from Lenin, 'Under Socialism, antagonism disappears, but contradiction exists' (p. 69).

2. IN THE PERIOD OF TRANSITION

In 1952 the Central Committee of the Chinese Communist Party declared that the revolution in China had reached the stage of building a socialist society. In January 1953, the first five-year plan was launched. The Constitution of 1954 called for the 'socialist transformation of agriculture, handicrafts and capitalist industry and commerce'. By 1956, the Communists noted with satisfaction that farming had in the main been organized into co-operatives or collectives, that private industry and commerce had been 'transformed' into state or semi-state enterprises, that capitalism was definitely on its way out, and that China was entering a new era of 'socialist construction'.

The important ideological question now arose: whether or not class contradictions still existed in the current stage of the revolution and whether the class struggle should still continue. Discussion of this question appeared frequently in Chinese Communist publications in the latter part of 1956. That it was debated in public forums as well as articles published in newspapers leaves no doubt that the discussion was authorized by the Party.

The specific question discussed in the latter part of 1956 was whether or not after the 'socialist transformation' of private enterprises there still existed class contradictions between the bourgeoisie and the working class, and, if so, whether these remaining contradictions were antagonistic in nature. This was not a purely academic question, because its answer would determine the nature of the 'struggle' to be waged against the bourgeoisie. If there were no more contradictions, there would be no further need of a 'bitter class struggle'. If there were remaining contradictions but they were non-antagonistic in nature, it would be possible to 'resolve' them by 'peaceful methods of struggle', namely, by 'persuasion' and 'education'. If, however, the contradictions were antagonistic, then they would be contradictions between the working class and its enemy, and more drastic, even violent, methods of struggle would be in order.

A mere listing of the titles of some of the articles and reports published in newspapers in 1956 will give some idea of the attention given to this question of contradictions.

'Are the contradictions between the national bourgeoisie and the working class in our country today antagonistic in nature?'—*Ta-kung-pao*, Peking, September 8, 1956.

'The transformation of the class relations in the period of transition in our country.'—*Ta-kung-pao*, Peking, September 16, 1956.

'Has there been any change in the nature of class contradictions today?'—*Ta-kung-pao*, Peking, October 6, 1956.

'The form of struggle and the nature of contradictions between classes in China today.'—*Ta-kung-pao*, Peking, October 13, 1956.

'A tentative discussion of the nature of contradictions between the proletariat and the bourgeoisie of our country in the period of transition.'— *Jen-
min jih-pao*, September 7, 1956.

'On Antagonism.'—*Jen-min jih-pao*, September 13, 1956.

'The antagonistic contradictions between the working class and the
bourgeoisie in our country are being eliminated.'—*Jen-min jih-pao*, September
14, 1956.

'Do contradictions between materialism and idealism continue to exist in
Communist society?'—*Jen-min jih-pao*, November 17, 1956.

'The contradictions between the working class and the national bourgeoisie
in our country do not have a dual character.'—*Kuang-ming jih-pao*, December
12, 1956.

All these writers followed the leading ideas set forth by Mao in
1937 in his treatise *On Contradiction*. All started from the premises
that contradictions are either antagonistic or non-antagonistic and
that one kind of contradiction may in time become the other kind.
They also accepted the current Party line on the dual character of
the Chinese bourgeoisie, its positive side and its negative side. The
question, then, was to what extent the positive side of the bourgeoisie
had increased and to what extent its negative side had diminished.
If its positive character was dominant, the non-antagonistic nature
of the class struggle between the working class and the bourgeoisie
would outweigh its antagonistic characteristics.

In a forum organized by the Institute of Philosophical Research
of the Academy of Sciences in which more than a hundred scholars
took part, the topic of the discussion was 'The nature of the
contradictions between the national bourgeoisie and the working
class'. While some participants maintained that the contradictions
were still antagonistic, others held that the positive side of the dual
nature of the bourgeoisie had been so strengthened since the high
tide of socialism that the contradictions had become non-antagonistic. Ai Ssu-ch'i, a high priest among the thought reformers,
expressed the view that antagonistic contradictions still remained
but 'we have adopted the policy of peaceful reform' toward the
national bourgeoisie.[6]

Members of the 'democratic parties' were naturally much
interested in this question. A forum on 'The question of evaluating
the Chinese national bourgeoisie at the present time' was sponsored
by the Chinese Democratic National Construction Association,
whose members were in large part industrialists, business people
and intellectuals engaged in industry and commerce. They admitted the dual character of their own class; its positive side was in its
support of the People's Democratic Dictatorship and its negative
side stood for profit and habitual exploiting of the working class.

The positive side progressively was becoming stronger and the negative side steadily receding. Although much of the surviving 'bourgeois ideology and working-style' remained to be overcome, they contended that after the transformation of private enterprises into enterprises jointly operated by the state and the capitalists a 'fundamental change' had taken place in the production process of the bourgeoisie and consequently the major contradictions had already been resolved.[7]

The way was now prepared for Mao's speech of February 27, 1957. The pros and cons were presented by different speakers and writers, but no one was in a position to say the final word. The Communist Party itself had not yet given out the official line on this question; it remained for Mao to make the final pronouncement by bringing up-to-date his 1937 exposition *On Contradiction* and applying it to the new conditions of 1956–1957.

In recent years, Mao had more and more freed himself from the routine of governmental affairs or the day-to-day execution of policy. He had assumed the role of a Head of State who intervenes at critical moments when important issues are at stake. This he did in his famous speech on agricultural co-operation on July 31, 1955. For some months, a debate had been going on among the Communist leaders concerning the speed of agricultural co-operation. Some advocated a policy of pushing ahead while others favoured caution to avoid the peasant opposition. Mao threw his weight on the side of speeding. Then, also, publication of the text of Mao's speech was withheld for a few months; not until October 11, 1955 did the Central Committee of the Communist Party publish a full statement of policy in line with Mao's ideas.

We find a comparable situation in regard to the 'hundred schools' policy. Although Chou En-lai announced a new policy towards the intellectuals on January 14, 1956, no mention was made of the idea of 'contending schools' until Mao's pronouncement at the Supreme State Conference on May 2, four months later. After Lu Ting-yi's fuller statement of May 26 on the 'hundred schools' policy, the intellectuals began to voice their criticism of past repressions and discuss ideas outside the strict Party line.

The new freedom of the intellectuals did not sit well with the orthodox-minded elements within the Party, who felt that the intellectuals were going too far and that the ideological basis of socialism was being endangered by a revival of bourgeois ideas. An example of their opposition to the new policy appeared in an article written jointly by five members of the Party and published in *Jen-min jih-pao* on January 7, 1957. Their criticism was specifically against writers and artists who were abandoning the 'narrow' scope of portraying the life and activities of workers, peasants and soldiers for 'broader subject-matter'. 'During the past year', they bewailed, 'fewer and fewer people advocate that literature and art should serve the workers, peasants and soldiers, and that social realism should be the method of producing literature and art. . . . Some people now say that socialist realism is not the only method of creative writing . . . others even go so far as to say that socialist realism is not necessarily correct'. The five authors blamed the policy of the 'hundred flowers' and 'hundred schools' for 'the increase of satirical writings full of discontent and despair'. They said:

> What has been the result? Some writers now no longer dare write to reflect the grave political struggles of today. A vast amount of stories based on family affairs, love and romance and adventure have taken the place of portrayals of epoch-making social reforms, of earth-shaking struggles for liberation, of heroic figures who win the peoples' respect and inspire them to follow their examples. Consequently, the fighting spirit of literature and art has been weakened, the face of our era has become blurred and its voice muffled. The splendour of socialist construction is darkened in the mirror of literature and art.   *JMJP*, Jan. 7, 1957

The airing of such views in the official organ of the Communist Party is evidence of powerful backing. Opposition within the Party to the new policy also appeared in the monthly journal devoted to ideological questions, *Hsüeh-hsi* (Study), in which on February 18, 1957, Ch'en Yi wrote: 'We cannot permit on our soil any propaganda inimical to socialist construction'. Some literary works, he maintained, had no 'educational value' and should not be allowed to 'blossom'. The 'leadership' of the Party was indispensable and in some cases 'interference' was necessary to stop unhealthy literary works being produced.

These reactions within the Party did not escape the notice of the intellectuals, who from the beginning had been more or less sceptical of the 'free discussion' permitted by the 'contending schools' policy. The *Jen-min jih-pao* article had aroused a good deal of discussion. Many feared that if emphasis were given to the viewpoint of the five writers it would nullify the 'contending schools' policy. One writer said that such attacks on the new policy were like cold water thrown on the newly aroused hopes of the intellectuals.[8]

The reactions of the intellectuals must have caused concern among the Communist leaders who were anxious to recruit them more fully for the tasks of 'socialist construction'. If the new inducements offered in 1956 failed to attract, the whole programme to recruit would be endangered. Something had to be done to reassure the intellectuals. Mao decided to step into the picture.

Mao's speech silenced, for the moment at least, the critics of the 'contending schools' policy. The *Jen-min jih-pao* swung around to support the leader of the Party; it published in March two articles expressing disagreement with the five writers. One was by Mao Tun, the well-known novelist and minister of Culture in the Communist government, who warned that petty-bourgeois influence in literature could not be wiped out by returning to the methods of suppression and doctrinairism.[9] On April 4, the *Jen-min jih-pao* published a summary of articles from newspapers in various cities on the viewpoint of the five writers. On April 10, it came out with an editorial bluntly condemning their views as 'an extreme distortion of facts'.

Under the title 'Continue to let go, thoroughly implement the policy of letting the hundred flowers blossom and the hundred schools contend', the editorial frankly admitted that 'quite a few comrades within the Party' were opposed to the policy of the 'contending schools'. It censured them as guilty of 'anti-Marxist doctrinairism and sectarianism'. The policy of 'hundred flowers' and 'hundred schools', it declared, would help the development of Marxism and was in no way contradictory to the indisputable 'ideological leadership of Marxism'; for 'it is a basic historical fact that our country is a socialist state led by the working class . . . and Marxism, the ideology which guides the socialist construction of the working class, must inevitably assume a position of leadership in the realm of thought'.

If in his speech of February 27 Mao Tse-tung sought primarily to alleviate the misgivings of the intellectuals, he must have been influenced also by some other factors. The restlessness among the intellectuals had spread to other sections of the population. Students, who in the earlier years of the regime seemed to have responded enthusiastically to its call for service and for active participation in the revolution, were now restive under the rigid regimentation of Communist thought and behaviour. They disliked being assigned to studies, to jobs, and to places of work without reference to their personal desires and plans. They objected to an education with an inflexible prescription of studies, with the compulsory political, social and athletic activities, and with the

fixed schedule which specified, to the last minute, the amount of
time a student was to spend in 'self-study' for each subject, and the
exact time he must begin and stop.[10] After a few years of quiescence,
student disturbances and student strikes again began to appear on
the Chinese scene.

Even more disturbing to the Communists must have been the
signs of peasant unrest. They had depended on the peasants as
the chief ally of the working class in China's proletarian revolution;
and they had been proud of what they considered signal success in
organizing the peasants into co-operatives and collectives. But the
co-operatives were not functioning smoothly and the peasants
disliked having to give up the land they had acquired through the
land reform only a short time ago. The peasants were not co-operat-
ing to meet the production quotas; many even lost interest in
farming, deserted their farms and drifted to the cities, creating a
new problem of unemployed migrants in the urban areas. It must
be remembered that although the Chinese Communists call themselves the vanguard of the working class, they realized that no
revolution in China can succeed without the support of the
peasants, who are China's 'masses'. Widespread peasant discontent
was something they could not afford to ignore.

The general political and economic unrest in China was accen-
tuated by a shortage of consumer goods. The five-year plan had
given top priority to the development of heavy industry; and
Communist propaganda had told the people that they must
further tighten their belts for the sake of a 'glorious future'. This
was beginning to sound hollow in the midst of severe privations
and daily hardships. Worst of all, there was a general shortage of
food. While grain and oil bearing crops were exported to serve
political ends or in exchange for machinery,[11] people were starving
at home and even the lowly *hua-sheng*, or peanut, was no longer
available in the people's market.[12] This food shortage was accen-
tuated by disastrous floods.[13] The pinch of food may have been a
reason for the nation-wide campaign for birth control and deferred
marriages; it may explain, partially at least, why the Communists
recently issued exit permits more readily for Hong Kong or other
places.

The workers themselves, supposedly the mainstay of the
proletarian revolution, were showing signs of discontent. The
Communist leaders talked much of 'labour discipline' and complained that too many workers had been 'lax' and had not worked

as hard and as enthusiastically as they ought to. Production was lagging and the workers were not fully awake to their responsibilities. Taking advantage of the opportunity for open criticisms in 1956, many reports and 'letters to editors' appeared in the Communist press to complain of labour conditions and the acute housing needs of the working class. The workers' discontent showed itself in absenteeism and other forms of passive resistance, in strikes and even open riots.[14]

If the Communists had closed their eyes to such unpleasant realities on the Chinese mainland, the Hungarian revolt must have opened them to the danger of widespread discontent even in a country where the Communist methods of control were supposed to have suppressed all 'counter-revolutionaries'. Mao Tse-tung referred more than once in his speech to the 'Hungarian events' and their echoes in China. With discontent spreading among the intellectuals, the students, the peasants, the workers, and in the general population, unless something was done to rectify the situation and to release to some extent the mounting pressure of repressed disgruntling, the Chinese Communists began to realize they might find themselves in a crisis not unlike the Hungarian uprising.

3. THE 27TH OF FEBRUARY 1957

Mao on February 27, 1957 at the session of the Supreme State Conference spoke to an audience of 1,800 people.[15] His title was 'The correct handling of contradictions among the people'. What he proposed was not so much a new approach but a change of approach in handling the unchanging policy of the Party. He spoke on the same subject a few days later, March 12, at a National Conference convened by the Propaganda Department of the Party's Central Committee.

In brief, Mao tried to do two things: first, to recognize the realities of widespread discontent and internal conflicts which had now come out so open that they could not be ignored any more; and, secondly, to show how these difficulties must be met by methods other than undisguised suppression and hard punishment. In the Communist view, they arose from conflicts, or, to use the Communist terminology, contradictions. The two basic questions then, were (i) what were the contradictions, and (ii) how to deal with them.

The contradictions, Mao said, were tensions growing out of the class differences, chief among which were the 'contradictions between the working class and the peasantry on the one hand, and the intelligentzia, on the other' and the 'contradiction between the working class and the national bourgeoisie'.[16] To translate these words into non-Communist language, we may substitute the words 'Communist Party' for 'working class' or 'alliance between workers and peasants'. The 'contradictions', then, were the conflicts between the Communists and the intelligentzia, and those between the Communists and the bourgeoisie. They were manifest in the resistance of the intelligentzia and the bourgeoisie to the Marxist remoulding that had been imposed on them.

But class conflicts were not the only source of tensions in Chinese Communist society. Mao recognized that apart from the contradictions between classes, there existed tensions within each class. So he spoke of 'contradictions within the working class, contradictions within the peasantry, contradictions within the intelligentzia . . . contradictions within the national bourgeoisie, and so forth'.

Moreover, Mao admitted, there was a wide gulf between the people and government in the 'people's democracy'. People did not yet identify themselves with the state or the collective group. They resented the new bureaucrats and the overbearing cadres. Mao described such conditions as 'contradictions between the government and the masses'; 'these included contradictions between the interests of the state, collective interests, and individual interests; between democracy and centralism; between those in positions of leadership and the led; and contradictions arising from the bureaucratic practices of certain state functionaries in their relations with the masses'.

It could not be denied that the state did not have the full support of the people. 'While the broad masses of the people weclome the new system they are not yet quite accustomed to it'. There was opposition to the co-operatives. 'Some things did go wrong', in the organization of co-operatives, but 'the movement on the whole is healthy'. 'Yet some people have stirred up a miniature typhoon. They are complaining that co-operative farming will not do, that it has no superior qualities'. Actually, 'only a very small minority are really dissatisfied. But quite a number of persons have failed to analyse the situation.' Unfortunately, the shortcomings could not be immediately overcome; 'this will probably take five years or a bit longer'. Here is a passage from the speech which is candid not only in the acknowledgement of troubles but also in the admission of fault.

In 1956, small numbers of workers and students in certain places went on strike. The immediate cause of these disturbances was the failure to satisfy certain of their demands for material benefits, of which some should and could be met, while others were out of place or excessive and therefore could not be met for the time being. But a more important cause was bureaucracy on the part of those in positions of leadership. In some cases, responsibility for such bureaucratic mistakes should be placed on the higher authorities, and those at lower levels should not be made to bear all the blame.

It was necessary to take warning of such expressions of popular dissatisfaction because the 'lesson of the Hungarian events deserves our attention'. The 'Hungarian events' had had their effect in China; they had 'caused some of our intellectuals to lose their balance a bit'. Moreover, 'certain people in our country were delighted when the Hungarian events took place. They hoped that something similar would happen in China, that thousands upon thousands of people would demonstrate in the streets against the People's Government'.

To forestall such a possibility, it was necessary to deal wisely with the existing contradictions. Would the harsh methods of suppression eliminate the contradictions? Mao did not think so. To justify his position, he drew on his old ideas on contradiction and again distinguished between two types of contradictions which needed different handling. 'We are confronted by two types of social contradictions: contradictions between ourselves and the enemy and contradictions among the people. These two types of contradictions are totally different in nature.'

Who were the 'people' and who were the 'enemies'? Mao gave a clear answer. 'At this stage of building socialism, all classes, strata, and social groups that approve, support and work for the cause of socialist construction belong to the category of the people, while those social forces and groups that resist the socialist revolution and are hostile to and try to wreck socialist construction are enemies of the people.' In plainer words, all who supported the programme of the Communist Party were the 'people' and any 'contradictions' arising from them were non-antagonistic in nature and could be dealt with by mild methods; but all those who resisted the Communist programme had to be considered as enemies and suppressed as ruthlessly as before.[17] 'After liberation, we rooted out a number of counter-revolutionaries. Some were sentenced to death. . . . This was absolutely necessary; it was the demand of the people'.[18] To be sure 'mistakes have been made' and 'there were excesses in some cases and in other cases counter-revolutionaries were overlooked'. Such mistakes should be avoided in the future, but 'we must . . . not pour cold water on the large number of functionaries and activists who took part in the work [of suppressing counter-revolutionaries]. It is not right to dampen their spirits'. It would be folly, even today, to relax the vigilance. 'Even when all the counter-revolutionaries in existence have been rooted out, new ones may emerge. If we drop our guard, we shall be badly fooled and suffer for it severely. Whenever counter-revolutionaries are found making trouble, they should be rooted out with a firm hand'.

As long as a person accepted socialism and supported the programme of the Communist Party (including its efforts to remould his thought and ideological outlook) he was not to be considered an 'enemy' even though he might be critical and dissatisfied. He was one of the 'people'. It was here that the new policy of moderation was to be applied and the method of coercion and indiscriminate suppression avoided in favour of 'democratic methods of discussion, of criticism, of persuasion and education'. Contradictions arising 'within the ranks of the people', however, did not spring from any opposition to basic policies, because all the 'people' accepted socialism and supported the Communist Party. This is what Mao meant when he said, 'Underlying the contradictions among the people is the basic identity of the interests of the people'.

4. THE INTELLECTUALS

Naturally, Mao devoted an important part of what he said to the 'question of the intellectuals'. The basic policy remained unchanged. 'They must *continue to remould themselves*, gradually shed their bourgeois world outlook and acquire a *proletarian, Communist world outlook* so that they can fully meet the needs of the new society and closely unite with the workers and peasants'.[19] The question was how to accomplish this. Past methods of thought reform had not been altogether successful; a modification of methods was now necessary. The new method was that of 'letting a hundred flowers blossom and letting a hundred schools contend'. Since many intellectuals had not yet embraced Marxism, there remained contradictions between them and the working class, but these contradictions were non-antagonistic in nature as long as no one came out in opposition to socialism. A long-term ideological struggle was necessary before Marxism became generally accepted. This struggle 'will still be long and devious and at times may even become very acute'.

This struggle, however, should not be carried on by 'crude coercive methods'. It called for 'the method of painstaking reasoning'. 'Any attempt to deal with ideological matters or questions involving the distinction between right and wrong by administrative orders or coercive measures will not only be ineffective but harmful. We cannot abolish religion by administrative orders; nor can we force people not to believe in it. We cannot compel people to give up idealism, any more than we can force them to believe in Marxism.' Wrong ideas, of course, must be combated. But ideas cannot be changed by edict. 'You may ban the expression of wrong ideas, but the ideas will still be there. Wrong ideas must be brought into the open and changed by the "methods of discussion, criticism and reasoning".'

The new policy was dictated by hard realism and not moved by sentimental ideas about freedom and democracy. 'Democracy . . . is only a means'. Bourgeois concepts of freedom and democracy could not be tolerated. What was advocated was 'freedom with leadership' and 'democracy under centralized guidance'. Everything must be under control. People must realize that 'they have to keep themselves within the bounds of socialist discipline'. Those who trespass the prescribed bounds were counter-revolutionaries and 'we simply deprive them of the freedom of speech'. There were limits to the 'flowers' and 'schools' that were permitted to flourish.

The central purpose was 'to make our new system secure and build up our new state'. To encourage the 'hundred schools' was to bring out the non-Marxist ideas for criticism and reasoning and show the superiority of Marxism. Marxism was not merely one of the contending schools, it was *the* correct ideology that all must study and eventually accept. 'Both students and intellectuals should study hard . . . they should study Marxism-Leninism, current events and political affairs in order to progress ideologically and politically'.

The 'hundred flowers' did not really mean flowers of all kinds. A distinction had to be made between 'fragrant flowers' and 'poisonous weeds'. Needless to say, the weeds must be uprooted, but they were hard to detect as long as they lay concealed beneath the surface. The better strategy was to allow them to come into the open to be identified and rooted out. How did one distinguish between 'fragrant flowers' and 'poisonous weeds'? Mao suggested six criteria. Words and actions were good, he said, if they:

> *i.* help to unite the people of our various nationalities, and do not divide them; *ii.* are beneficial, not harmful, to socialist transformation and socialist construction; *iii.* help to consolidate, not undermine or weaken, the people's democratic dictatorship; *iv.* help to consolidate, not undermine or weaken, democratic centralism; *v.* tend to strengthen, not to cast off or weaken, the leadership of the Communist Party; *vi.* are beneficial, not harmful, to international socialist solidarity of the peace-loving peoples of the world.

The last was given further emphasis at the end of Mao's long address. He was speaking of 'China's path to industrialization'. 'In order to transform our country into an industrial power, we must learn from the advanced experience of the Soviet Union'. He saw no contradiction between this reliance on the Soviet Union and the new 'hundred schools' policy. 'It is perfectly true that we should learn from the good experience of all countries, socialist or capitalist, but the main thing is still to learn from the Soviet Union'. This policy of 'indestructible friendship' with the Soviet Union, specifically stipulated in the preamble of the Constitution of Communist China, was re-affirmed in the concluding paragraph of Mao's speech: 'To strengthen our solidarity with the Soviet Union, to strengthen our solidarity with all socialist countries— this is our fundamental policy'.

CHAPTER XV

THE RECTIFICATION CAMPAIGN

MAO'S speech revealed the undercurrent dissatisfaction in Communist China and the danger of an explosion of pent-up resentment similar to the Hungarian revolt. The naked methods of suppression and the past methods of thought reform had not been successful; more effective corrective measures had to be found.

Briefly speaking, the corrective methods adopted in 1956–1957 fell under three general categories: (i) the improvement of living conditions, for the masses as well as for the intellectuals; (ii) a rectification campaign within the Party to correct 'leadership errors'; and (iii) a re-affirmation of the 'blossom and contend policy' to permit criticism and thereby some release of pent-up emotions.

1. IMPROVEMENT OF LIVING CONDITIONS

The Party had been telling the people that the central aim of all effort must be to industrialize China, to increase production, and to build for a bright future. It emphasized that all must be ready to sacrifice the present for the future and that the duty of all patriotic citizens was to tighten their belts and forego the luxuries and comforts of life in the hard work of fulfilling the state plans. The first five-year plan gave priority to heavy industry and paid secondary attention to light industry and agriculture. This policy was re-affirmed in the proposed second five-year plan submitted to the Eighth National Congress of the Communist Party in September, 1956.

After the uprisings in Poland and Hungary, the Party decided to make some concessions to the demand of the people for an amelioration of their miserable living conditions. As a major source of widespread discontent was the scarcity of consumers' goods, it was necessary to modify the policy of heavy industrialization in order to give more attention to light industry.

The relative importance of heavy versus light industry or industrialization versus consumers' goods had been the topic of numerous articles in Communist newspapers. As late as November 27, 1956, the *Jen-min jih-pao* still stood by the policy of unequivocal priority to heavy industry and of sacrificing the present for the future. It editorialized as follows:

> Since the improvement of living conditions can only come gradually, the present-day difficulties cannot be quickly overcome. Such conditions as crowded housing, crowded tramcars, and insufficiency of meat and edible oil cannot be eliminated right away. After a few years, our production will be increased, and the foundation of our economy will be more secure, but even then it will be possible to raise the standard of living by gradual degrees only. . . . One thing we must know: at any given time, the standard of living cannot possibly be raised more quickly than the rate of production.

But, alarmed by what happened in Eastern Europe, the Central Committee of the Chinese Communist Party finally deemed it wise to modify its policy and ordered a revision of the proposed second five-year plan and to give more attention to light industry. The *Jen-min jih-pao* reflected the new position in an article on December 7, 1956, in which the author stressed the importance of paying due regard to the people's livelihood problems and pointed out the fallacy of 'absolute' priority of heavy industry. He said that past thinking on economic development had been 'enslaved' by the theory that since heavy industry was the foundation of better livelihood, an all-out effort must be made to develop it as quickly as possible. He warned against neglecting agriculture and light industry which might result in 'having heavy industry but losing the people or even losing both heavy industry and the people'.

The new concern about rural restlessness was expressed not only in an increase of investments in agriculture, irrigation, water conservancy and related projects in the revised second five-year plans, but also in doing something to reduce the widespread dissatisfaction within the co-operatives, where the cadres who took no part in farming acted like bureaucrats imposing their ideas on the peasants. A directive of the Central Committee of the Party prescribed three specific reforms: (i) 'open knowledge' of financial income and disbursements; (ii) joint discussion of problems by cadres and the peasants; and (iii) actual participation in production by the cadres. Subsequent directives ordered an overhauling of co-operatives to correct glaring errors. A temporary retreat in the ruthless march towards collectivization was made by reducing the size of the co-operatives by fifty per cent, viz. from an average of 200 families in an agricultural producers' co-operative to 100 families.[1]

2. RECTIFICATION WITHIN THE PARTY

As many complaints voiced in 1956 were directed against the imperious and bureaucratic cadres and lower-echelon Party members, a rectification campaign in the Party was ordered. In his opening address at the Eighth National Congress of the Party in September 1956, Mao Tse-tung specified three Party shortcomings:

> Among many of our comrades there still are standpoints and styles of work which are contrary to Marxism-Leninism, namely, subjectivism in their way of thinking, bureaucracy in their way of work, and sectarianism in organizational questions. Such standpoints and such styles of work alienate us from the masses. . . . They . . . must be vigorously corrected by strengthening ideological education in the Party.[2]

The call for 'rectification' was made also by Liu Shao-ch'i in what was certainly the most important address of the Eighth National Congress. He assailed bureaucracy as 'arm-chair leadership which doesn't understand and which suppresses the opinions of subordinates and the masses, and pays little attention to the life of the masses';[3] he exposed subjectivism and doctrinairism as ideological violations of the Marxist-Leninist teaching of observing and knowing the actual conditions and problems of life.[4] The resolution passed by the Eighth National Congress urged an intensified effort to correct these 'many shortcomings in our work'. To do so, 'members of the whole Party, and especially our high-ranking cadres, must constantly deepen their Marxist-Leninist understanding, and wage a continuous struggle against bourgeois and petty-bourgeois ideological tendencies'.[5]

The Party leaders had not planned to have a full-scale rectification campaign till 1958, but the mounting criticisms which appeared in late 1956 and early 1957 convinced them that the situation called for earlier action. Even before the Central Committee of the Party issued a formal call for a nation-wide rectification campaign, Party organizations in different parts of the country had launched small-scale campaigns at local levels. On February 17, 1957, appeared in the *Jen-min jih-pao* an article by the secretary of the Heilungkiang Party organization in Manchuria reporting the progress of a rectification campaign in the province. The three major reasons which he gave for the campiagn were: (i) the Party had many new members who needed more systematic ideological indoctrination; (ii) the remaining influences of petty-bourgeois ideology; and (iii) the serious shortcomings in the working-style of the cadres, which the intellectuals had brought to light in their criticisms.

In the following month, commemorating the fifteenth anniversary of the rectification campaign of 1942 for ideological remoulding, Lu Ting-yi again stressed the necessity of combating subjectivism, bureaucracy and sectarianism which cut the Party away from the masses and from objective realities. 'The contradictions among the people', he added, 'are not a matter of relations between the enemy and ourselves; they must be solved by the long-term, patient and delicate method of persuasion, and not by the crude, violent and simple method of administrative orders'.[6]

The official directive for a nation-wide 'anti-bureaucratism, anti-sectarianism, and anti-subjectivism rectification campaign'[7] was issued by the Central Committee of the Chinese Communist Party on April 27, 1957.[8] The 1957 campaign was to be guided by the two speeches of Mao Tse-tung on the correct handling of contradictions. The major shortcomings to be overcome were 'bureaucratism, which alienates masses of workers, peasants, soldiers, students and intellectual elements; sectarianism, which neglects the unity of the 600,000,000 people, the unity of all nationalities and political parties, the unity of the masses outside the Party, and the unity of the Party; and subjectivism, which ignores the actual objective conditions'. The campaign should be one of 'ideological education' and its principal method that of criticism and self-criticism, with preference for small discussion groups and personal interviews.

The primary purpose was to remove the sources of friction between the Party and the people, or, to use the Communist terminology, to resolve the contradictions between the leadership (i.e. the Party) and the masses. The goal was to strengthen the Party leadership and to hasten the pace of socialist construction. In its editorial of April 11, 1957, the *Jen-min jih-pao* said:

> . . . if the masses get no support in their criticism of bureaucratic tendencies, the problems may be hidden from view for a time and the people may appear to be calm. But if, over a long time, the masses are prevented from presenting correct views and justified demands, a moment will come when, their patience exhausted, they will resort to extreme and violent measures in their fight against bureaucracy. They may then even demand the immediate solution of problems that cannot be adequately solved for the time being.

The campaign would be a purge of anti-Marxist ideas and practices, but not the physical purge of the guilty. The slogan was to 'cure the disease and save the patient'. The emphasis was laid on 'study', which meant a thorough understanding of Mao's speeches on contradictions and other 'ideological remoulding documents'. All Party members were urged to combat by a more intensive study of Marxism-Leninism the 'petty-bourgeois ideology' which was at the root of bureaucratism and related evils.

The order given to the cadres to take part in the production activities of the agricultural co-operatives grew into a general movement to bring the bureaucrats into closer contacts with the people. Cadres were told 'to take off their shoes and work on the farms'.[9] Government officials were asked to go to the farms and factories and take part in labour. A directive of the Central Committee of the Party ordered all Party leaders and government officials to set aside a definite time each year to take part in physical labour and to engage in such activities as weeding, harvesting, street cleaning, road repair, feeding pigs, digging ditches, etc.[10] The 'mass line' of the Party was given a new emphasis, and government officials and Party members were to avoid appearing as bureaucrats who kept themselves aloof from the masses. Mao Tse-tung, Liu Shao-ch'i, Chou En-lai and Chu Teh made personal inspection tours to different parts of the country and talked with the workers in the factories.

The Communist leaders now declared that they would listen to criticism from the public and invited the 'democratic parties' to suggest ways for improving Party leadership in the period of socialist reconstruction. This gave the intellectuals, who in China had always been the mouthpiece of public opinion and who con-stituted the bulk of the membership of the 'democratic parties', an additional impetus to speak their mind.

In the first phase of the 'hundred flowers and schools' policy of 1956, the intellectuals had been sceptical and reluctant to test the new 'freedoms' promised. When they did speak, they kept their 'contending' to the meaning and value of the policy, and spoke of their hard living and working conditions. Compared to the previous eight years their criticisms were bold, but still moderate in language so as to avoid possible Communist ire. After Mao's speech of February 1957 they continued in the same trend, even if in some respects they were bolder than in 1956; but they reiterated their support of socialism and the Communist Party. In general, there was much hesitation among the intellectuals. The playwright Ou-yang Yü-ch'ien said that there still were Party members who were unwilling to implement the new policy and were placing restrictions on the 'blooming' and 'contending'.[11] Annoyed with the little enthusiasm the intellectuals had shown, the Communists made new advances, which in May were to open wide the flood-gates and to dismay them with torrential criticism.

To get the intellectuals going, the Communists organized forum discussions on the question of contradictions in the ranks of the people. A feature of these forums was the 'relay report' on the gist of Mao's February 17 speech. In Peking 350,000 members of the 'democratic parties' had participated in such discussions by the end of April. In the interior province of Yünnan, during the fortnight of late March and early April, 6,000 persons had heard 'relay reports' of Mao's two February pronouncements and reports on 'the spirit of the conference on propaganda work of the Central Committee of the Communist Party'.[12] In these discussions, though the intellectuals expressed gratification with the new policy, they said that they had been hesitant to take advantage of the new policy because of severe restrictions in the past. One participant in a Shanghai forum cited the case of an intellectual who had written a volume of several hundred thousand characters but was afraid to submit it for publication; he said that other authors used pseudonyms for fear of becoming a target of 'rectification'.[13]

3. THE FIRST RUMBLINGS

The 1957 March session of the National Committee of the Chinese People's Political Consultative Conference gave the intellectuals and members of the non-Communist political parties an opportunity to test the new policy laid down by Mao. Two of the speakers deserve mention because later they were made targets of attacks as 'Rightists' and 'anti-socialists'. Both were leading figures of the Democratic League and were well-known non-Communists who early decided to cast their lot with the Communist regime. One was Chang Po-chün, who was educated in Germany and was associated with leftist groups for a long time before the Communist conquest. He was a vice-chairman of the Democratic League, chairman of the Peasants and Workers Democratic Party and minister of Communications in the government. Speaking in the CPPCC, he said that the 'democratic parties' had no reason to be timid any more. Since the Communist leaders had promised the 'long-term co-existence' of various political parties, the 'democratic parties' might well plan to expand their influence and to draw young people into their ranks instead of limiting their activities to the older intellectuals. Moreover, the various 'democratic parties' might well enter into closer co-operation to further the common cause of socialism.[14]

Obviously dissatisfied with the unimportant role of the 'democratic parties' and with the practice of assigning non-Communists to high government posts but without real authority, Chang proposed to put into actual practice the high-sounding Communist slogan of 'long-term co-existence and mutual supervision' of political parties. 'Mutual supervision is necessary', he said, 'in order to achieve mutual trust and to vest office holders with real authority. I hope that the democratic parties and those who do not belong to political parties will demand that our Communist friends carry out criticism in various appropriate ways in order to correct certain improper methods of work'. He was in favour of full freedom of discussion. 'To club the head of intellectuals who seek progress and improvement as soon as they begin to talk, is to block the channel of contending and is obviously wrong'.

Nevertheless, this was still a time of cautious probings. The critics took care to use mild and indirect language. It is not surprising, therefore, that Chang concluded his remarks with a pledge of loyalty. 'Because I love and support the Communist Party as well as the democratic parties and because I love socialism as well as democracy', he concluded, 'I have made bold to express my personal and crude ideas. . . . I invite your criticism and advice'.

The other outspoken critic in the March session of the CPPCC was Lo Lung-chi, another vice-chairman of the Democratic League. A political scientist with a doctor's degree from Columbia University, he was known for his leftist and pro-Communist views before the Communist regime. When speaking in the CPPCC, he took pains to voice his support of the views of Mao Tse-tung and Chou En-lai, and made his criticisms indirectly, prefacing them with 'some people say' and adding that some of the criticisms arose from misunderstanding of government policies. Nevertheless, he gave vent to complaints which had been in the minds of many intellectuals.[15]

In spite of recent improvement, Lo said, the intellectuals were still enmeshed in difficulties. The question of adequate employment remained unsolved. 'There are returned students from Britain who make a living pulling carts, and there are returned students from the United States who sell cigarettes at street stalls'. Moreover, the Communist Party had since 1956 begun to pay attention to the higher intellectuals but had neglected the intermediate and lower ones. He called attention to the plight of the elementary school teachers, who had to run errands for the cadres, copy documents for government offices, help to sell books for the state-owned bookstores, and perform such menial tasks as digging wells and building dykes in the countryside. 'If they are too exhausted to obey the orders, they become victims of unjust attacks'.

'The key problem of today', Lo continued, 'is still how to close the chasm between Party and the non-Communists'. Intellectuals and college teachers suffered from discriminatory practices in the preferential treatment accorded to Party members in promotion and in opportunities for further study. Almost a year had gone by since the announcement of the 'hundred flowers' and 'hundred schools' policy, but so far there had been very little 'blossoming' and very little 'contending'. 'The basic reason is that the higher intellectuals are hampered by numerous misgivings and deep suspicions and do not dare to blossom or contend'. He placed the blame on Party cadres who posed themselves as defenders of orthodoxy against the heresies that might appear under the guise of contending schools. Such cadres, he charged, were guilty of doctrinairism and were alienating and not leading the intellectuals.

Pleading for a better understanding of the psychology of the intellectuals, Lo said that the scholars of China had not always been aloof from politics. Through China's long history they had maintained that 'every individual must accept responsibility for the rise or fall of his nation'. But the scholars, Lo warned, were proud people; their slogan had been: 'If I am treated as a scholar of the state, I respond as a scholar of the state; if I am treated as a commoner, I respond as a commoner'.

He quoted two well-known sayings from China's intellectual heritage. One was: 'Just as a woman beautifies herself for the one who loves her, so a scholar would give his life for some one who understands him'. The other was: 'A scholar would rather accept death than humiliation'. Intellectuals could not be won by material inducements alone; they must be 'understood' and treated with due 'courtesy'.

4. THE SCHOLARS CRITICIZE

Scholars who were concerned chiefly with their academic pursuits spoke up against the limitations imposed on them. In an article written in most tactful terms, sociologist Fei Hsiao-t'ung said that although the new policy had brought improvement in the material conditions of their living, it had not done much to enable them to pursue their academic interests without restraint or worry. The intellectuals, he said, were experiencing the uncertain weather of early spring when it would turn cold as suddenly as it would turn warm.[16] Many, he added, were still hoping to attain the simple goal of 'one room and two books' so that they might carry on without interruption.

The scholars were more specific in their criticisms and more blunt than in 1956. Under the title 'Why do intellectuals have the feeling of early spring?' a scholar explained that 'early spring' was merely a 'poetic' way of saying that many intellectuals were feeling the 'chill' of early spring, or, in plainer language, they felt that the 'leadership comrades' were not quite ready yet to allow free 'blossoming' and 'contending'.[17] Many intellectuals felt that the slogan of 'letting a hundred flowers blossom and a hundred schools contend' was like the thunder making a lot of noise but producing little rain. He demanded that the Party leadership produce some real 'rain' in order to encourage the intellectuals to 'blossom' and 'contend'; for all the talk about 'hundred flowers' and 'hundred schools', the 'free discussion' of historians was limited to five major topics; in other words, the 'blossoming' was limited to five flowers. There were numerous other topics worth the study and research of historians, but they had not yet been sanctioned by the 'leadership'.

Criticisms came from scholars in various fields of study. For example, in a forum of college professors in Tientsin, a professor of political science said that scholars in sociology, political science, law, and other social sciences had become so discouraged under the Communists that many had decided to give up their academic careers; in consequence there were few people engaged in research on problems of population and social thought. Courses of study in the university curriculum had been abolished simply because they were not being offered in the Soviet Union.[18] Important books of reference published in the Western countries were condemned as 'reactionary'. He pleaded for a more rational policy in regard to the social sciences.

Another scholar[19] who took part in the same forum severely criticized the limitation of all social sciences to Marxism. The social sciences, he said, were born after the rise of capitalism and Marx and Engels actually built their new interpretation of the social sciences on the foundation of the capitalist social sciences. Moreover the Marx-Engels interpretation ceased to develop after the death of Engels in 1895; since then the Marxist school had failed to produce any new understanding of human history or new theories of the social sciences. Those who thought that Marx and Engels had settled all problems of the social sciences or that the social sciences could not advance beyond the theories of Marx and Engels had committed a serious error. He further argued for the study of the social sciences of the capitalist countries because 'there are social scientists in the capitalist countries who are not consciously serving the cause of capitalism'.

Although the *Jen-min jih-pao* published these criticisms, it added an editorial note indicating strong objection to such an unflattering opinion of the latter-day Marxists. The editor observed that it was all right to ask for the continued development of the social sciences but 'contrary to fact' to say that Marxism failed to grow after 1895. Such a statement, he said, ignored the valuable contributions of Lenin in regard to imperialism, the proletarian revolution, and the proletarian dictatorship, without which there could have been no October Revolution in Russia. The editor invited further discussion of this point of view. This was an early indication that the 'contending' of schools would not be permitted to question the fundamental validity of Marxism-Leninism and the Communist ideology.

Other scholars joined the chorus of complaints against the stifling of academic life by Party cadres. They reported that scholars had been afraid to speak or write, for the slightest 'error' might invite the charge of 'reactionary thinking' and cause many sleepless nights, and that even though there were English periodicals in the library, no one would go near them for fear of incurring official displeasure.[20] They echoed Lo Lung-chi's declaration that 'scholars would rather accept death than humiliation' and that the Party could only win the intellectuals by according them due respect and appreciation.[21] They raised the question whether the 'leadership' of the Communist Party was essential in such technical academic questions as the reform of the written language[22] or the nature of scientific research.[23] They pointed out how academic learning had been hurt by the doctrinairism of Party cadres, who held that all discussions of physiology must conform with the theories of Pavlov, and that the theories of Michurin constituted the biology of the proletariat while those of Morgan represented the biology of the bourgeoisie.[24] One after another expressed the fear that even after Mao's reassurance there were Party cadres ready to pounce upon the intellectuals with charges of idealism and reactionary ideology if they should really 'blossom' or 'contend'.

5. THE MAY EXPLOSION

Such were the ominous signs preceding the bursting of the dam in May 1957. The month of May has always been a month of explosive developments in contemporary China. Its calendar is full of highly emotionalized anniversary dates.[25] It is the month of patriotic demonstrations, of strikes and riots, of mass emotions which easily get out of control. Now it has acquired a new meaning in the minds of the thinking people of China. It will be remembered as the month in 1957 when courageous intellectuals 'would rather accept death than humiliation' and persons who prized freedom of the mind above material things spoke out against the Communists. The small safety valve to release the pressure of mounting popular discontent proved ineffectual and the flood-gates of pent-up criticism against the Communists were pushed wide open. The torrents burst with such violence that the Communists got alarmed and rushed to dam up the swelling waters.

CHAPTER XVI

MAY BLOSSOMS

MAY 1957 was a month of resplendent blossoming in Mao's garden, but the variety of blossoms did not quite fit into the Communist colour scheme. The Communists were willing to see 'a hundred' flowers, but they wanted all of them to be red. They did not want any flowers that destroy the 'unity' of this red colour. Whatever interfered with this 'unity' must be rooted out as 'poisonous weeds'.

The first buds to burst open in this short-lived spring were the new and bold criticisms of the leaders of the 'democratic parties'. The democratic parties had been told by the Party that they had their place in Chinese politics in the era of social construction. The slogan of the moment was 'Long-term co-existence and mutual supervision'. The Communist Party's Central Committee had set up a 'United Front Department' to foster the activities of the 'democratic parties'; it convened their leaders in a series of forum meetings. Its director gave repeated assurances that the Communist Party welcomed the criticisms and the assistance of the 'democratic parties' and promised them freedom of 'blossoming'. Thus emboldened, the intellectuals in leading positions of the various parties seized the opportunity to speak their minds.

Chang Po-chün and Lo Lung-chi, the two vice-chairmen of the Democratic League who had already shown themselves bolder than other critics, proceeded to make even more daring criticisms and proposals. Chang sought to elevate the position of the non-Communist parties. In the past, he said, criticisms and suggestions made by the non-Communist parties had been ignored by the Communist Party and the parties actually had little opportunity to make their contribution. Communist cadres received frequent promotion while the non-Communists had little chance of it. In practice, he said, everything was controlled and decided by the Communist Party organization.[1] He again criticized the practice of putting non-Communists in high government positions and not giving them any real authority and responsibility. Thus a non-Communist department head of a government office who was supposed to be in charge of (economic) planning, had been excluded from the conferences convened by the State Planning Commission to which only members of the Communist Party were admitted.[2] Important government policies, he maintained, should be determined by legally established administrative agencies, not by the Party organization. Before political questions were settled, the non-Communist parties should be consulted and invited to make suggestions. To facilitate co-operative planning, Chang proposed the establishment of a Political Planning Board in which political and civic groups would be broadly represented. With an implied criticism of the harshness of the 'three-anti' and 'five-anti' campaigns and the campaign for the suppression of counter-revolutionaries, he suggested a 'thorough review' and early settlement of cases and problems which had not been adequately solved.[3]

Lo Lung-chi also pleaded for a more active role for the non-Communist parties. At present, he said, the 'democratic parties' existed in name only; all problems of major policies were discussed by the Communist Party before they were submitted for 'consultation' to the 'democratic parties'. One of the difficulties confronting the non-Communist parties was the membership problem. They were not allowed to recruit members from the workers and peasants, because these lay in the exclusive territory of the Communist Party. They were supposed to draw members from the 'old-time intellectuals', that is, intellectuals over thirty years old, and thus they were cut off from the young. Even among the older intellectuals, the recent drive for the recruitment of intellectuals into the Communist Party had made intellectuals hesitate to join the non-Communist parties for fear that such membership might be taken as an indication of political 'backwardness' and so increase the difficulty of eventually becoming members of the Communist Party.[4]

Lo attacked the use of Party Commissioners in schools and universities as 'incompatible with the Chinese political system and spirit'.[5] It meant monopolizing the control of education by the Communist Party without the 'democratic parties' participating. On a later occasion he voiced dissatisfaction with the purges of the past few years and proposed the establishment of an appeal board to which those who had grievances could turn for redress. Such a board, composed of non-Communists as well as Communists, would review the 'deviations' perpetrated during the 'three-anti' and 'five-anti' campaigns and the campaign for the suppression of counter-revolutionaries; its existence would also give further encouragement to 'blossoming' and 'contending' and allay fears of unjust punishment.[6]

1. AN INCREASING VARIETY OF FLOWERS

Many other members of the non-Communist parties spoke boldly in the forum discussions of May. Chang Nai-ch'i deserves mention because he represented the intellectuals associated with private industry and commerce. He was a banker and college professor before World War II, and was arrested by the Nationalist Government in 1936 as a leftist engaged in pro-Communist activities. As vice-chairman of the China Democratic National Construction Association and as minister of Food in the Communist government, he, too, complained of 'position without authority' and blamed the sectarianism of the Communists as the source of this hardship. Many Communists, he said, were unwilling to accept the criticisms of non-Communists even when correct. If a non-Communist made a proposal entirely in line with Party policy, and the 'responsible Party comrade' shook his head, there would be no chance of the proposal getting further hearing.[7]

Chang Nai-ch'i openly criticized an editorial of the *Jen-min jih-pao* of April 22, 1957, in which it was said that although industrialists and merchants had made progress, yet they still had a 'negative' and 'conservative' attitude that needed further remoulding. Chang refuted this and accused the paper of sectarianism. He rejected its editorial statement that 'private industrialists and merchants must obey the leadership of the representatives of the state'. In a joint public-private enterprise where the private capitalist was the manager and the state representative the deputy manager, he pointed out, the 'one-sided' demand for obedience to the state would again put in a 'position without authority' the non-Communist. The industrialists and merchants, he said, had gone through repeated 'regenerative transformations' in the agrarian reform struggle, the three-anti, the five-anti and other remoulding campaigns, and any talk of further remoulding would only cause endless worries and misgivings.

In the *Jen-min jih-pao* of May 14, Chang Nai-ch'i further aired his views on the cause of the 'wall' and 'chasm' between the Communists and non-Communists. The foundation of the wall, he said, lay in the Communists' arrogance and self-complacency which were traceable to Stalin's statement, 'We Communists are people of a special mould. We are made of special stuff'.[8] Chang condemned this as unscientific and dangerous. Since Stalin's statement appeared in the *History of the Communist Party of the Soviet Union,* now used in ideological indoctrination classes all over China, its influence must be great. Even if no more than one per cent of the 12,000,000 Communists should be guilty of such arrogance, Chang pointed out, the 120,000 would still be doing immense damage in their 'leadership' position. To eliminate the 'wall' and the 'chasm', this 'doctrinaire' view of Communists as people specially endowed had to be attacked. Chang criticized the usurpation of governmental power by the Communist Party and wanted a clearer recognition of the authority of state organs as apart from the Communist Party.

Ch'eng Min-shu was another critic who later got reprimanded for his openness. He had taken part in the revolt against the Nationalist Government and the establishment of the short-lived 'people's government' in Fukien in 1933. He was now a member of the Standing Committee of the Kuomintang Revolutionary Committee, and had held different positions in the Communist government. His criticism was centred on the Party Commissioners in positions of control in every educational institution. He stood for a larger voice for the faculty members and students in educational affairs. He sought for a broader participation of the non-Communists in policy making of state organs.[9] He took issue with the censuring of the critics who spoke of the shortcomings of the Communist cadres and not enough of their accomplishments. To rectify, he argued, was to expose the faults; it was quite in harmony with the spirit of the campaign to dispense with unnecessary praise of good points.

Another critic of the Party Commissioners in educational institutions was Yeh Tu-yi, a leading figure of the Democratic League. They had too much power, he said, and needlessly controlled all matters. Relations in the schools and universities would be more cordial and less complicated if each person was known simply as professor or president without the complicating consideration of his Party status.[10] He pleaded for a clearer recognition of the problem of intellectuals and for the establishment of a specialized agency by the Chinese People's Political Consultative Conference (in which all parties have representation) to take charge of such matters. He made an even bolder proposal: to merge the Democratic League, the Association for the Promotion of Democracy, the Peasants and Workers Democratic Party, and the Chiu-san Society into one political party of intellectuals.[11]

2. ONE MONTH OF FLORAL SPLENDOUR

These few bold leaders of the non-Communist parties struck a responsive chord in the hearts and minds of numerous intellectuals. College professors, secondary school teachers, journalists, writers and artists now really seized the opportunity to 'blossom' and 'contend'. It is unnecessary to name them all or summarize the ideas presented by each of them. The most frequent criticisms were:

i. The role of the 'democratic parties' was too narrow and restricted. They existed only as appendages of the Communist Party with no programme of their own. They were not free to recruit members and because of their unimportant role they had no prestige which might attract promising members.

ii. The non-Communists and members of non-Communist parties were given in the government high-sounding positions which carried no authority or responsibility. Where a non-Communist was in charge of a state organ or an educational institution, he was always assisted by a deputy head or vice-principal who was a Communist Party man; this Party man had the real authority and knew much more about state plans and policies than the titular head. The so-called democratic representation of non-Communists in the government had thus become a farce.

iii. There existed a high 'wall' or a deep 'chasm' between the Communist and the non-Communist. In schools, in government offices, in factories, and in all phases of social and political life, there was discrimination against the non-Communist. The Party men formed an inner circle of trusted cadres to which non-Communists were not admitted. They were given privileges, such as priority in promotion and in opportunities for study. Many facts and important information about state plans and policies were kept back from non-Communists for reasons of 'security'. The Communists did not trust the non-Communists, even those who supported socialism and the Communist Party. All non-Communists were treated as outsiders.

iv. The Communist Party identified itself with the state to such an extent that the Party and the state had become one. Decrees and directives which should come from government agencies were issued by the Central Committee of the Communist Party or jointly by the Party and the state organ concerned. The relations between the Party and the state had not been defined and clarified.

v. There was no system of law to guide the nation. Past purges and the injustices in the 'three-anti' and 'five-anti' campaigns showed the need for a well-defined legal system which everyone could understand.

vi. The control of educational institutions by Party commissioners had done much harm. It had taken educational administration and planning out of the hands of the faculty and educators. Party members with no special ability and no understanding of educational matters had exercised power over the non-Communist scholars and educators. Since they represented the 'leadership of the Communist Party', their words and their authority could not be questioned. They looked down on the intellectuals.

3. MANY FORUMS

Such were the criticisms aired in the China mainland press in the month of May 1957. They were heard in forums which were held within individual colleges and universities, or organized by special groups such as writers and artists or journalists, or sponsored by the various non-Communist parties. The *Kuang-ming jih-pao*, a daily newspaper representing the interests of the 'democratic parties', instituted a series of forums in different parts of the country which gave the intellectuals in major cities a chance to be heard.

A Shanghai correspondent of the *Kuang-ming jih-pao* interviewed a number of university professors on the 'hundred flowers' and 'hundred schools'. Several expressed the prevalent scepticism of the intellectuals. One said that the new policy might turn out to be a bait and any one biting the bait would be headed for trouble.[12] Another said that the fear of being branded as 'idealist' had held back many an intellectual from saying anything at all.

In a forum in the Academy of Sciences, a number of scientists complained that bureaucratism had hampered their work, and the 'leadership' had become an unwieldy organization wasting time and energy.[13]

Participants, in a forum in Changchun (Manchuria) under the auspices of the local branch of the Democratic League, declared that there could be no 'blossoming of fragrant flowers' unless the Party sincerely and effectively relaxed its rigid control. This would have to be evident not only at the top but also at the local levels, and it should guarantee that 'blossoming' would not bring reprimand or reprisal.[14]

In a forum of the Democratic League in Sian, a professor of Northwest University stressed the need of reviewing the past record of punishments administered in the various purges. In the 'three-anti', he reported, there were people who could not sleep nights, and after the campaign for the supression of counter-revolutionaries people had been altogether afraid to speak. Without a review of past cases it would not be easy to dispel misgivings and to set people at rest.[15]

Ch'en Ch'i-yu, chairman of the Chih-kung-tang, was for the early promulgation of a civil and criminal code and for conducting affairs strictly according to legal procedure. He complained that during the campaign for the suppression of counter-revolutionaries, members of the 'democratic parties' in government offices were arrested without the knowledge of their parties and without giving reasons for their arrest.[16] This need of a system of law was also emphasized by Huang Shao-hung, a leading figure of the Kuomintang Revolutionary Committee. He pointed out that the government still had not promulgated a civil code, a criminal code, or regulations governing the punishment of public functionaries. A clear legal system would avoid the present condition of 'positions without responsibility' for non-Communists in the government; a system of laws and regulations on economic development was needed. He also urged a review of heavy sentences condemning persons to corrective labour or imprisonment.[17]

In a forum of journalists, the complaint was that reporters could not gain admittance to government offices and were not permitted in conferences; the only source of news was the New China News Agency, which, having no competition, chose to release news any time it saw fit, often after long delays. Even then, news releases were often given to Party papers first or with the instruction that the non-Communist papers were to withhold publication to after the publication in the Party organs. In some important press conferences, only the privileged correspondents of the Party papers were invited.[18]

4. PARTY CONTROL OF EDUCATION

'Democratic administration of schools' was the subject of many a forum.[19] Teachers of secondary schools and higher institutions expressed their dissatisfaction with the domineering role of the Party Commissioners. A professor of biology in Peking University reported that the harmless remark about the Communist vice-president of the university making too long a speech had brought down on the critic an official censure of hostility toward the Party leadership. When criticisms were made of the non-Communist president or other non-Communist administrators, the Communists would make no objection at all, but might even join in.[20]

A professor of Northwest University and a member of the China Association for the Promotion of Democracy reported that department heads in the university merely rubber-stamped the decisions made by Party members in key positions. The dominant psychology of faculty members, he said, was one of fear: fear of offending the Party commissioners, fear of saying the wrong thing, fear of being reported to the Party leadership by activists and informers in their midst. To avoid suspicion, most people cautiously avoided close contacts with one another. A person who had casually remarked that 'one must be careful what one says these days', was reported by an unknown informer and confronted with the question whether he was planning a revolt.[21]

Wu Yi-fang, a well-known feminine educator who for many years was president of Ginling (Women's) College in Nanking and now a member of the Association for the Promotion of Democracy, cited the example of a non-Communist school principal who received a letter officially addressed to the school, and as he was about to open the letter, saw it snatched out of his hands by the Communist vice-principal, who happened to be standing by and claimed the letter.[22]

In a forum of faculty members of Wuhan University held under the auspices of *Kuang-ming jih-pao*, many examples were given of domineering by Party cadres and their disdainful attitude toward the intellectuals.[23] Party cadres in the university acted as if they owned the place and had authority over all and sundry. When a message or report came to the university, the Party members would be the first to know about it, then the members of the Youth League, and the non-Communists would be the last to be informed, if at all. In the appointment of assistants and the selection of students for study in USSR, all decisions were made by the Party men, and priority went to Party and Youth League members. Believing themselves to be 'made of special stuff', Party members set themselves apart from the people. They talked about 'Red experts' with obvious disapproval of experts who were not Party men. In their eyes the intellectuals were persons to be reformed

and they the reformers with the right—which they often exercised
—to call any faculty member out of the classroom any time and
demand of him a satisfactory 'self-examination' before permitting
him to return to his teaching duties. It was also said that the
personnel department of the university, controlled by Communists,
was virtually an 'independent kingdom' in the university. Its
actions were based solely on the opinions of Party members. Once
a student, judged scholastically deficient and unworthy of graduation by the faculty, was allowed to graduate on the insistence of the
personnel department simply because he was a member of the
Party or the Youth League. Another student much disliked by the
faculty was appointed as assistant after graduation despite the
objection of the dean's office. The 'Party leadership' people looked
down on the scholars and haughtily referred to them as 'you
intellectuals'. Any personal disagreement with them might result
in the accusation of ideological deviation. When faculty members
signed a petition to retain a co-operative store of the faculty residen-
tial area about to be abolished, they were accused of opposing the
Party and its leadership.

The situation in Wuhan University was not unique as may be
seen from the statements of Tsinghua University professors. The
Party organization controlled everything in the university. The
Dean of Studies had no authority, for the real power rested in the
hands of the 'Secretary' to the Dean, who was a Communist. The
words of the secretary carried much more weight than those of the
Dean, who, like other non-Communists, occupied a position with
little authority.[24] The Party members were so aloof that they did
not stop to greet people on the campus. Their excuse was that
they were so busy with work and so occupied in thinking that they
did not really see the people they met on the way.[25] Names of
students recommended for study abroad did not come from the
Dean's office, but from the Party leadership. Faculty members
were not allowed to talk with foreign visitors in a foreign language.
A senior professor said that although he had been at the university
for many years, he felt now more and more like a stranger, because
the professors were never consulted and not respected by the new
leadership. He said that teacher-student relations had greatly
deteriorated; how one could teach the young people when they
could turn around and wage a 'struggle' against the teacher? In the
'three-anti' and the anti- counter-revolutionary campaigns, he also
recalled, students dug out minute details of their teachers' personal

lives to expose their faults. When teachers knew that what they said might be used against them, they became extremely wary in their speech.[26]

The principal of the Nanking School of Physical Education said that he was actually no more than a 'clay idol', in a nominal position with no authority; the real power in the school was the Communist vice-principal. Official documents were sent out in the name of the principal, but they were prepared by the Party leadership. His task was merely to carry out the Party orders.[27]

A scientist complained that scientific work was greatly hampered by the Communists in high positions who knew no science and were unwilling to learn. They exercised their 'leadership' in military fashion and looked down on the scholar and the expert. Party leadership, he continued, actually amounted to Party control of all matters.[28]

In a forum of workers in the Ministry of Posts and Telecommunications it was brought out that the vice-minister and the Party organization in the ministry superceded the non-Communist minister in authority. All matters were discussed in Party meetings before they came to the attention of the non-Communist staff. It often happened that a new development was well known to the Communist departmental heads and section chiefs but unknown to the non-Communist minister. Even in matters of technical improvement, the Party members without any technical knowledge still had the final say.[29]

Party control came under severe criticism even from the faculty of the Chinese People's University, which was specially founded on ideological orthodoxy. Between Communists and non-Communists, they said, there was nothing to talk about except the weather. Some Party members told the scholars, 'When we were engaged in guerilla war, you were merely scholars of the bourgeoisie class'. The only courses of study considered important were the 'political study' courses, and the teachers of these courses were the only faculty members that commanded attention.[30]

According to a professor in the Central China Normal College, the Communist vice-president once told non-Communist teachers, 'Do not think you are indispensable. In three years we shall have a new crop of experts and we shall not need you any more'.[31]

In another forum of Democratic League members, the story was told of the non-Communist vice-principal of a school who was so accustomed to the exertion of high authority that before he left on a trip he put up a notice informing the public that in his absence the principal of the school would be in charge.[32] Another participant said that the Communists were deliberately building a wall between themselves and the people in various ways. He cited the example of Chou En-lai, who began his address in the People's Political Consultative Conference with 'Comrades and friends'. Evidently Chou was calling his fellow Communists comrades and the non-Communists friends. If all were working for the same cause of socialism, why could not the non-Communists be considered as comrades too?[33]

At a forum under the auspices of the Chinese Peasants and Workers Democratic Party, a professor of education in the Peking Normal University stated that educational statistics had suffered a violent death and that he had no knowledge of what was going on in the secondary schools. Any attempt to get data from the Ministry of Education was foiled by 'security regulations' which kept all kinds of information from non-Communists. Another said: 'I am a professor but I do not do the work of a professor. My assistant is a Party member; formerly a student of mine, he was quickly promoted to be a lecturer and now he is my leader'. Another well-known professor said that the moment he saw a Party member he would tremble with fear.[34]

These few examples show that in May 1957, 'blossoming' and 'contending' became a good deal more advanced and less inhibited. The intellectuals voiced their discontent not only with conditions of work, but also with the personal relations and attitudes of the Communists toward them. They placed the blame squarely on the Communists. Nevertheless, except for the suggestion that Party control of education should be replaced by a more democratic administration of schools and universities, none directly attacked the Communist Party and its programme of socialism. The critics freely condemned the cadres at local levels and the Party leadership in educational institutions and government offices, but they did not assail the top leaders of the Communist Party.

5. THE PARTY'S UNEASINESS

The Communists were no doubt becoming uneasy for they found themselves in a dilemma. They had given repeated assurances that the newly granted 'freedom' of discussion was genuine and that those who took part in it would not be persecuted. Now they began to consider the eventual necessity of stopping the blossoming season. This is clear from Mao Tse-tung's address before the Third National Conference of Representatives of the Communist Youth League on May 25, 1957. At a time when intellectuals in different parts of the country were warming up for energetic 'contending', Mao told the youth conference that the Communist Party must always be the 'centre' of the Chinese people and socialism could not be achieved without this 'centre'. 'Any speech or action which deviates from socialism must be considered entirely wrong', he warned.[35]

Despite this uneasiness, the Communists still wanted to avoid the official abandonment of their 'blossoming-contending' policy, so much advertised at home and abroad. They continued to permit the expression of frank views and the publication of these views in the press. They were uneasy and unhappy. Their alarm and the subsequent reaction were to appear in the first week of June.

CHAPTER XVII

FRAGRANT FLOWERS OR POISONOUS WEEDS?

1. 'KILL THE COMMUNISTS'

THE outburst in the last days of May and first week of June revealed how irksome the Communist Party with its monopoly of power had become not only to the 'democratic parties' but even to intellectuals within the Party's institutions.

It is ironic indeed that one of the most trenchant critics to arouse Communist ire came from the faculty of the Chinese People's University, established by the Communists to foster a 'new-type' intelligentzia firmly rooted in proletarian ideology. This critic, Ke P'ei-ch'i, unleashed a most severe attack on the Communists in a forum of the university, when he declared that the people had come to hate the Communists and did not want their leadership. The economic policy of 'planned purchase and supply' had increased the sufferings of the people, the campaign for the suppression of counter-revolutionaries had been a 'mess', and the guilty Communists ought to submit themselves for punishment. He continued:

> There is a shortage of pork and the people cannot get it. Some call this a higher standard of living, but who are the people who enjoy the higher standard? They are the Party members and cadres who used to wear worn-out shoes but now ride in luxury cars and wear woollen uniforms. . . . Where has all the pork gone? The shortage is not due to the consumption of the people but to the mistakes committed by persons in charge of the planned purchase and supply of food, and the consequent unwillingness of the people to rear pigs. *JMJP*, May 31, 1957

Ke went on to say that the common people of China had welcomed the Communists in 1949 but now had turned against them, just as they had at first welcomed and later rebelled against Chiang Kai-shek, and as they had done to other rulers in China's long history. The so-called leadership of the Communist Party, he said, amounted to the surveillance of the masses by plain-clothes police, whose main job was to make all kinds of 'intelligence reports' to the Party organization. The Party members should not be blamed for this; the responsibility lay with the Party organization which assigned such duties to its members. He minced no words in addressing himself directly to the Communists.

> The 'I-am-the-state' attitude you hold cannot be tolerated. . . . You must not be arrogant and conceited, you must not distrust the intellectuals. If you do well, fine; if not, the masses will knock you down, will kill the Communists,

and overthrow you. And they cannot be considered unpatriotic, inasmuch as the Communists no longer serve the people. The downfall of the Communist Party will not be the downfall of China. Those who reject the leadership of the Communist Party are not guilty of treason.   Also *JMJP*, May 31, 1957

It is evident that this kind of scathing attack was very different from the criticisms of May, bold and revealing as they had been. But Ke's was not a lone voice, neither was the attack an impulsive act representing a momentary emotional outburst. Five days later, Ke defended his views in a forum convened by the Party Commissioners of his university in which a number of speakers criticized him for what he had said. 'I repeat', he insisted, 'that the masses want to overthrow the Communist Party and kill the Communists. . . . If you do not reform . . . the day will surely come when you will meet this end. This is in conformity with the socialist law of development; loud shouts of 'long live' are not going to help'. He went on to describe the ruthlessness of the Communists in the following words:

> Last year the Central Committee issued a directive for a better treatment of the intellectuals and provided functionaries in schools to serve meals and drinking water to the intellectuals, but this year they have been abolished in the name of economy. When the Party wants to use a person, he is highly prized even if he has murdered friends, comrades, and people within the Party. But when the person is no more useful to the Party, he is dropped cold even if he has sweated and shed blood for the Party. There are Party members who have forsaken their kin and relatives, even their own fathers. A son addressed his mother as comrade when he wrote to her after joining the Party. These instances help to explain why the common people, with good reason, have come to distrust the Communist Party.   *JMJP*, June 8, 1957

2. 'THE PARTY IS THE STATE'

Chu An-p'ing, the editor of *Kuang-ming jih-pao*, also emphasized that the people of China who had once supported the Communists had become disillusioned after seven years of the new regime. In a forum of the 'democratic parties' on June 1, Chu blamed the 'Party-is-the-state' or 'this-is-the-Party's-world' outlook of the Communists. 'In my opinion', he said, 'the leadership of the Party in the state does not mean that the state belongs to the Party and when people support the Communist Party they do not forget that they themselves are still the masters of the state'. He assailed the all-pervasive system of Party control whereby 'through the length and breadth of the nation, in every unit, big or small, down to the smallest government department or bureau, there is always a Party man to be the boss, and all matters big or small must have the approval of the Party man'. Many Party men, he pointed out, occupied important positions for which they had not commensurate abilities. 'They neglect their work, bringing loss to the state, and they do not have the confidence of the people, thus aggravating the tension between the Party and the masses.' In almost the same words used by Ke P'ei-ch'i, he laid the blame at the door of the Party, which had placed unqualified Party members in key positions.

Chu also criticized the monopoly of power by the Communists as an indication of the 'the-Party's-world' thinking. And he was bold enough to address his criticism to the highest authorities.[2] He said:

> I now have something to say to Chairman Mao and Premier Chou. Before liberation we heard Chairman Mao propose the organization of a coalition government in co-operation with non-Communists. When the new regime was established in 1949, provision was made for six vice-chairmen of the Central People's Government and three of them were non-Communists. There were four deputy-premiers among whom two were non-Communists. There was at least the appearance of a coalition government. Later on, however, the government was reorganized. There is now only one vice-chairman of the Chinese People's Republic,[3] and all the non-Communist vice-chairmen lost their positions and were shifted to the Standing Committee of the National People's Congress. That is not all. Among the twelve deputy-premiers of the State Council today, there is not a single non-Communist. Is this because there is not a single person outside the Party who is qualified for the high post or not a single person who may be so nurtured to take up the office?   *KMJP*, June 2, 1957

3. 'CLASS DISTINCTIONS UNNECESSARY'

Chang Nai-ch'i, vice-chairman of the Democratic National Construction Association, whose previous criticisms were reported in the last two chapters, came up with some more unorthodox blossoms in the first week of June. Reacting against pressure for the 'reform' and 'ideological remoulding' of industrialists and merchants, he said:

> Formalism has no place in the reform of industrialists and merchants. There are people who pride themselves on their firm ideological stand and shout slogans with gusto. They brand industrialists and merchants with ideological deviations. . . frightening the industrialists and merchants to such an extent that they do not dare pursue their work. Still others avoid contacts with industrialists and merchants for fear of being contaminated. This is metaphysics, very different from the consideration of problems from the standpoint of the real interests of the working class. *JMJP*, June 2, 1957

Although Chang said that he was not urging a return to capitalism, he criticized socialism and named some of the good points of private capitalism. Bureaucratism, he said, is 'a more dangerous enemy than capitalism. . . . If bureaucratism grows in the socialist enterprises, their efficiency will be lower than those of the capitalists'. 'Why is it' he asked, 'that some socialist enterprises

today are not so well managed as the modernized private enterprises
of the past? It is because the capitalists, working for profit, made
good use of personnel and exercised fairness in the cultivation
and promotion of talented personnel, for only in this way could
they compete with others. This is something some socialist enterprises have not been able to do.'

In further defence of private industrialists and merchants he
objected to a continued emphasis on the class nature of the
bourgeoisie. This, he maintained, had changed and had lost its
importance and it was no longer necessary to insist on a differentiation between the private and the public sectors, or between the
Party and the non-Communists. All should work together, and
duties and positions should be assigned on the basis of ability
without regard to class differentiation. If there were vestiges of
past class origins to be overcome, this could be achieved by 'study'
and thought reform. Even then, the circumstances of each person
should be the guide; repetition of the same theme again and again
or trying to force all persons into the same mould would not be
successful.

He challenged the use of the word 'exploitation' to describe the
industrialists and merchants and their activities, and the practice
of setting the 'exploitative bourgeoisie' apart from the 'exploited
working class'. He argued that current differences between the
bourgeoisie and the working class should be considered as differences in degree, not in kind, and that only such a view could
harmonize with the contention that contradictions in present-day
China were non-antagonistic in nature. For example, the interest
being paid to private industrialists for transforming their enterprises into joint public-private operations should not be considered
as exploitation.[4]

4. 'GET OFF THE HIGH CHAIR'

Another stinging criticism was made in a forum of the Political
Science and Law Association by an editor of a law journal, Yang
Yü-ch'ing. The rectification campaign, he said, should be named
the 'campaign for getting off the sedan-chair'. He explained that
the Communists had been riding high on sedan-chairs, holding
themselves aloof from the masses, and for eight years they had
been studiously cultivating one type of people, namely, those who
were willing to serve as chair-bearers. In demanding that the
Communists come down from the sedan-chairs, he argued that it

was incorrect to say that the top Communist cadres were good
men and that only the lower echelon of cadres were bad. The
source of evil, he boldly asserted, was in Peking, and the top cadres
in Peking must be the first to get down from their sedan-chairs;
indeed, some of them must 'get off the stage' completely. As a
concrete example he named the editor of the *Jen-min jih-pao* as
one of those who must be ejected 'in order to pacify the indignation
of the people'. For several years, he said, this editor of the Party
paper had been singing the praises of the new regime; this continual
eulogy was not consistent with the spirit of 'blossoming'.[5]

5. 'IS THE SOVIET UNION REALLY FRIENDLY?'

Lung Yün—former governor of Yünnan province and then vice-
chairman of the Kuomintang Revolutionary Committee and vice-
chairman of the National Defence Council—had, in an earlier
forum of the Kuomintang Revolutionary Committee, expressed
dissatisfaction with the lack of enthusiasm of the participants, who
hampered by worries and reservations had spoken in conciliatory
tones.[6] In a subsequent forum he supported the views of Chang
Po-chün, Chang Nai-ch'i and other critics. He repeated that participants in forums still could not get rid of their fears and worries
as they had been cowed by the various purge campaigns.[7] He urged
that all the shortcomings of the present regime should be fully
exposed; he criticized the confusion of system in which state organs
and Party organizations exercised 'dual leadership' and both sent
directives to the local bodies; and he proposed that more of the
work in the regions of the minority groups should be done by their
own cadres rather than by Han cadres[8] sent into the areas from
outside. Then, as his boldness increased, Lung Yün attacked the
very heart of the Communist ideology—the Party policy with regard
to Soviet relations and land reform.

On the question of Soviet relations, Lung Yün questioned the
'friendliness' of the Soviet Union toward China. He asked why a
friendly nation had stripped the Manchurian factories of their
valuable equipment at the close of World War II; why China had
had to shoulder the expenses of the Korean War without substantial
aid from Russia; and why in giving economic aid to China the
Soviet Union should ask for payment of interest. He proposed
that China should postpone for 20 or 30 years the repayment of
the Soviet loans contracted since 1950. Lung Yün even had the

audacity to compare the Soviet Union unfavourably with the United States. Recalling how the United States had cancelled the loans she made to her allies during World War II, Lung Yün pointed out that the Soviet Union had insisted on the repayment of all loans to China, plus interest.[9]

With regard to the agrarian reform, Lung Yün said it had caused a collapse of the rural economy. He even questioned the benefit of socialism and of the numerous projects of national construction. The more projects for construction, he averred, the more waste of money and the more acute the problem of unemployment.

6. 'WORSE THAN THE KUOMINTANG'

These were not the only blossoms in the final period of 'blossoming-contending'. There were other less well-known intellectuals who were just as frank and open in their criticisms. Under the heading 'Who said there are no Rightists today?' the *Jen-min jih-pao*, on June 12, 1957, reported a number of 'fantastic and crazy ideas' expressed by various persons in the course of 'blossoming-contending' in Tientsin. A secondary school teacher had proposed that the Communists allow the 'democratic parties' to take turns in running the government. A bureau chief in the city government had suggested the experiment of assigning some province or city for the 'democratic parties' to rule and giving them authority over police and law enforcement. An industrial leader had assailed the Communist worship of Marxism-Leninism, saying that Marxist-Leninist principles did not fit Chinese conditions, and the Communist use of Marxism-Leninism as the guide in all matters had caused much harm. And an outspoken engineer added the following daring 'blossom'.

> When the Communists first came to Tientsin, they said, 'This is a revolution; our revolution is not a change of dynasties'. Now we find that the new regime is worse than a change of dynasties. It is disheartening to live in such a society. The intellectuals are becoming more scared and jittery day after day and they do not have as much peace of mind as they did under Japanese occupation or under Kuomintang rule.

The last example again came from the citadel of Communist higher education, the Chinese People's University, and was published in the *Chung-kuo ch'ing-nien pao* (Chinese Youth Journal) which, like *Kuang-ming jih-pao*, later became a target of rectification on the charge of spreading anti-Party ideas. Here are the words of a young man who had been subjected to intensive Communist indoctrination:

The Party has come before a situation where it confronts a dangerous crisis. . . . Speaking of pork, in a certain lane twelve butcheries have been reduced to two. When pork is unavailable, it is difficult to convince people that living standards have improved. Vegetable prices have increased by 600 per cent compared with the previous year. The common people begin to *lose confidence* in the *Central Committee*, saying that in some matters the situation is *worse as compared with the days of the Kuomintang*. . . . To say that the Party has divorced itself from the masses is not so true as to say that the masses have divorced themselves from the Party. *The Party will collapse soon.* . . . At any time might overcomes might. It is possible to mount machine guns to deal with trouble, but what is to be feared is that the machine guns may be turned around for action.[10]

CHAPTER XVIII

THE COMMUNIST REACTION

FROM the beginning the Communists had made clear that 'blossoming' and 'contending' were not to be without bounds and qualifications. Mao Tse-tung, in his speech,[1] set six criteria for distinguishing 'fragrant flowers' from 'poisonous weeds'. 'Of the six criteria', said Mao, 'the most important are the socialist path and the leadership of the Party'. At no time did he or any of the Communist leaders suggest that people would be free to discuss whether or not China should adopt socialism or whether the Communist Party should yield any part of its power and authority in the new state.

Though determined to stop the alarming outburst of unproletarian thinking which manifested itself in early June the slogan-minded and propaganda-conscious Communists did not want to announce openly that they were throwing out the policy which they had made so much of. They characteristically accused the critics of sabotaging their policy and declared their determination to smash such acts in order to assure its continuation free from malicious misinterpretations and dangerous abuses.

The occasion seized by the Communists to launch their 'counter attack' against the outspoken critics was an anonymous letter alleged to have been received by a person who had defended the Communists against them. In a forum on May 25, Lu Yu-wen, an assistant to the Secretary General of the State Council, had asserted that there was no chasm between the Communists and the non-Communists, but if closer relations were desired, the responsibility should be borne by both sides, for it was unfair to blame the Communists solely for everything. He opposed Chang Po-chün and other critics who assailed the system of Party Commissioners in schools and the assumption of government power by Party organizations. In the midst of 'blossoming' and 'contending', he argued, no one should forget that the entire nation was committed to socialism under the leadership of the Communist Party.[2]

On June 7, the *Jen-min jih-pao* published the story that Lu Yu-wen had received an anonymous letter calling him a 'shameless rascal' and accusing him of 'abetting the ferocious tiger'. The letter exhorted Lu to 'turn back before it is too late' and warned that men of his ilk would simply hasten the downfall of the Communists. The next day, the *Jen-min jih-pao* came out with an editorial which marked the official beginning of the anti-Rightist campaign. The anonymous 'letter of intimidation', said the editorial, was evidence that some people were 'taking advantage of the rectification to wage an acute struggle', and it should serve as a 'warning to the broad masses of people' that 'the class struggle has not died down, especially on the ideological front'. In other words, the editorial was saying that it was not the Communists, but their opponents, who were reviving the class war. Confronted with Rightist elements who wanted to 'overthrow the Communist Party and the working class' and who 'hanker after capitalism and the political system of Europe and America', the Communists had no choice but to hit back in order to safeguard the proletarian-socialist revolution. Despite the clamour that the Communists should 'get off the stage' and the attempt to intimidate their supporters, declared the editorial, the Communist Party and the masses would remain unshaken.

Pursuing this argument, the paper published an editorial on June 9 with the title 'There must be constructive criticism and there must be correct counter-criticism'. The gist was that under the policy of 'blossoming-contending' the Communists had as much right of 'counter-criticism' as the anti-Communists had of criticizing; but the anti-Communists were trying to stop the counter-criticism by such methods as anonymous letters of intimidation and by condemning any attempt at counter-criticism as an indication of unwillingness on the part of the Communists to permit criticism. In the same issue, the paper published the story of a forum in Futan University in Shanghai in which a defender of the Communists was subject to rude heckling. Such acts, contended the editorial, were attempts to deprive the people of free speech.

Posing as the champion of free speech, 'above all, the socialist freedom of speech of the working people', the paper declared that 'any speech in the interests of the people and beneficial to socialism' must be given full freedom without interference. But it distinguished between two kinds of criticism: 'well-intentioned criticism' whose purpose was 'to strengthen the socialist cause, to strengthen the people's democratic dictatorship, and to strengthen the unity of the Party and people' and the 'malicious criticism' which was intended 'to destroy the socialist cause, to destroy the people's democratic dictatorship, and to destroy the unity of the

Party and the people'. The latter, of course, must be subjected to vigorous 'counter-criticism'.

1. THE CAMPAIGN AGAINST RIGHTISTS

As usual, the Communists did not want to do all the work of counter-attacking. They stirred up another 'mass campaign' so that the attack against the 'Rightists' appear to come from the 'people'. At the same time, they urged each group—each 'democratic party' and the students and faculties of each school and university—to chastise its own recalcitrant members and to undertake a 'voluntary' and 'self-initiated' house-cleaning of the 'Rightists' in its midst.

On the day the *Jen-min jih-pao* condemned the anonymous 'letter of intimidation', it also reported an indignation meeting of the workers of a steel factory at which the workers protested against anti-socialist speakers and denounced the 'despicable' act of an anonymous letter of intimidation. In the ensuing days, the Communist press abounded in headlines reporting other 'protest meetings' of workers and peasants. These headlines gave the impression that the 'masses' had risen to defend the socialist cause and the Communist Party, and a strong and articulate public opinion had appeared to demand firm action against the 'Rightists'.

'The workers speak up', said the *Jen-min jih-pao* editorial on June 10; they had risen in wrath to denounce the Rightists. It declared that a wave of mass emotions had swept the workers of the country and rallied them against the anti-socialist enemies. A factory worker in Shenyang was reported to have declared, 'I am an ordinary worker, I am not a member of the Communist Party, but I know that we workers and the Communist Party are of one heart and one life. . . . Whoever opposes the Communist Party is our enemy'.[3] The firm stand on the part of the workers, said the paper, carries great educational significance for the intellectuals of the entire country.

The peasants were also enlisted to join the nation-wide campaign against 'Rightists'. They too 'spoke up' to defend the policy of 'planned purchase and supply' and to praise the benefits of the agricultural co-operatives.[4] But the rallies of workers and peasants were intended only to create a general climate of public opinion and to support the propaganda line of a 'people's democracy founded on the alliance of workers and peasants'. The direct attacks on individual 'Rightists' were to be made by their very friends and acquaintances in their own groups. Thus the faculty and students

of the People's University held special forums to denounce Ke
P'ei-ch'i; industrialists and merchants tore apart Chang Nai-ch'i's
criticisms; and each of the 'democratic parties' encouraged its
members to analyse the mistakes of Chang Po-chün, Lo Lung-chi,
Ch'en Ming-shu and others. Just as intellectuals had earlier
joined the campaign to attack the ideology of Hu Shih, Hu Feng
and their other colleagues, so well-known non-Communists who
had been cautious in the 'blossoming' season of May and June or
who had made border-line statements and stood in danger of
being labelled as anti-socialist and anti-Communist, now hastened
to dissociate themselves from the leading 'Rightists'. One after
another they rose in forums to voice their disagreement with the
outspoken criticisms of their discredited colleagues.

2. THE FORMAL CHARGES

The Communist change of mood and of policy appears in the
difference between Chou En-lai's speech on the problem of the
intellectuals in January 1956,[5] and his report to the National
People's Congress on June 26, 1957. While the former was marked
by confidence and a desire to win over the intellectuals, the latter
was defensive in tone and sought to explain away the shortcomings
which had been exposed by open critics. What he said about the
Rightists deserves quoting directly because it reveals what were the
vulnerable spots the critics had hit and why the stick replaced
carrot fare. Chou said:

> Certain right-wing elements have come out with quite a number of utter-
> ances of a destructive nature, on the pretence of helping the Communist
> Party with its rectification campaign. Not a few such views are aimed against
> the basic state system of our country. These people have taken their stand on
> bourgeois democracy to attack our state system. They slander the people's
> democratic dictatorship, describing it as the root of all mistakes and short-
> comings. They attempt to set up apart from the National People's Congress
> . . . certain other organs of state power, such as what they call a 'political
> planning council', a 'rehabilitation committee' and such like. What they are
> really trying to do is to divorce our state power from the leadership of the
> working class and of its vanguard—The Communist Party. . . . We welcome
> criticism of shortcomings and mistakes offered with the aim of perfecting and
> developing our socialist system. But what the right-wing elements are in fact
> trying to do is to divert our country from the socialist road to the capitalist
> road. The broad masses of the people will not permit this. . . . The right-
> wing elements say there is too little freedom in our country, and speak as if
> there would be freedom only when the state granted facilities and provided
> guarantees to those who opposed the basic state system laid down in the
> Constitution, and opposed socialism in words and deeds. It is quite clear that
> the people will not agree to give them this sort of freedom.
> The right-wing elements have also chosen to attack our electoral system.
> They say that only direct elections of the kind held in capitalist countries can
> be described as the most democratic. . . .

The leading role of the Chinese Communist Party in the political life of the state is set out in clear terms in our Constitution. The Communist Party is the vanguard of the working class, and the leadership of the Communist Party is the embodiment of the leadership of the working class. . . . It is the unshakable purpose of the Communist Party to lead the entire Chinese people to build a prosperous and happy Communist society. . . .

But the right-wing elements have put forward preposterous demands, such as 'Let Communist Party organizations quit state organs and schools!' 'No recruitment of new members by the Communist Party among intellectuals!' 'There must be no Party system running things apart from the state apparatus!' 'Let the Communist Party get out of office!' etc. . . .[6]

Since Lu Ting-yi of the Propaganda Department of the Party's Central Committee was responsible for the first statement on the new policy in 1956, it is of interest to hear what he had to say a year later. The problem of the Rightists he officially related to that of the intellectuals, saying:

The rightists actively disseminated ridiculous anti-socialist views. They attempted to seize leadership in the democratic parties and among educationists, writers, artists, journalists, scientists, technicians, jurists, industrialists and business men, as a step prior to seizing leadership of the whole country. They tried to provoke students to disturbances and judged that the 'student question' thus created had reached the point of explosion. They thought that once the students went on to the streets and the rightists stirred people up at the lowest levels, factory and office workers would join the students in making trouble; and then they could come out and 'clean up the mess'!

. . . The rightists centred their hopes on the higher intellectuals. They shouted demagogic slogans about 'protecting the scientists' and 'letting the professors run the schools'.[7]

What Lu considered the most reprehensible in the Rightists was that they 'provocatively said that the movement to suppress the counter-revolutionaries was "rotten to the core", and the ideological remoulding movement a total mistake'; that they maintained that 'the Communist Party, the political party of the working class, should not lead the state', and to do so would mean 'the monopoly of the state by the Party'; that they proposed 'government by turns' and a 'two-party system'.

Lu defended Stalin's statement that 'Communists are made of special staff'. 'What's wrong with that?' he asked. Another unpardonable offence of the Rightists was that they had tried to 'stir up the masses' by an appeal to nationalism and they had tried to 'sow discord between China and the Soviet Union'. Alliance with the Soviet Union, he declared, was a basic policy of the state written into the preamble of the Constitution. 'Without a solid unity between China and the Soviet Union, there would be no reliable guarantee for world peace and mankind might suffer terrible disasters. That is why we advocate absolute devotion to this unity'.

That the stinging criticisms of May and June had hurt is evident from the intense feeling of Lu's words. 'Our struggle with the Rightists', he said, 'is one between two roads and is a matter of life and death for the nation. To reject socialism, to reject the leadership of the working class, to reject the people's democratic dictatorship and democratic centralism, and to reject alliance with the Soviet Union can only destroy the country'. And, returning to the rigid dogmatism of pre-hundred-schools days, he repeated that 'it is impossible to have a middle road'. In other words, one is either a supporter of the Communists or their enemy; a neutral position cannot be tolerated.

The intellectuals did not surrender immediately. Despite his colleagues in the People's University who had been led to criticize his views, Ke P'ei-ch'i stood by his guns and maintained that the Chinese people distrusted and disliked the Communists.[8] Though made the target of criticism in a number of forums, Chang Nai-ch'i answered his attackers without flinching. In a written statement he denied disloyalty to the Communist Party, and argued that his criticisms were constructive and of assistance to the Communists in their rectification.[9] He accused his critics of excessive name-calling, of using without any discrimination such labels as 'resisting reform', 'departing from socialism', and 'abandoning the leadership of the Party'. He said that they should read more carefully his original statements and asked whether those who had added to his own words were deliberately lying or just weak in memory. There were still people, he said, who did not yet understand the policy of 'hundred flowers and hundred schools' and the meaning of the 'long-term co-existence and mutual supervision' of various political parties. There were others who sought to advance their personal interests by appearing to be the sole supporters of the Communist Party. Some had indulged in plain vilification and did not even deserve an answer.

But a dauntless few could not withstand the overwhelming might of the Communist Party and its all-powerful state, which had the means to direct the activities of all organized groups and to mould public opinion to suit their purposes. One after another the critics were silenced, and the Communists announced publicly that the 'hundred flowers, hundred schools' policy would continue, confident from now on that all flowers in their garden would bloom red and all schools would uphold in their contentions the infallibility of the Party's socialism and Marxism-Leninism.

3. GROUP PRESSURE

One of the methods of thought reform was to place the individual under the surveillance of the group to which he belonged, as we have seen in Chapter VIII. The pressure of one's colleagues and personal acquaintances is harder at times to resist and consequently more effective than the naked coercion of the Party or state. Since the bold critics were mostly members of the 'democratic parties' or deputies to the National People's Congress, these two media were made the chosen instruments for bringing the Rightists to their knees (see p. 184f on the NPC session).

Chang Nai-ch'i was chastised by Ch'en Shu-t'ung, the chairman of the Federation of Industry and Commerce, which had been organized in 1955 under Communist initiative to facilitate the transforming of private enterprises into socialist enterprises. Since Chang Nai-ch'i was one of the vice-chairmen of the Federation, Ch'en felt the need of washing himself and his Federation from any guilt by association. In a long statement expressing complete acceptance of the 'leadership of the working class' over the bourgeoisie, Ch'en censured Chang for spreading the bourgeois ideology under the cloak of 'blossoming-contending'. He supported the Communist line concerning the dual character of the bourgeoisie; though the socialist nature of the latter was increasing and its capitalist nature waning in the high tide of socialism, yet it had not completely ridden itself of its capitalist and exploitative nature, and still needed continued efforts to reform. He opposed prolonging the period of paying the capitalists annual interest for turning their assets into public use, and upheld the Communist contention that such interest was a vestige of capitalist exploitation.[10]

Chang Nai-ch'i was also criticized by a fellow leader of the Democratic National Construction Association and another vice-chairman of the Federation of Industry and Commerce. Speaking on 'Fragrant flowers or poisonous weeds?' he said Chang's ideas were 'poisonous weeds'. To clear himself and his colleagues, he denied Chang the right to speak on behalf of private industry, and challenged his criticism of Communist doctrinairism. He emphasized his own acceptance of Marxism-Leninism as the indispensable guide for building a socialist society.[11]

The Federation of Industry and Commerce and the Democratic National Construction Association jointly sponsored successive forums to oppose Chang Nai-ch'i and to restate their emphatic support of the Communist policy.[12] In a joint directive they called upon 'industrialists and merchants throughout the country and all members of the Democratic National Construction Association to make a determined struggle with the anti-social utterances of Chang Nai-ch'i' and urged that appropriate disciplinary action be taken by the two organizations.[13]

Following the pattern of group pressure, the denunciation of Ch'en Ming-shu and Lung Yün was carried out by the Kuomintang Revolutionary Committee, while the opposition to Chu An-p'ing was channelled through the Chiu-san Society, of which he was a member, and through the sponsors of *Kuang-ming jih-pao*, of which he was editor.

4. THE CHANG-LO ALLIANCE

A well-organized campaign was launched against the so-called 'Chang-Lo Alliance'. According to the Communists, Chu An-p'ing and many other prominent Rightists were connected with this alliance, whose objective was to seize control of the Democratic League and to use it for anti-socialist and anti-Communist activities. Chang Po-chün and Lo Lung-chi were not only attacked for their views in the 'blossoming-contending' season but also accused of plotting over a number of years against the 'leadership of the working class'. In successive forums sponsored by the Peasants and Workers Democratic Party, of which Chang Po-chün was chairman, and the Democratic League, of which Lo Lung-chi was vice-chairman, leaders and members of the two parties took turns in exposing the reactionary thinking of these two men in the past. The newspaper reports of the forums gave the impression that the preponderant majority in the two parties supported the Communist Party and were anxious to prove their strong opposition to the reactionary views and the wicked plots of the two Rightists.

Parroting the Communist accusations, the secretary-general of the Democratic League issued a long statement 'exposing' the 'Chang-Lo Alliance'.[14] He called the two men 'bourgeois middle-of-the-roaders' who intrigued among those 'bourgeois intellectuals' who vacillated between socialism and capitalism. He said that Chang Po-chün had joined the Communist Party in his student days and had been infected with 'the anti-Communist views of the renegade Kautsky', while Lo Lung-chi was 'one of those bourgeois intellectuals, mainly holding British and American university degrees' who 'flirted with the U.S. imperialists', and sought to foster a 'Chinese third force'. Both men were charged with 'middle road' dreams and of making the Democratic League a 'third force' in the Kuomintang-Communist struggle prior to 1949. The article continued:

> What is the real aim of the Chang-Lo Alliance? Judging from facts that have already come to light, those intriguers have a clear-cut programme. They hoped first to shake the proletarian dictatorship in China, then replace it by the dictatorship of the capitalist class. They wanted to replace the people's congress system with a parliamentary system of the Anglo-American type, democratic centralism by a two-party system. . . .
>
> In foreign policy, the Chang-Lo Alliance was anti-Soviet. They did not like to see the unity of the socialist camp headed by the Soviet Union. With regard to culture and education, both Chang and Lo have consistently opposed Communist Party leadership in these fields. . . . Both have, in effect, denied that culture and science exist in the Soviet Union. They declare that, in science, China should learn from Britain and the United States.

Chang and Lo were accused of rallying 'intellectuals who are dissatisfied with the Communist Party . . . who were not yet remoulded ideologically, who were . . . even resentful towards the new socialist system'. They were charged with calling a meeting of 'six Rightists professors' on June 6 in which they expressed the hope that popular discontent had reached a point where 'something like the Hungarian events' might be instigated in China. One of the participants[15] was alleged to have said 'it is in the tradition of Chinese intellectuals to stir up disturbances' and to lead revolutionary movements.

5. ACTION AGAINST NEWSPAPERS

Two newspapers were charged with falling under the control of Rightists and with spreading anti-socialist views: the *Kuang-ming jih-pao* in Peking and the *Wen-hui-pao* in Shanghai. Both were published under the auspices of the 'democratic parties' and had catered to the interests of the intellectuals. Although all newspapers in Communist China depend on the government news agency for news and all are expected to propagate the line laid down by the Party and its *Jen-min jih-pao*, these two papers publish more and fuller reports on the activities of the various non-Communist parties and they print more news in the cultural and educational field. They discuss problems of special interest to intellectuals. During the 'blossoming-contending' season of May and June, they carried full reports of the various forums and helped publicize the bold criticisms which alarmed the Communists. Actually, what they printed was not so very different from what was found in the

Jen-min jih-pao, and in some instances the *Jen-min jih-pao* reported the criticisms even more fully than the two papers. Nevertheless, there were indications of differences in editorial policy and the Communists hastened to make the two papers toe the line.

The *Kuang-ming jih-pao* got into trouble not only because its editor, Chu An-p'ing, had dared to criticize the 'Party's world' view of the Communists but also because its managing director was Chang Po-chün and Chang Nai-ch'i a member of its board. Each represented his own party on the board of directors of the *Kuang-ming jih-pao*. All the three were dismissed and new representatives were appointed to replace them.

The 'self-examination' of *Kuang-ming jih-pao* began about the middle of June. Its staff and its board members held meetings to review their past work and to pinpoint their mistakes. They vigorously denounced Chu An-p'ing and Chang Po-chün for making use of the paper for political intrigue against the 'people'.[16] Under the title 'No more to be tricked by the Rightists' a *KMJP* editorial on June 17 declared that to protect socialism and to repel the attack of the Rightists was a grave ideological struggle of great significance for the nation, and it called upon all patriots to continue to expose the Rightists and refute their views. After a month of 'soul-searching', the editorial department came out on July 15 with a long statement entitled 'An examination of the errors committed by this paper during the unlawful alteration of its political course by Chang Po-chün and Chu An-p'ing'.

The *Kuang-ming jih-pao* statement amounted to a confession on the part of its editorial staff. It acknowledged that both it and the *Wen-hui-pao* had become tools of the Chang-Lo Alliance and had engaged in seditious and agitating activities. To have sponsored forums in major cities, at which 'Rightists' and disgruntled persons were encouraged to expose the faults of the Communist Party, was now conceded to have been a mistake. Detailed charges against its discredited editor were, we quote:

> After Chu An-p'ing became editor of this paper he followed the journalistic policy of the Chang-Lo Alliance. He held that the newspapers of today must learn from the old newspapers of the Kuomintang areas before liberation . . . that editorials should be more critical and perform the function of 'supervising'. . . . He maintained that any news was worth printing as long as it was true. He liked scoops, 'exclusive news' and 'inside stories'. He wanted the editorial staff and the reporters to be unafraid of getting into trouble. He said that there existed a basic contradiction between the newspapers on the one hand and the Communist Party and the people's government on the other, because there were news items which the newspapers wanted to publish but the Party and government wanted to withhold. In reporting international

news, he wanted to use the dispatches of the capitalist news agencies. . . and he wanted to print more reports on the activities of socialist parties in the capitalist countries. He criticized current reporting of international views on the ground that it did not suit the taste of the intellectuals. . . .

In this period, because Chu An-p'ing carried out the intrigue of the Chang-Lo Alliance, our newspaper attacked Party leadership in cultural and educational enterprises; it distorted the policy of the Party, stirred up enmity between the Party and the intellectuals, and spread dissatisfaction with the Party. It advocated absolute democracy and individualistic freedom. It incited student riots. *KMJP*, June 17, 1957

After a lengthy and detailed account of the various offences committed by the newspaper under Chu An-p'ing's editorship, the statement of self-examination concluded with a pledge of strict observance of the policies laid down by the Communist Party. It said:

On the basis of this bitter lesson, we solemnly point out that any departure from the leadership of the Communist Party will surely lead to serious mistakes. A newspaper like the *Kuang-ming jih-pao*, published under the auspices of the democratic parties, is a revolutionary socialist paper. The democratic parties of China are socialist democratic parties under the leadership of the Communist Party. Consequently, we must more fully accept the leadership of the Party. . . . Unless the intellectuals undertake a thorough thought reform, unless they change their fundamental stand to that of the working class, unless they unite with the workers and peasants, they are bound to commit serious mistakes.

The Shanghai *Wen-hui-pao,* in pre-Communist days, was known as a Leftist newspaper and had been popular with radical-minded youth and intellectuals before 'liberation'. After 1949, it naturally followed the Communist line completely but retained its policy of paying special attention to problems of interest to intellectuals. In May and June, the paper had published reports of forums containing bitter attacks on the Communists. Now, in the period of the 'counter-attack' against Rightists, the paper came under severe reprimand for having adopted an editorial policy of maximizing the faults and minimizing the merits of the new regime.

The *Jen-min jih-pao* on June 15, in an article by its editorial department, condemned the 'bourgeois tendencies' of *Wen-hui-pao*. The 'fundamental direction' of non-Communist newspapers, it argued, must be the same as that of the Party newspapers, because the press was, after all, 'an instrument of the class struggle'. Presently various newspapers in Shanghai joined in the exposure of bourgeois tendencies among journalists and the staff of *Wen-hui-pao* promptly began a self-examination and self-correction. The paper now published editorials to voice its enthusiastic acceptance of the supervision and help of the Party and to acknowledge its past mistakes and shortcomings. It admitted the error of 'unconditional blossoming and contending' and of publishing articles full of bourgeois viewpoints and of inflammatory nature.[17] It declared the new determination of the paper to serve the cause of the class struggle and to propagate the ideology of the proletariat, realizing that any policy of 'objective news reporting' would only benefit the bourgeoisie in the class struggle.

The *Jen-min jih-pao* on June 14 said that the *Kuang-ming jih-pao* and the *Wen-hui-pao* were not the only two newspapers exhibiting 'bourgeois tendencies'. This evil was found in other newspapers, in periodicals, and in the journalism departments of some universities. Even the *Chung-kuo ch'ing-nien-pao*, official organ of the Communist Youth League, fell under official censure. A drive was launched to purge all newspapers and publications of anti-socialist and anti-Communist tendencies, through forums and 'self-examination' meetings, and it reaped new pledges of loyalty by journalists, writers and publishers.

6. PRESSURE ON THE NON-COMMUNIST PARTIES

The Communists had no intention of liquidating the 'democratic parties'. The 'blossoming-contending' policy would continue, but it must be correctly followed. The only requirement was that all must uphold socialism and the Communist Party leadership. To do so the parties must rid themselves of Rightist elements and all remnants of bourgeois ideology.

Beginning in June rectification campaigns were launched within each party; they were marked by vigorous denunciations of the exposed 'Rightists' elements and reaffirmations of loyalty to socialism and to the Communist Party. Outwardly at least, and for the moment anyway, the non-Communist parties gave up the role of opposition parties they had tried so briefly and unsuccessfully to assume. They reverted to their passive role of existing under the unquestioned 'leadership' of the Communist Party.

In its editorial of August 29, 1957, the *Jen-min jih-pao* declared the 'democratic parties' should continue to support socialism and to undertake 'self-reform' so that they might become 'in fact as well as in name a political force truly serving the cause of socialism, so that they may win the confidence of the people and justify the hope of the Communist Party for long-term co-existence and mutual supervision'.

CHAPTER XIX

THOUGHT REFORM, REVISED EDITION

1. 'AN UNUSUAL SPRING'

'THE spring of 1957', the *Jen-min jih-pao* editorialized on June 22, 'is an unusual season for the political life and the intellectuals of our country'. In the swelling tide of contending schools and blossoms, the Communists, strong in their physical control of the country, were confident of turning to their advantage the movement which they had started to weed their garden of 'poisonous weeds'. 'If the people with erroneous or even reactionary thoughts had not been given full opportunity to express themselves, how' asked the editorial, 'would the masses be able to recognize their face so clearly and how would they be able to rectify and refute the errants?' 'The bourgeois Rightists' said the paper, 'are not willing to see China march toward socialism. The Hungarian affair had strengthened their dream that in a country in which the system of ownership had been placed on a socialist basis, it was still possible to overthrow it and change its character. . . . In their view, opponents of the Party were rising from all quarters and China was on the eve of a Hungarian affair.'

Unlike the campaigns against landlords, counter-revolutionaries, and the bourgeoisie, the 1957 campaign against Rightists was specifically a phase in the thought reform of intellectuals and its methods were those of reform instead of severe punishment or physical elimination.

2. THE 'SCHOOLS' CONTEND NO MORE

The courageous fighters for freedom nevertheless began to succumb one after another. On June 13, Chang Po-chün made a preliminary statement confessing that he had 'committed a grave ideological error', and that his proposal for a political planning board and other ideas he expressed had been caused by 'my un-certain stand, my lack of clear understanding, and a very flippant liberalist attitude'.[1] 'I have proved unworthy,' he said, 'of the guidance and confidence which the Communist Party and Chairman Mao have given me in the past years. I feel deeply ashamed.'

Lung Yün, in an attempt to pacify his accusers, expressed his gratitude to them for having called attention to his mistakes. If he had admired such bold critics as Chang Po-chün, it was for their spirit, not what they said; and now after a more careful reading of the Constitution he realized that Chang Po-chün's proposals were entirely out of place.[2]

Yang Yü-ch'ing, who had demanded that the Communists get down from their high sedan-chairs, confessed that his views were really anti-socialist and anti-Party and stemmed from a deeply in-grained feudalistic and bourgeois ideology. In the same forum, Fei Hsiao-t'ung admitted that his statements reflected 'an inaccurate estimate of the intellectuals'; he declared his determination to fight against the Rightists under the leadership of the Communist Party.[3]

3. THE 1957 CONFESSIONS

Fuller confessions were made in the National People's Congress, which was in session from June 26 to July 15. Many of the bolder critics were members of the Congress; and if the wave of increas-ingly severe attacks had not been checked before its convening, the NPC session might have turned out to be dangerously rebel-lious. In timing their 'counter-attack' before the NPC session, the Communists wanted through the NPC to bring group pressure upon the non-conformists and thereby compel Congress members, who had been denounced as Rightists, to clarify their position.

To report in full the confessions made in the NPC is neither feasible nor necessary. To summarize the declarations of a few leading persons will be sufficient. The confessions were not confined to the statements made in the 'blossoming-contending' season, but went far back into past personal history. In many cases the 'self-examination' began with birth and class origin, conforming to the pattern of the 1952 confessions. This was all the more necessary because the Rightists had been attacked for their personal morals and connections in pre-Communist days. In 1957, as in 1952, the confessors expressed their disgust with themselves and hatred for their personal reactionary past; they were grateful to the Communists and the 'people' for opening their eyes and giving them a chance to start anew. Some carried their self-depreciation to ridiculous extremes, when recounting their past 'crimes' and the heinous motives for every action they had taken. The discredited Rightists, moreover, started to denounce each other, in mutual abhorrence of their 'reactionary ideas and proposals'.

The entire session of the NPC was marked by loud and fiery denunciations, echoed all over the country in forums and gatherings. Finally the Rightists surrendered and confessed, particularly in the last days of the session on July 13 to 15.

'*I hate myself.*' Chang Po-chün's statement was entitled 'I bow before the people and admit my guilt'. Its opening sentences were: 'I am today a guilty person who has committed serious political errors . . . I admit my errors. I bow my head and admit my guilt, and I shall endeavour with the greatest determination to reform myself.'[4] The root of his faults was in his reactionary class origin and his feudal and bourgeois education. In his long list of ideological offences, he had advocated a middle-of-the-road course between the Communists and the Nationalists; he had gone too far in condemning Stalin's mistakes; he had neglected the study of Marxism-Leninism; he had considered socialism as opposed to democracy; he had planned to expand the influence of the 'democratic parties' and thus endanger the leadership of the Communist Party, etc. He gave details of his anti-Party plans and activities. He implicated Lo Lung-chi, Fei Hsiao-t'ung, and other 'Rightists'. He concluded his long confession thus:

> . . . In the past year or so, my political thinking degenerated in a shameful and alarming manner . . . my political ambitions steadily increased. I plotted to expand and realize my reactionary political programme by utilizing my official position, and by means of such methods as conferences, forums personal talks. . . . All these erroneous utterances and actions . . . were completely anti-Party, anti-people, and anti-socialist. I cannot shirk the responsibility for my heinous crime. I ask the people of the whole nation, the Party, and the government to give me due punishment. . . . I hate my own depravity. I want to destroy my old reactionary self and I shall not permit it to come to life again. I want to join the people of the whole country in a solemn struggle against the Rightists, including myself. . . . I hope to attain a new life under the leadership and education of the Party and Chairman Mao.

'*I am a bourgeois individualist.*' Chang Nai-ch'i confessed his 'bourgeois individualistic thinking and working style'.[5] He now renounced the views he had expressed in the previous month: that the capitalists taking fixed interest for their assets were not exploitors; that class distinctions between the bourgeoisie and the working class had become unimportant; that bureaucracy was more dangerous than capitalism, etc. Chang nevertheless managed to preserve a small part of his integrity, for he did not go the whole way to denounce himself and still denied some of the statements attributed to him. Such stupid statements he could not have made, for he had always been loyal to the Communist Party and never unfriendly to the Soviet Union, so he argued. No wonder his confession was considered unsatisfactory, and he remained a major target of attack in forums throughout the country.

'*I am ashamed of myself.*' Lo Lung-chi called his confession a 'preliminary accounting'.[6] He went as far as Chang Po-chün in acknowledging guilty actions against the Party and against socialism. The eight specific offences he had committed were: *i.* by proposing that persons unjustly punished in the past purges be given a chance to appeal, he had given comfort to the reactionary and counter-revolutionary elements; *ii.* he had blamed the Party for failure to win over the intellectuals, instead of stressing their need of self-reform; *iii.* he had co-operated with Chang Po-chün in an attempt to swing the Democratic League over to the Rightist path; *iv.* he had associated with anti-Party bourgeois intellectuals who had been poisoned by Anglo-American education; *v.* his understanding of the international situation had been influenced by English and American newspapers and periodicals and so he had misjudged the significance of such events as the 20th Soviet Congress, and the Polish and Hungarian incidents; *vi.* he had used his influence in the *Wen-hui-pao* to encourage an editorial policy favouring the Rightists; *vii.* he had neglected his official duties as minister of Timber Industry; and *viii.* he had not 'studied' enough or tried hard enough to reform himself.

The eight faults were not the whole list of his sinful activities, he said, and he retold the story of his life with its feudal and bourgeois influences, and of his ideological degeneration which had been exacerbated by his American education. He had entertained selfish motives for speaking on behalf of intellectuals. In currying favour with bourgeois intellectuals he was merely trying to expand the influence of the Democratic League. He concluded:

> I have come to you to admit my guilt, not to explain it away . . . . My errors are serious, my guilt is grave. I am so ashamed of myself that I cannot find a hiding place. I have been untrue to Chairman Mao, to the leading Party, to the tens of thousands of my comrades in the Democratic League, to the state, and to the people of the nation. . . . It is not enough for me merely to confess my sins . . . I must thoroughly reform myself so that from now on I may loyally and sincerely serve the cause of socialism and the people of China.

'*I am ashamed I did not love the Soviet Union,*' said Lung Yün, who had stirred up a hornet's nest by his criticism of the Soviet Union. He traced his mistakes to his class origin, to his birth in a feudal, landlord family, and to his infatuation with 'the ideology of bourgeois democracy and freedom'. He even confessed that he had exploited the people in the days when he was governor of Yünnan province. Then he specifically pointed out his errors about the Soviet Union, when he had said that it was unfair for China to bear the entire burden of the Korean War. He now saw that China was defending her own soil against American aggression and that the Soviet Union had really given much aid. To compare the Soviet Union with the United States was most reprehensible on his part; he had failed to 'distinguish between friend and enemy'. In the question of Soviet removal of machinery from the Manchurian factories, he had not seen that the Soviet Union had been rendering China really a great service by putting valuable equipment out of the reach of Chiang Kai-shek. Lung Yün continued:

> The Soviet Union is our great ally. If we do not rely on the Soviet Union we shall be isolated and without help. The Soviet Union and our country share the same fortunes and tribulations, common benefits and difficulties. . . .
> My utterances on recent occasions . . . produced adverse effects on international solidarity, on the socialist cause, and on the people's interests. Reflecting on these matters during the night, I feel ashamed and repentant. . . . I ask the Party and the government to give me due punishment.[7]

'*My whole life history is wicked and ugly*,' declared Ch'en Ming-shu, who had played a relatively minor role in the 'blossoming-contending' of May and June. His criticism of Party Commissioners in education had been comparatively mild. But he had been labelled a Rightist and found it necessary to clear himself. After confessing this one specific mistake, Ch'en went far afield to call himself all sorts of names. His whole life history reeked of 'reactionary acts' and 'dirty deeds'. He was 'an arrogant and conceited fortune-seeker'. He was a 'reactionary dyed-in-the-wool idealist', whom Marxism-Leninism could not countenance. His working style was characterized by 'self-approbation, subjectivity, one-sidedness, excessive emotionalism, sentimentalism, impetuousity and other bad habits'. Since no punishment could be too great for such a depraved personality, he asked the Congress to inflict on him the most severe punishment, and to dismiss him from all offices, so that he might thoroughly reform himself and start a new life.

'*I surrender to the people*,' cried Chu An-p'ing. When he accused the Communists of having a 'this-is-the-Party's world' attitude and of Party domination in all matters, he confessed he was lying and was trying to alienate the people from the Party. In his groundless criticism of the Party, 'my ugly face as a bourgeois Rightist and an opponent of the Party and socialism has been completely unmasked'.[8] He blamed Lo Lung-chi and Chang Po-chün for having induced him to use the *Kuang-ming jih-pao* for anti-Party propaganda, and he dug into his past to trace the 'historical root' of his errors. He well described the mental state which drove him and many others to surrender and to making the confessions, when he said:

> When the whole nation directed its solemn criticism to me, I began to see my own mistakes. I suffered intense anguish within me and felt that there was no more any place for me. Each day when the postman comrade brought newspapers and letters to my door, I was too ashamed to go to the door to get them. Week before last when I was ill and had to see a doctor, I did not dare give him my true name for fear that the doctor would identify me as the Rightist Chu An-p'ing.

Hemmed in from all directions, he saw no way to escape, and his only choice was to surrender.

Were this fiction, one might get a good laugh from such ludicrous antics of self-degradation. But this was not comic opera; it was the stark tragedy of real life, involving the destruction of the dignity and self-respect of living persons. When Chang Po-chün said that he detested his old self and wanted to destroy it, when Lo Lung-chi pledged that he would 'use the person that I am today to struggle against the person that I was yesterday', when Lung Yün and many others declared that they wanted to 'reform thoroughly' and start a new life, they were merely using the accepted vocabulary of the thought reform. For Communism requires a person to give up his all to serve the proletarian-socialist revolution and recognizes no middle course, no neutral position; one is either an active supporter or an enemy. Its 'ideological remoulding' demands a complete break with the past and a new start. The emotions of self-degradation and disgust pave the way to self-destruction and to rebirth as a 'new person'.

4. THE ANTI-RIGHTIST CAMPAIGN CONTINUES

The Communists broadened the campaign to weed out 'anti-socialist' and 'anti-Party' ideas and persons in all walks of life. Up to the time of writing in January 1958, no 'Rightist' intellectual has met with bodily harm; not one has yet been physically liquidated.[9] The editors of the denounced newspapers and periodicals were relieved of their posts, and the Rightists occupying leading positions in the non-Communist parties were ousted by their colleagues. The Communist Party and the state did not take any immediate disciplinary action beyond the denunciation campaigns and the pressure for self-examination and confessions.[10] Chang Po-chün, Lo Lung-chi and others retained their official positions in the government until January 1958 when they were dismissed. The effective authority in their ministries had always been in the hands of the Communist deputy-minister and the removal of the non-Communist titular head hence made no great administrative difference. But the Communists still could claim their method of persuasion was democratic, and moreover they avoided making outright martyrs. In keeping the Rightists around and not liquidating them, they kept personalized targets for their ideological struggle, which is an important factor in the 'education' of the masses.

To denounce a reactionary, a counter-revolutionary, a Rightist, etc. is in the Communist eyes an act of great 'educational significance', since the participant acquires thereby the outlook of the proletariat and the emotions of the class warrior. The masses react more readily to concrete matters than to abstract principles. Rural exploitation was too vague to arouse among the peasants mass reactions, but unpopular landlords were a target that all could attack. Counter-revolution was too abstract to 'struggle' against, but persons accused of espionage and sabotage could be used as tangible realities. This point of view was clearly presented by Ch'en Shu-t'ung, chairman of the Federation of Industry and Commerce. Speaking before a joint conference of the Executive Committee of the Federation and the Central Committee of the Democratic National Construction Association, he explained that disciplinary action against the Rightists had been withheld not out of kindness to the Rightists, but 'in order to strengthen the struggle against Rightists'.[11] The anti-Rightist struggle had just started, he said, and the masses would continue for some time to expose the Rightists, analyse their mistakes, and criticize their ideology. The Rightists were 'living teaching material' for the masses, and to withhold disciplinary action until the completion of the mass struggle was of definite benefit to 'the education of the masses'. The essence of the anti-Rightist campaign was the continuous exposure of Right elements. If quick disciplinary action were taken today, Ch'en continued to explain, the people would lose the opportunity of carefully investigating and analysing Rightist ideology, and many Rightists would escape detection, and the damage would be great.

Thus for months after their public confessions, the Rightists were on display to the whole nation as 'exhibits' of public enemies, cursed and castigated in forums and ideological struggle gatherings all over the country. This prolonged tribulation was extremely humiliating and more agonizing than direct punishment.[12]

5. RESULTS OF THE RECTIFICATION CAMPAIGN

The Communists charted out four stages of their rectification campaign. The first phase, they said, was the open airing of views in accordance with the 'hundred flowers' and 'hundred schools' policy. This made possible the detection of Rightist elements. The second stage was the anti-Rightist campaign. The third stage was marked by a positive programme of improving the work of the government and construction enterprises on the foundation of a victory over the Rightists. And the fourth stage would emphasize the 'study' of documents, the practice of criticism and self-criticism, and raising the level of ideological and political consciousness.[13]

The first stage had been concluded. The second stage overlapped with the third and the fourth. As a phase of the third stage, the sending of large numbers of government personnel and intellectuals into farms and factories was given a new emphasis.[14] Throughout the second, third and fourth stages, opposition to the Rightists constituted a major theme.

The material conditions of the intellectuals in China as compared with the pre-1956 days of the new regime are better. If not all the intellectuals have yet benefited from the improvements, at least the top-ranking personnel, the most needed by the new regime, has been given better housing facilities and more favourable working conditions, such as more hours for professional work, expanded library and laboratory facilities, and partial relief from political tasks. Substantial inducements have been offered to scientists and technologists, who now enjoy benefits and privileges not available to other intellectuals. The scientists are now permitted to study capitalist science and to read scientific journals from the capitalist countries and are not narrowly limited to Soviet theories.[15] They have obtained partial release from the rigid control and active interference of cadres. They must accept 'Party leadership' of course, but the Communists have realized that the interference of their cadres in purely scientific matters seriously hampered scientific progress and they have taken steps to avoid the stupid mistakes of past years.

As far as freedom of thought is concerned, the intellectuals are no better off than before. The pressure of thought reform is just as great as before 1956; there is no relaxation in the Communist demand that intellectuals must cast away their 'aloofness from policies' and 'aloofness from class' and must 'study' Marxism-Leninism to be able to serve the proletarian-socialist revolution. In some ways, however, the disillusionment, the frustration and discouragement of the intellectuals may be even more acute than before, for their hopes have been aroused and shattered.

Scholars in the social sciences have actually had their freedom reduced. Smarting under the criticisms of the social scientists, the Communists have become even more insistent that the social sciences must be purged of their bourgeois character.[16] Fei Hsiao-t'ung, Wu Ching-ch'ao and P'an Kuang-tan have been discredited as Rightists. Since the narrow scope of Marxist social science had been criticized, a special drive against the bolder Rightists was launched from among the social scientists, and many forums were organized to oppose the 'revival' of the 'bourgeois social sciences'.[17]

In this campaign, the *Jen-min jih-pao* published on September 21, 1957 an article titled 'We shall not permit the return of Ch'en Ta's *Labour Problems* and *Social Survey*'. Ch'en Ta, an eminent authority of national and international fame on Chinese population problems and other problems of sociological interest, was denounced as a typical example of the 'reactionary, anti-scientific, and anti-Marxist' bourgeois social scientist, whose methods and point of view were unacceptable in the new age. Ch'en qualified as a Rightist because during the brief 'blossoming' season he had made some caustic comments on Party leadership when, for instance, he had compared the Party to a chess player and the people to chessmen.[18]

Especially heart-breaking must have been the experience of the intellectuals who, honestly and earnestly, had cast their lot in with the Communist regime but were denounced as Rightists on account of over-enthusiastic 'blossoming'. In the long list of names, a few only need be mentioned. The experience of two persons will serve as examples of the plight of liberal intellectuals in China: Fei Hsiao-t'ung and Ch'ien Tuan-sheng. Both were well-known scholars in their respective fields; their books had been published in the United States; they were among the first intellectuals to rally the new regime and even accept its general ideology. Both had found it necessary to make public confessions of their 'Rightist' views.

Fei Hsiao-t'ung is a noted anthropologist-sociologist whose works are read in England and America. In the early days of 1949–50 he took an active and leading role in the 'reform of the old intellectuals', and was recognized as a 'progressive' intellectual who talked the language of the new society. He wrote articles reporting his 'study' and his gradual transformation,[19] and edited a volume titled *The reform of the old intellectuals*.[20] As an anthropologist, he was interested in research on China's racial minorities, and his service was enlisted by the Communists to help implement their policy in dealing with the minority groups. As vice-president of the Central Institute for Nationalities, he went many times to the areas of the minority groups to study their problems at first hand. To all appearances, he was a non-Communist intellectual who had won the respect and confidence of the Communists.

In June 1956, Fei published an article in English to assure his friends in England and America that all was well with him. 'We love our present-day work, we love New China', he declared.[21] 'All that I dreamed about in the past is now, or will soon be, reality'. He defended the Communist thought reform, maintaining that intellectuals were changing themselves by their own voluntary effort and no compulsion had been exerted on them. Citing the case of Liang Shu-ming, who had resisted thought reform but remained unpunished, he asked 'Who can say there is no freedom in a country like this?'

But Fei misjudged the Communist temper. He was in reality among the moderate critics of the 'blossoming' season, but what he said was enough to incriminate him. He was declared a 'Rightist', a master-mind of the Chang-Lo Alliance. He became a major target of the anti-Rightist campaign, condemned and cursed all over the country. What must have hurt him most deeply was that a close friend and associate who had co-operated with him in anthropological studies had joined this nation-wide attack and called him all sorts of cruel and humiliating names: 'a plotter', 'traitor', 'slave to imperialists', 'betrayer of peasants', etc.[22]

Fei also made his confession in the National People's Congress.[23] He admitted that he had reflected the views of backward intellectuals in his article 'Early spring weather for the intellectuals' (see p. 148). He had made a serious mistake when, in forums sponsored by the Democratic League, he encouraged intellectuals to air their criticisms freely so that the various opinions could be compiled and sent to the Party and government. In doing so, he indiscriminately spread the anti-socialist and anti-Communist views of backward discontented intellectuals. Among his reactionary ideas was his desire to restore the study of the old social sciences and his failure to realize that 'bourgeois social science cannot possibly be scientific, and my demand for its restoration was a reactionary political demand'. He confessed that his participation in the intrigues of the Chang-Lo Alliance was a 'treasonable crime' and he thanked the Party for 'clubbing me in order to awaken me in good time'. The root of his mistakes, he said, lay in his bourgeois reactionary stand and his failure to reform himself. 'I hate my past,' he declared. 'I confess my sins, I shall continue to reflect, to struggle against the Rightists, to study in the course of the struggle, in order to reform myself. I resolve to accept the education of the Party and to take the path of socialism under the leadership of the Party'.[24]

Ch'ien Tuan-sheng, an American-educated political scientist on the faculty of Peking University, was before 1949 much admired by Americans who did not think much of Chiang Kai-shek's government. After 1949, he was so active in 'self-reform' and in supporting the new regime that he was made head of the new College of Political Science and Law. During the thought reform of 1951, he had confessed many shortcomings arising from his bourgeois ideology: his selfish individualism, his inadequate teaching, his unwillingness to co-operate with colleagues, etc. He assailed the traditional 'freedom and licence' of Peking University and the reactionary ideology of Hu Shih and Ts'ai Yüan-p'ei. Even then he was already talking against the 'Rightists of the May 4 movement'. 'In order to improve ourselves,' he wrote, 'in order to reform higher education, in order to live up to the expectations of the people and of Chairman Mao, let us teachers of higher institutions plunge ourselves with the utmost enthusiasm into the high tide of self-education and self-reform, using the method of criticism and self-criticism'.[25]

In the following years Ch'ien continued to speak and write in praise of the political system of the new regime as 'democratic in spirit, suitable for present-day China, and a guarantee for the fulfilment of the great task of building a socialist society'. 'In China', he wrote in 1955, 'power now belongs to the people and the people alone'.[26] Nevertheless, during the 'blossoming' season he voiced dissatisfaction with the Party control of education and he was also denounced as a Rightist.

Ch'ien's new confession bears the title 'My criminal record'. 'Before liberation', he began, 'I was over a long period of time engaged in anti-Communist, anti-Soviet, pro-reactionary Kuomintang, pro-America, and worship-America activities'.[27] Then he retailed his recent 'anti-socialist and anti-Party' activities in connection with the Chang-Lo Alliance. He admitted that his recent criticisms had tended to weaken the leadership of the Party in education and in government. He had not been able to discard his bourgeois ideas about education, and he was an unscrupulous politician under the mask of a scholar. He was particularly ashamed of his connections with American imperialist and he named the Americans with whom he had foolishly maintained friendly relations. 'I now bow before the people to admit my guilt. I am determined to give a complete account of all my crimes, new and old'.

6. NO PEACE FOR THE INTELLECTUALS

If the intellectuals who had been labelled as Rights had no peace of mind, what rest could expect the intellectuals who had not been denounced? For if 'progressive' elements like Fei Hsiao-t'ung and Ch'ien Tuan-sheng who had early taken the lead in self-reform nevertheless ended up with being abused all over the country, what security could the less progressive and more indifferent intellectuals feel? If after their early confessions, two distinguished scholars still had to dig up their past to examine their criminal record of bourgeois ideology and reactionary background, does it not mean that the 'thought struggle' must go on indefinitely with its tensions and humiliations? Despite extreme caution can one feel sure that one might not be the next target of rectification?

The thought reform is not something which can be disposed of once for all in a single campaign. It is a never-ending process with recurrent demands for self-examination, for criticism and self-criticism, for new confessions and fresh pledges. It carries on under different slogans at different times but the some methods of group pressure are used, and the real objective is always the complete surrender of the individual to the Party and the state. Between each campaign, the breathing pauses are short-lived. There is no end to the strains and tensions for the harassed intellectuals.

What makes life even more precarious in the Communist state is that the line of orthodoxy is a narrow one and shifts from time to time. What is today the orthodox view may to-morrow become 'Rightist' or 'Leftist'.[28] It is not enough to be in favour of socialism, one must interpret it in exactly the way that the Party leaders consider correct at a given moment. When even high-ranking Communists fall by the wayside in ideological deviations, what assurances have the uninitiated non-Communists of not going astray? Under the ceaseless pressure for more 'study' and more 'self-examination' no peace of mind is left to anyone.

7. NO COMPLETE SURRENDER

Viewed from a certain angle, the experience of the 'Rightist' intellectuals gives a partial answer to a question which has been often asked: to what extent did the confessions of intellectuals express their inner thoughts and emotions? Some people concluded that the intellectuals of China had been so thoroughly 'brainwashed' and so completely 'conditioned' that they had come to a state of mental numbness, or even of mental vacuum, easy then to fill with indoctrination. From the abject confessions and sweeping pledges it might seem that the intellectuals surrendered unreservedly to the pressures of thought reform.

But recent events point to a different conclusion. If after seven or eight years of thought reform, the intellectuals of China did seize the first opportunity to attack the Communists in their most vulnerable points and to express ideas which had been suppressed for so long, they could not have lost entirely their mental alertness or sense of values. They must have managed to keep inviolate a small sector of their mind and heart. It may be a very small domain, and in a society built upon mutual spying and informing, its presence would not be revealed even to the most intimate member of the family. This little sanctuary of unexpressed and unexposed thoughts and emotions for many an intellectual was a secret spring of pure water upon which he could draw in times of great thirst and a hidden reservoir of courage which enabled the intellectuals to speak with the power which they showed in May and June of 1957.

The May 'blossoming' of 1957 was a Chinese version of the Hungarian affair. The fight of the Chinese intellectuals was not wasted for it left an indelible mark on China's millions. It had reseeded many a heart with hope. As leaders of rebellions against unpopular government the Chinese intellectuals had maintained their long tradition.

Students of Chinese civilization and Chinese society have often pointed out that the Chinese lived as members of the family and other groups rather than as discret individuals. But there is also a definite tradition of individualism in the Chinese intellectual heritage. The classic statement so often quoted by the outspoken critics of 1957 to the effect that scholars would rather accept death than humiliation implies a strong sense of individual dignity and self-respect. There are many sayings by China's revered thinkers of the past which reflect this sense of personal dignity. 'The scholar is not a utensil', said Confucius (*Analects* II, 12); he also said that the man of virtue would not seek to live at the expense of virtue (or principles) but would readily sacrifice his life for the sake of virtue (XV, 8). Mencius made many similar statements. 'When people are subdued by force', he said, 'they do not submit in heart. They submit because their strength is not adequate to resist. But when they are subdued by virtue, they are pleased in their inner hearts and they submit sincerely' (*Mencius* II, i, 3). And every Chinese intellectual is familiar with Mencius' definition of a strong man as one whom riches and position cannot corrupt, whom poverty and lowliness cannot swerve, and whom power and violence cannot break (*Mencius* III, ii, 2). With such powerful ideas in their heritage, the intellectuals of China may yet prove that they possess a strength of inner resources which no amount of coercive persuasion or group pressure can completely subdue.

The critics have been muzzled and the 'Rightists' pledged to mend their ways, but Communist troubles are not over. For seven or eight years, the Communist press and other propaganda media had spread glowing reports of the enthusiastic support of the Party and state by the masses, and Communist leaders confidently boasted of their success in 'remoulding' the entire population. But the events of the 'unusual spring' must have unnerved them. They must have found it hard to believe their ears when they heard the intellectuals publicly state that their regime was worse than Kuomintang rule, and that some people wanted to 'kill the Communists'.

The bold attacks did not come from a limited few. A Hong Kong newspaper published a list of 476 top intellectuals who had been denounced as Rightists by the end of July 1957.[29] More names have been added since then. By November 1957, the anti-Rightists campaign was reported to have ferreted out 1,400 anti-Communists among the members of the non-Communist parties.[30] While this alleged exposure was undoubtedly in part motivated by a new drive to chastise the non-Communist parties and force them into submissive position, it also showed that the leading 'Rightists' had many supporters.

Another piece of evidence that the bolder intellectuals expressed views which were shared by many people, is that in the Communist 'counter-attack', in forums convened for the express purpose of castigating the critics, there were still persons who stood up and spoke in defence of the critics. For instance, in a forum of the Chiu-san Society, against three persons who spoke against Chu An-p'ing, five persons rose in his defence.[31]

Moreover, the 'Rightists' were found not only among the non-Communists. There were 'Rightist' elements within the Party itself allegedly in league with the anti-socialist anti-Party non-Communists. Lu Ting-yi frankly stated that 'Rightists inside and outside the Party hope for a Hungarian incident in China, they plot first of all to seize the leadership over the intellectuals and the industrial and commerical circles, and later to seize the leadership of the whole country'.[32] So important a person as the vice-president and vice-editor-in-chief of the People's Publishing Company, Tseng Yen-hsiu, was discovered to be a Rightist.[33] Calling for a determined fight against the Rightists within the Party as well as without, the *Jen-min jih-pao* editorial of September 11, 1957, stated that even some veteran Party members, of ten to twenty years' standing, had turned Rightists.

The extent of the anti-Communist sentiment in China may be judged from the fact that the Communists have uncovered Rightists in all walks of life. Among them are writers, editors, publishers, cartoonists, industrialists, government officials, leaders of women's organizations, leaders of trade unions, etc. Especially astonishing was the exposure of the well-known Left-wing feminine writer and novelist Ting Ling as a Rightist. Once highly honoured by the Communists as one of the brightest lights on their intellectual horizon and recipient of the Stalin award in 1952, Ting Ling was also accused of anti-socialist, anti-people and anti-Party activities. Her denunciation began in the Writers Association, of which she was vice-chairman, and was carried on by forums all over the country. Among other Rightists in key positions were an editor of

the Foreign Lauguages Press, a member of the editorial board of
the *Chinese Youth*, the editor-in-chief of the *Ta-kung-pao* in
Tientsin, and others. Rightists have also been found in the army
and the church organizations.[34]

Student riots and strikes must have come as an even greater
shock to the Communists, who had subjected the young students
for seven or eight years to the most carefully planned political
indoctrination, and still found among them enough contrary-
minded individuals to start disturbances. Student strikes, which
did so much to undermine the morale of the Nationalist regime
in the post-war years, had disappeared from the Chinese scene
after the Communist takeover. Now they were re-appearing and
the Communists were finding that 'methods of persuasion'
had not been altogether successful.

In the post-war years student dissatisfaction with the Kuomintang was often expressed on the 'democratic wall'. On certain
sections of campus walls the students posted their bulletins and
miniature 'newspapers' in which they openly criticized the *status
quo*. They claimed that it was their democratic right to express
their views freely. After some blank years, the 'democratic wall'
came again to life in Chinese schools and universities with criticisms
which were directed against the Communists. One of the charges
against the *Wen-hui-pao* was that it published a 'democratic wall'
story of the Peking University which encouraged the anti-Party
Rightist students.[35]

Student dissatisfaction was in large part caused by the system of
Party and state education which put a premium on indoctrination
and conformity and made no provision for the development of
individual interests. It was a reaction against the regimentation of
education and the mechanization of school life in the name of
collective learning and collective living. It was a rebellion against
the absolute power of the state, which dictated what and where a
student should study and where he should serve after graduation.
These undercurrents of student dissatisfaction were given a strong
impetus by the revolts of students in Poland and Hungary. Despite
strict censorship, Chinese students were getting factual reports of
the situation in Eastern Europe and they were encouraged to raise
their voice of protest. They saw their opportunity in the 'blossoming-contending' policy of the Communists and started their own
'blossoming' and 'contending'.

Mao Tse-tung had frankly admitted in his February speech that 'in 1956, small numbers of workers and students went on strike'. More reports of student disturbances began to drift out in April 1957. Students of two colleges in Peking organized massed demonstrations to register their protest against the arbitrary assignment of jobs by the state and to demand fuller news reports of foreign events. To quell the disturbances, the Communists suspended classes in the two colleges for two weeks in order to give the students an intensive dose of political indoctrination and reclarify their erroneous thinking.[36]

Student unrest continued to spread in spite of suppressive measures. The outside world heard little of the disturbances and they were not reported in the Communist press until the situation had become serious and required official action.

One of the more serious student riots took place in June 1957, in the city of Hanyang in Central China, but the news was suppressed for two months. The story finally came out in connection with the new drive against Rightists and counter-revolutionary elements in schools. One thousand students of the Hanyang First Middle School staged extensive demonstrations against the government on June 12 and 13. They boycotted classes, they wrecked Party offices and government offices, and they plastered the city with daring posters demanding the resignation of Mao Tse-tung and welcoming the return of the Kuomintang. This ugly story was not known until August 8 when the New China News Agency reported a mass meeting in Hanyang 'to expose and accuse a gang of counter-revolutionary elements who utilized the demand of the students of the Hanyang First Middle School for higher education, and incited and organized nearly a thousand students to go on strike and to engage in parades and other violent disturbances'.[37] It was charged that the instigators spread the preposterous views of the Chang-Lo Alliance and organized a ferocious attack on the Communist Party. Under their influence, the students made many posters reading 'The Communist Party is going downhill', 'Mao Tse-tung will fall', 'Down with the Party organization', 'We welcome the return of the Kuomintang', etc. Besides smashing the office of the local Party organization and beating up the cadres, the students attempted to seize the arms stored up in the army recruitment office. The Party authorities tried to mollify them, but the next day the students attacked again the office of the Party organization and beat up a number of cadres.

Student leaders and faculty members, including the vice-principal, were arrested. In September it was announced that the ringleaders had been subjected to a mass trial and three had been sentenced to immediate execution.[38] But this was not the end of the troubles. Student disturbances have taken place in other cities,[39] and increasing student unrest will continue to harrass the Communists as much as the non-conformity of the intellectuals.

8. COUNTER-REVOLUTIONARIES

Mao Tse-tung had warned that the 'hundred flowers-hundred schools' policy did not mean that counter-revolutionary elements would be given lenient treatment. An important function of the democratic dictatorship set by the Communists is to wipe out counter-revolutionaries promptly and without mercy as soon as they are detected. How many of the 'Rightist' intellectuals will eventually be put in the counter-revolutionary category and punished as 'enemies of the people' still remains to be seen. The charge against the Chang-Lo Alliance comes very closely to the charge of counter-revolution.

However, anti-Communist uprisings in China have occurred which do come under the Communist category of counter-revolution. These show that opposition to the Communists is not confined to the intellectuals and students. According to a United Press report,[40] the Chinese Communists admitted in August 1957 that organized revolts in different parts of the country had necessitated punitive measures against their leaders. In Tsinghai province, a number of intellectuals had been arrested for inciting peasant revolts. In Nanking, the vice-president of the Normal College confessed a plot to organize the students for a Hungarian revolt. In Kuangtung, nineteen persons were given death sentences for rioting and murdering seven Communists. In Szechwan the Communists reported the discovery of an organization aiming to incite peasant revolt and the seizure of arms and ammunition. Leaders of a 'freedom army' in Kwangsi, leaders of a 'China Liberty Party' in Shantung, and leaders of a 'Chinese Justice Salvation Army' in Shensi had been arrested.

Rioters in Kwangtung attacked a government food station, a tax office and other buildings. They killed five Communist officials, and twenty-four rioters were 'virtually eliminated the same day'.[41] There were other reports on the sabotage and seditious activities of the 'agents of American imperialism and the Kuomintang reactionaries'. The Communists have in recent months announced the discovery of a number of anti-Communist organizations such as *Chung-hua Chien-kuo tang* (Chinese National Construction Party) in Nanking,[42] a 'counter-revolutionary' group in Tsinghai province 'backed by intellectuals and capitalists from elsewhere in China',[43] an organized group in Hunan and Hupeh plotting the overthrow of the Communist Party and its regime[44] and a group who attempted to set up an independent government in the province of Fukien. One of the most ominous movements was a group in Kweichow province that had the characteristics of a religious cult. The leader called himself 'Emperor' and declared that the aim of his organization was to overthrow the Communists.[45] Thus after eight years of rigid control and ruthless suppression there are still many anti-Communist activities, some of which seem to be fairly well organized.

A major source of trouble besetting the Communists is their double-talk. They talk democracy but practise dictatorship; they stress voluntarism and exercise compulsion; and they preach freedom while they apply rigid control. Theirs is the double-talk of democratic dictatorship, the people's democratic state, and freedom of speech in a people's democracy. This Communist double-talk inevitably increases the inner contradictions of their regime. It is in the nature of the Communist ideology to try to ride horses racing in two opposite directions, the horse of 'democracy' and the horse of 'democratic dictatorship'. This may well unsaddle them.

Freedom, democracy, public opinion, mass movements . . . these are powerful forces which, once released, are apt to gain momentum. They cannot be casually released and suddenly shut off to suit the purposes of the manipulators. They have a way of resisting manipulation and running tbeir own course. Even in the introduction of universal education, the Communists may finally be confronted with this kind of problem. Will a literate population always read and think what is decreed by the rulers?

The unexpected blossoms of the 'unusual spring' of 1957 show that 'freedom of discussion', though designed to be limited in scope, could easily get out of hand. In the end, however distant that may be, the Communists may find themselves engulfed by the powerful forces they release but cannot permanently control. If this should prove to be true, we might well say that Communism contains within itself the seeds of its own destruction.

DRAMATIS PERSONÆ

Ai Ssu-ch'i
艾 思 奇

Communist theoretician; director, department of philosophical teaching and research of the Marxism-Leninism Institute.

Chang Chung-yi
張 重 一

Professor of economics, Fu Jen University.

Chang Po-chün
章 伯 鈞

Educated in Germany; one of founders of Democratic League; chairman of the Chinese Peasants and Workers Democratic Party; minister of Communications.

Chang Te-hsing
張 德 馨

Vice-president, Northeast Normal College.

Chang Wei
張 維

Professor of mechanical engineering, Tsinghua University.

Chao Ch'eng-hsin
趙 承 信

Professor of labour relations, Yenching University.

Chao K'e-tung
趙 克 東

Associate professor of architecture, Tungpei College of Engineering.

Ch'en Ho-ch'in
陳 鶴 琴

Graduate, Teachers College, Columbia University; educationalist and psychologist; professor, Nanking Normal College.

Ch'en Yüan
陳 桓

President, Fu Jen University.

Ch'en Yung-ling
陳 永 齡

Dean, College of Engineering, Lingnan University.

Chi Hsien-lin
季 羨 林

Head, department of oriental languages, Peking University.

Chiang Yin-en
蔣 蔭 恩

Graduate, University of Missouri; former editor, *Ta-kung-pao;* head, department of journalism, Yenching University.

Ch'ien Chün-jui
錢 俊 瑞

Communist Party member; former political commissar of New Fourth Army; former managing editor of New China News Agency and vice-minister of Education; now deputy director, Second Office, State Council.

Ch'ien Tuan-sheng
錢 端 升

Political scientist, educated in United States; author, *The Government and Politics of China* (Cambridge, Harvard University Press, 1950).

Chin Yüeh-lin
金 岳 霖

Dean, College of Arts, and professor of philosophy, Tsinghua University.

Chou Chin-huang
周 金 黃

Head, department of pharmacology, Peking Medical College.

Chou P'ei-yüan
周 培 源

American-educated physicist; dean of studies and professor of physics at Tsinghua University after the Communist conquest; now vice-president of Peking University.

Chou Yang
周 揚

Studied in Japan; former secretary, Left-wing Writers League; now vice-minister of Cultural Affairs and deputy director of the Propaganda Department of the Central Committee of the Chinese Communist Party.

Chung Hsin-hsüan
鍾 心 煊

Professor of biology, Wuhan University.

Chung Hsing-cheng
鍾 興 正

Professor of agriculture, Shantung University.

Fan Wen-lan
范 文 瀾

Communist historian; former president, Central Research Institute, Yenan; former president, *Pei-fang Ta-hsüeh* (Northern University); now director, research institute of modern Chinese history, Academy of sciences.

Fei Hsiao-t'ung
費 孝 通

Sociologist; professor at several Chinese universities; now president of College for National Minorities; author, *Earthbound China* (Chicago, University of Chicago Press, 1945).

Feng Hsüeh-feng
馮 雪 峯

Communist writer; former editor, *Literary Gazette*.

Feng Yu-lan
馮 友 蘭

Philosopher educated in U.S.; one-time dean, College of Arts, Tsinghua University; now professor of philosophy, same institution; author: *History of Chinese Philosophy*, 2 volumes. (Vol. 1, first ed., Peking, Henri

	Vetch; re-issued by Princeton University Press, 1952; Vol. II, Princeton 1952). Usually spells his name Fung.
Ho Lin 賀　麟	Professor of philosophy, Peking University.
Ho Ting-chieh 何 定 傑	Educated in France; dean of studies and professor of biology, Wuhan University.
Hsia K'ai-ju 夏 開 儒	Professor of geography, Northwest University.
Hsiao Ch'ien 蕭　乾	Graduate, Yenching University; London correspondent, *Ta-kung-pao*.
Hsüeh Mu-ch'iao 薛 暮 橋	Left-wing economist; director, National Statistical Bureau.
Hu Ch'iao-mu 胡 喬 木	Graduate, Tsinghua University; former editor, *Hsin-ch'ing-nien* (New Youth); one-time political secretary of Mao Tse-tung; former director, Information Administration; now vice-minister of Propaganda and president of *Jen-min jih-pao;* author: *Thirty Years of the Communist Party of China* (Peking, Foreign Languages Press, 1951).
Hu Chih-pin 胡 志 彬	Professor of chemistry, Peking Normal University.
Hua Kang 華　崗	Former deputy director, Propaganda Department of Communist Party; now president of Shantung University.
Hua Lo-keng 華 羅 庚	Mathematician; professor, Tsinghua University; lectured in U.S. and England.
Huang Chu-feng 黃 祝 封	Head, department of veterinary medicine, Northeast College of Agriculture.
Huang Nien-t'ien 黃 念 田	Associate professor of Chinese literature, Szechwan University.
Huang Yü-shan 黃 玉 珊	Professor of aeronautical engineering, Nanking University.
Ke T'ing-sui 葛 庭 燧	American educated physicist; professor, Nankai University.

K'o Chao 柯 召	Professor of mathematics, Chungking University.
Kuo Mo-jo 郭 沫 若	Writer; graduate, Tokyo Imperial University; vice-premier; president of Academy of Sciences, vice-president of Sino-Soviet Friendship Association, president of the All-China Federation of Art and Literature, and vice-chairman of the Standing Committee of the National People's Congress.
Lei Hai-tsung 雷 海 宗	Former head of history department, Tsinghua University; educated in U.S.; now professor of history, Nankai University.
Li Fang-hsün 李 方 訓	Former chairman, administrative committee, University of Nanking; now vice-president, Nanking University.
Li Pao-chen 李 寶 震	Former vice-president, Chingku University, Tientsin.
Li Ta 李 達	Educated in Japan; former president, Hunan University; now president, Wuhan University.
Liang Ssu-ch'eng 梁 思 成	Educated in United States; head, department of architecture, Tsinghua University.
Lin Ch'uan-ting 林 傳 鼎	Assistant dean of studies, Fu Jen University.
Lin K'ung-hsiang 林 孔 湘	Professor, Hua Nan College of Agriculture, Canton; educated in U.S.
Liu Hsien-chou 劉 仙 洲	Graduate, Hong Kong University; former president, Peiyang University; now vice-president, Tsinghua University.
Lo Ch'ang-p'ei 羅 常 培	Philologist; professor of linguistics, Peking University; member, Language Reform Committee.
Lo Lung-chi 羅 隆 基	Political scientist, educated in U.S.; former professor, Southwest Associated Universities; vice-chairman, Democratic League.
Lu Chih-wei 陸 志 韋	Psychologist; educated in U.S.; former president of Yenching University.

Lu Ting-yi 陸 定 一	Studied in Soviet Union; member, Central Committee of Communist Party; minister of Propaganda.
Ma Hsü-lun 馬 叙 倫	Leader, China Association for Promoting Democracy; one-time minister of Education; now member, Standing Committee, National People's Congress.
Ma Yin-ch'u 馬 寅 初	Noted economist; educated in U.S.; president of Peking University.
Mao Tun 矛 盾	Pen-name of Shen Yen-ping, *q.v.*
Mao Yi-sheng 茅 以 昇	Engineer; educated in U.S.; former president, Chiaotung University (Tangshan).
Ou-yang Yü-ch'ien 歐 陽 予 倩	Educated in Japan; playwright and actor; now head, Central School of Drama, Peking.
Pai Shou-yi 白 壽 彝	Head, history department, Peking Normal University.
P'an Kuang-tan 潘 光 旦	Sociologist; educated in U.S.; former dean, College of Arts, Kuanghua University (Shanghai); now professor, Tsinghua University.
P'eng Ti-hsien 彭 廸 先	President, Szechwan University; educated in Japan; member, Democratic League.
Shen Yen-ping (Mao Tun) 沈 雁 冰（矛 盾）	Novelist; Chairman, Federation of Literary and Art workers; minister of Cultural Affairs.
Sun Hua 孫 華	Head, department of horticulture, Northwest College of Agriculture.
Tai Fang-lan 戴 芳 瀾	Professor, Peking College of Agriculture.
T'ang Yung-t'ung 湯 用 通	Philosopher; graduate of Tsinghua and Harvard; vice-president, Peking University.
T'ao Hsing-chih 陶 行 知	Educator, (1891–1946); studied at Columbia; famous for his popularization of science and mass education.
Teng Chia-tung 鄧 家 棟	Head, department of internal medicine, Peking Medical College.

T'eng Ta-ch'un 滕 大 春	Professor, Hopei Normal College.
Teng Tzu-hui 鄧 子 恢	Vice-premier; head of the rural department of the Central Committee of the Communist Party.
Ts'ai Ch'iao 蔡 翹	Physiologist; dean, College of Medicine, Nanking University.
Ts'ai Ch'u-sheng 蔡 楚 生	Motion-picture director and producer.
Wang Chia-chi 王 家 楫	Director, Institute of Marine Biology, Academy of Sciences.
Wang Yi-chai 王 毅 齋	Secretary-general, Honan University.
Wen Kung-yi 溫 公 頤	Head, department of Chinese language and literature, Hopei Normal College.
Wu Ching-ch'ao 吳 景 超	Sociologist; educated in U.S.; professor, Tsinghua University.
Wu Ta-k'un 吳 大 琨	Professor of economics, Chinese People's University; former research associate and assistant professor of economics, University of Washington, Seattle.
Wu Yao-tsung 吳 耀 宗	Christian leader and YMCA worker; studied at Columbia; leader, Chinese Christian Three-self movement; member, Standing Committee of National People's Congress.
Wu Yü-chin 吳 于 廑	Head, history department, Wuhan University.
Yü Te-yüan 喻 德 淵	Vice-president, Northeast College of Geology; chairman, Changchun branch of Democratic League.
Yüan Shui-po 袁 水 拍	Poet; editor-in-chief, *Jen-min jih-pao*.

TITLES OF PUBLISHED CONFESSIONS

The confessions examined in this study were published in various Communist newspapers and periodicals. Twenty-eight were compiled in two volumes of *Chiao-shih ssu-hsiang kai-tsao wen-hsüan* 教師思想改造文選 (Selected Documents on the Thought Reform of Teachers) published by the Chung-nan jen-min ch'u-pan-she 中南人民出版社 in March, 1953. Another compilation *Ssu-hsiang-kai-tsao wen-hsüan* 思想改造文選 (Selected Documents on Thought Reform, referred to in the Notes as *Documents*) was published in 5 vols. by the Kuang-ming jih-pao she 光明日報社 in January, 1952. Fifty-five confessions are contained in the 5 volumes.

The following list is, of course, incomplete. The titles may give some idea of the content of the articles.

CHANG Chung-yi 張重一 : 我在學習中的初步認識 *Wo tsai hsüeh-hsi chung ti ch'u-pu jen-shih* (What I learned from preliminary study)

CHANG Te-hsing 張德馨 : 徹底清算我的資產階級思想 *Ch'e-ti ch'ing-suan wo-ti tzu-ch'an-chieh-chi ssu-hsiang* (To liquidate thoroughly my bourgeois ideology)

CHANG Wei 張維 : 我所看到的清華大學的一些問題 *Wo so-k'an-tao-ti ch'ing-hua ta-hsüeh-ti i-hsieh wen-t'i* (A few problems of Tsinghua University as I see them)

CHAO Ch'eng-hsin 趙承信 : 批判我的「國際學者」思想 *P'i-p'an wo-ti kuo-chi hsüeh-che ssu-hsiang* (Criticism of my idea of becoming a scholar of international fame)

CHAO K'e-tung 趙克東 : 批判我的錯誤教學觀點和個人主義思想 *P'i-p'an wo-ti ts'o-wu chiao-hsüeh kuan-tien ho ko-jen-chu-i ssu-hsiang* (Criticism of my erroneous concepts of teaching and my individualistic ideology)

CH'EN Yüan 陳桓 : 自我檢討 *Tzu-wo chien-t'ao* (My self-examination)

CHIANG Yin-en 蔣蔭恩 : 我要徹底改造我的思想 *Wo-yao ch'e-ti kai-tsao wo-ti ssu-hsiang* (I have to reform thoroughly my thought)

CH'IEN Tuan-sheng 錢端升 : 爲改造自己更好的服務祖國而學習 *Wei kai-tsao tzu-chi keng-hao-ti fu-wu tsu-kuo erh hsüeh-hsi* (Study in order to reform myself and serve the fatherland better)

CH'IEN Wei-ch'ang 錢偉長 : 我跳出了帝國主義的陷阱 *Wo t'iao-ch'u-liao ti-kuo-chu-i-ti hsien-ching* (I escaped from the imperialist trap)

CHIN Yüeh-lin 金岳霖 : 批判我的唯心論的資產階級教學思想 *P'i-p'an wo-ti wei-hsin-lun-ti tzu-ch'an-chieh-chi chiao-hsüeh ssu-hsiang* (Criticism of my idealistic bourgeois pedagogical ideology)

CHOU Chin-huang 周金黃：徹底剷除崇拜美帝國主義的思想 *Ch'e-ti ch'an-ch'u ch'ung-pai mei-ti-kuo-chu-i-ti ssu-hsiang* (To root out thoroughly my ideology of admiring American imperialism)

CHOU P'ei-yüan 周培元：批判我的資產階級的腐朽思想 *P'i-p'an wo-ti tzu-ch'an-chieh-chi-ti fu-hsiu ssu-hsiang* (Criticism of my decadent bourgeois ideology)

CHUNG Hsin-hsüan 鍾心煊：清算我的親美崇美思想 *Ch'ing-suan wo-ti ch'in-mei ch'ung-mei ssu-hsiang* (To liquidate my pro-America admire-America mentality)

CHUNG Hsing-cheng 鍾興正：檢討我的腐朽的資產階級教育思想 *Chien-t'ao wo-ti fu-hsiu-ti tzu-ch'an-chieh-chi chiao-yü ssu-hsiang* (Examination of my decadent bourgeois concepts of education)

FEI Hsiao-t'ung 費孝通：我這一年 *Wo che-i-nien* (My past year)

FENG Yu-lan 馮友蘭：我參加了革命 *Wo ts'an-chia-liao ke-ming* (I took part in the revolution)

Ho Ting-chieh 何定傑：讀「中國社會各階級的分析」後的自我分析 *Tu 'chung-kuo she-hui ko chieh-chi-ti fen-shih' hou ti tzu-wo fen-shih* (My self-analysis after reading Mao Tse-tung's 'Analysis of Classes in Chinese Society')

HSIA K'ai-ju 夏開儒：批判我的崇美思想 *P'i-p'an wo-ti ch'ung-mei ssu-hsiang* (Criticism of my admire-America ideology)

HU Chih-pin 胡志彬：檢討我的錯誤思想 *Chien-t'ao wo-ti ts'o-wu ssu-hsiang* (Examination of my erroneous ideology)

HUA Lo-keng 華羅庚：我們祇應當有一個傳統──爲人民服務的傳統 *Wo-men chih-ying-tang yu i-ko ch'uan-t'ung—wei-jen-min fu-wu-ti ch'uan-t'ung* (We should have only one tradition—the tradition of serving the people)

HUANG Chu-feng 黃祝封：清算我的名利思想 *Ch'ing-suan wo-ti ming-li ssu-hsiang* (To liquidate my 'fame and gain' ideology)

HUANG Nien-t'ien 黃念田：批判我的「人生如夢」的錯誤觀點 *P'i-p'an wo-ti 'jen-sheng-ju-meng' ti ts'o-wu kuan-tien* (Criticism of my erroneous ideology of 'life is like a dream')

HUANG Yü-shan 黃玉珊：批判我的「知識商品化」的思想 *P'i-p'an wo-ti 'chih-shih shang-p'in-hua' ti ssu-hsiang* (Criticism of my ideology of commercialized knowledge)

KE T'ing-sui 葛庭燧：批判我的崇美思想 *P'i-p'an wo-ti ch'ung-mei ssu-hsiang* (Criticism of my admire-America ideology)

K'o Chao 柯召：批判我的純技術觀點 *P'i-p'an wo-ti shun-chi-shu kuan-tien* (Criticism of my purely technical viewpoint)

LI Fang-hsün 李方訓：批判我的政治思想 *P'i-p'an wo-ti cheng-chih ssu-hsiang* (Criticism of my political ideology)

LI Pao-chen 李寳震：我的反動思想危害了人民教育事業 *Wo-ti fan-tung ssu-hsiang wei-hai-liao jen-min chiao-yü shih-yeh* (My reactionary ideology has jeopardized the people's educational enterprises)

Liang Ssu-ch'eng 梁思成：我爲誰服務了二十餘年 *Wo wei-shui fu-wu-liao erh-shih yü nien* (Whom I served for more than twenty years)

Lin Ch'uan-ting 林傳鼎：我的反省 *Wo-ti fan-sheng* (My self-reflection)

Lu Shu-yü 盧書愚：批判我盲目崇拜羅斯福的錯誤思想 *P'i-p'an wo mang-mu ch'ung-pai Lo-shih-fu ti ts'o-wu ssu-hsiang,'* (Criticism of my blind worship of Franklin D. Roosevelt)

Mao Yi-sheng 茅以昇：我的檢討 *Wo-ti chien-t'ao* (My self-examination)

Sun Hua 孫華：批判我著作中的資產階級思想 *P'i-p'an wo chu-tso-chung-ti tzu-ch'an-chieh-chi ssu-hsiang* (Criticism of the bourgeois ideas in my published works)

Tai Fang-lan 戴芳瀾：從頭學起從新做起 *Ts'ung-t'ou hsüeh-ch'i ts'ung-hsin tso-ch'i* (To learn from the beginning, to learn anew)

Teng Chia-tung 鄧家棟：我們要批判過去「協和」的一切 *Wo-men yao p'i-p'an kuo-ch'ü 'hsieh-ho' ti i-ch'ieh* (I must criticize the past of Peking Union Medical College)

T'eng Ta-ch'un 滕大春：我對敵友認識的檢討 *Wo tui ti yu jen-shih-ti chien-t'ao* (Examination of my understanding of friend and enemy)

Ts'ai Ch'iao 蔡翹：和資產階級思想劃清界限 *Ho tzu-ch'an-chieh-chi ssu-hsiang hua-ch'ing chieh-hsien* (Drawing a clear demarcation line with bourgeois ideology)

Wang Chia-chi 王家楫：批判我的舊思想 *P'i-p'an wo-ti chiu ssu-hsiang* (Criticism of my old ideology)

Wen Kung-yi 溫公頤：檢討我過去的宗派主義思想 *Chien-t'ao wo kuo-ch'ü-ti tsung-p'ai-chu-i ssu-hsiang* (To examine my factionalism in the past)

Wu Yü-chin 吳于廑：我認識了自己的虛僞性 *Wo jen-shih-liao tzu-chi-ti hsü-wei hsing* (I have recognized my hypocrisy)

Yen Kuai-yü 嚴怪愚：批判我的個人主義與自由主義 *P'i-p'an wo-ti ko-jen-chu-i yü tzu-yu-chu-i* (Criticism of my individualism and liberalism)

Yü Te-yüan 喻德淵：批判我的「名流學者」思想 *P'i-p'an wo-ti 'ming-liu hsüeh-che' ssu-hsiang* (Criticism of my idea of becoming a famous scholar)

NOTES

[1] Derk Bodde, *Peking Diary*, New York, Henry Schuman, 1950, p. 23-24.

[2] Wu Ching-ch'ao 吳景超, 參加土地改革工作的心得 'Ts'an-chia t'u-ti-kai-ke kung-tso ti hsin-te' (Lesson learned through participation in the agrarian reform), 人民日報 *JMJP*, April 1, 1951.

[3] Huang Chia-te 黃嘉德, 批判我辦西風雜誌替美國帝國主義做宣傳工具的反動買辦思想 'P'i-p'an wo pan hsi-feng tsa-chih t'i mei-kuo ti-kuo-chu-i tso hsüan-ch'uan kung-chü ti fan-tung mai-pan ssu-hsiang' (A criticism of my reactionary compradore ideology in founding and editing the *West Wind Monthly* to serve as a propaganda instrument for American imperialism), 光明日報 *KMJP*, July 11, 1952.

[4] T'eng Ta-ch'un 滕大春, 我對敵友認識的檢討 'Wo tui ti yu jen-shih ti chien-t'ao' (An examination of my understanding of friend and enemy), 光明日報 *KMJP*, Dec. 31, 1951.

[5] Lo Ch'ang-p'ei 羅常培, 我究竟站在什麼立場爲誰服務 'Wo chiu-ching chan-tsai she-mo li-chang wei shui fu-wu' (Where did I stand and whom did I serve), in 知識份子的思想改造問題 *Chih-shih-fen-tzu ti ssu-hsiang kai-tsao wen-t'i* (The problems of the thought reform of intellectuals) compiled by the Propaganda Committee, Southern Branch of the Democratic League, Canton 1952, p. 93-94.

[6] Yü Te-yüan 喻德淵, 批判我的名流學者思想 'P'i-p'an wo-ti "ming-liu hsüeh-che" ssu-hsiang (A criticism of my thought of becoming a famous personality and a scholar), *TPJP*, May 19, 1952, reprinted in 思想改造文選第五集 *Ssu-hsiang kai-tsao wen-hsüan* (Selected documents on thought reform) Peking, 光明日報社 Kuang-ming-jih-pao she *V*, p. 42-46. Hereafter referred to as *Documents*.

[7] Feng Yu-lan 馮友蘭, 發揮知識份子潛在力 'Fa-hui chih-shih-fen-tzu ch'ien-tsai-li' (Bring out the latent strength of intellectuals) in 人民日報 *JMJP*, Jan. 15, 1956.

[8] Chi Hsien-lin 季羨林, 我對知識份子問題的看法 'Wo tui chih-shih-fen-tzu wen-t'i ti k'an-fa' (How I look at the problem of intellectuals), 人民日報 *JMJP*, Jan. 13, 1956.

[9] Chang Wei 張維, 在新的形勢下看知識份子 'Tsai hsin-ti hsing-shih-hsia k'an chih-shih fen-tzu' (A look at the intellectuals in the new situation), 人民日報 *JMJP*, Jan. 18, 1956.

[10] Mao 毛澤東, 目前抗日統一陣線中的策略問題 'Mu-ch'ien k'an-jih t'ung-yi-chan-hsien chung-ti ts'e-lüeh wen-t'i' (The problem of strategy in our present anti-Japanese united war front) in 毛澤東選集 *Mao Tse-tung hsüan-chih* (Selected works of Mao Tse-tung, Peking), 人民出版社 Jen-ming ch'u-pan-she, 1952, Vol. II, p. 724; see also *ibid*, p. 522.

[11] English translation of resolution in Conrad Brandt *et al.*: *A documentary history of Chinese communism*. Harvard University Press, Cambridge 1952, Document 31, p. 349-351.

[12] *Ibid.*, p. 350-351.

[13] Ma Fu-yao 馬伏彞, 我與共產黨 'Wo yü kung-ch'an-tang' (The Communist Party and I). 自由出版社 Freedom Press, Hong Kong 1952, p. 8.

[14] 毛澤東在延安文藝座談會上的講話 'Mao Tse-tung tsai Yen-an wen-yi tso-t'an-hui shang-ti chiang-hua' (Mao Tse-tung's address at the Yenan conference of writers and artists) in 整風文獻 *Cheng-feng wen-hsien* (Ideological remoulding documents) 新民主出版社 Hsin-min-chu ch'u-pan-she, Hong Kong 1949, p. 267.

[15] *Ibid.*, p. 271.

[16] Mao Tse-tung 毛澤東, 整頓學風黨風文風 'Cheng-tun hsüeh-feng tang-feng wen-feng' (On the rectification of education, party work and literature) in 整風文獻 Cheng-feng wen-hsien (Ideological reform documents), 新民主出版社 Hsin-min-chu ch'u-pan-she, Hong Kong 1949, p. 11-12.

[17] Ibid., p. 12.

CHAPTER II   [p. 7-11]

[1] 中共中央中原區關於爭取團結改造培養知識份子的指示 'Chung-kung chung-yang chung-yüan-ch'ü kuan-yü cheng-ch'ü t'uan-chieh, kai-tsao, p'ei-yang chih-shih-fen-tzu ti chih-shih' (Directive of the Central Plain Bureau of the CCP to win over, unite, reform and cultivate intellectuals) in Chih-shih-fen-tzu yü chiao-yü wen-t'i (Problems of intellectuals and education), p. 34-39. Hsin-hua shu-tien, Fukien 1949.

[2] Ibid., p. 35-36.

[3] Hsüeh Mu-ch'iao 薛暮橋, 知識份子的思想改造 'Chih-shih-fen-tzu ti ssu-hsiang kai-tsao' (The thought reform of intellectuals) in 確立爲人民服務的人生觀 Ch'üeh-li wei jen-min fu-wu ti jen-sheng kuan (Establish the outlook in life to serve the people), 重慶青年書店 Ch'ing-nien shu-tien, Chungking 1952, p. 14-15.

[4] Mao Tse-tung 毛澤東, On People's Democratic Dictatorship. July, 1949. (Translation from the Chinese text).

[5] Mao Tse-tung 毛澤東, 反對自由主義 'Fan-tui tzu-yu-chu-yi' (Opposing liberalism) in 整風文獻 Cheng-feng wen-hsien, p. 163.

[6] Liu Shao-ch'i 劉少奇, 論黨內鬥爭 'Lun tang-nei tou-cheng' (On inner-party struggle).

[7] Report of Kuo Mo-jo 郭沫若, Chairman of the Committee of Cultural and Education Affairs of the Government Administration Council in a session of the National Committee of the Chinese People's Political Consultation Conference on June 17, 1950. English translation published by the Foreign Language Press in Peking under the title Culture and Education in New China, Foreign Language Press, Peking.

[8] Loc. cit.

CHAPTER III   [p. 12-20]

[1] Mao was quoting Lenin.

[2] A daily schedule for work and 'study' announced by the government, see Ta-kung-pao 香港大公報, Hong Kong, April 15, 1952.

[3] A formal announcement of the hospital appears in KMJP 光明日報, November 26, 1951.

[4] KMJP, October 16, 1949.

[5] KMJP, October 30, 1949.

[6] KMJP, November 29, 1949.

[7] KMJP, January 1, 1950.

[8] Time, May 26, 1952, p. 41.

[9] Edward Hunter, Brainwashing in Red China, Vanguard Press, New York 1953, p. 25.

[10] Fei Hsiao-t'ung, 費孝通, 思想陣線的一角 'Ssu-hsiang chen-hsien ti yi-chiao' (One corner of the ideological battlefront), 學習 Hsüeh-hsi II, I, March 16, 1950, p. 17-19.

[11] KMJP, October 12, 1949.

[12] Lan Kuang et al, 藍光, 等, 思想問題 Ssu-hsiang wen-t'i 北京, 三聯書店 San-lien shu-tien, Peking 1950, p. 181.

[13] Edward Hunter, op. cit., p. 115.

[14] KMJP, October 25, 1949.

[15] KMJP, June 2, 1950.

[16] The term 'organization' usually means the Party organization; it may also mean the collective unit to which the individual belongs.

[17] *KMJP*, June 4, 1950.

[18] A report on the first year of political education in institutions of higher learning in Peking and Tientsin, submitted to the National Conference on Higher Education, *KMJP*, June 2, 1950.

[19] Fei Hsiao-t'ung 費孝通, 大學的改造 *Ta-hsüeh ti kai-tsao* (Reform of the universities), Shanghai Publishing Co., 1950, p. 97.

[20] *KMJP*, January 6, 1950.

[21] Kuo Mo-jo 郭沫若, 'Report on Cultural and Educational Work', *Culture and Education in New China*, Foreign Language Press, Peking, undated, p. 2-4.

[22] Kuo Mo-jo, 郭沫若, 一年來的文教工作 'Yi-nien-lai ti wen-chiao kung-tso' (Cultural and educational work during the past year), 新華月報 *Hsin-hua yüeh-pao II*, 6, October 1950, p. 1404.

[23] Lu Ting-yi, 'Education and Culture in New China', *People's China*, I, 8, April 16, 1950, p. 26.

[24] See article by Lu Ting-yi in *Jen-min chiao-yü* (People's education), I, 6, October 1950.

[25] Yüeh Fung, 'Ke-ta—A furnace of revolution', *People's China*, I, 8, April 16, 1950, p. 18.

[26] Southwest Operational Committee of the New Democratic Youth League (ed.) 確立為人民服務的人生觀 *Ch'üeh-li wei jen-min fu-wu ti jen-sheng-kuan* (To establish firmly the philosophy of serving people), 重慶, 西南青年出版社 Hsi-nan ch'ing-nien ch'u-pan-she, Chungking 1952, p. 1-10.

[27] Yüeh Fung, *op. cit.*, p. 17.

[28] A detailed report on the process of learning in the North China People's Revolutionary University is given by Li Tzu-ying 李子英 in 我的思想是怎樣轉變過來的 *Wo-ti ssu-hsiang shih tsen-yang chuan-pien kuo-lai-ti* (How my thought was changed), 北京, 五十年代出版社 Wu-shih nien-tai ch'u-pan-she, Peking 1951, p. 93-109.

[29] *Loc. cit.*

CHAPTER IV [p. 21-29]

[1] Teng Tzu-hui 鄧子恢, 關於土地改革的幾個基本問題 'Kuan-yü t'u-ti-kai-ke ti chi-ko chi-pen-wen-t'i' (Several fundamental problems relating to the agrarian reform) in 一九五零年中國經濟論文選 *Yi-chiu-wu-ling nien chung-kuo ching-chi lun-wen hsüan* (Selected essays on Chinese economy, 1950), Vol. II. Part I, 北京, 三聯書店 San-lien shu-tien, Peking 1951, p. 188.

[2] Ou-yang Tsai-wei, 'Intellectuals and Land Reform', *People's China* II, 3, August 1, 1950, p. 22-23.

[3] 'Scholars and Land Reform', *People's China*, I, 8, April 16, 1950, p. 24.

[4] Ou-yang Tsai-wei, *op. cit.*

[5] Kuo Mo-jo, 連繫着武訓批評的自我檢討 *Lien-hsi che Wu Hsün p'i-p'an ti tzu-wo chien-t'ao* (Self-examination in connection with the criticism of Wu Hsün) *Ta-kung-pao*, Shanghai, May 15, 1950.

[6] Among such books are: Wu Ching-ch'ao, Lei Hai-tsung *et al*: 吳景超, 雷海宗, 等: 土地改革與思想改造 *T'u-ti-kai-ke yü sus-hsiang-kai-tsao* (Land reform and thought reform), *KMJP* she, Peking, 1951; Tientsin land reform visiting team; 我們參觀土地改革以後 *Wo-men ts'an-kuan t'u-ti-kai-ke yi-hou* (After we have seen the land reform), 北京, 五十年代出版社 Wu-shih-nien-tai ch'u-pan-she, Peking 1951; P'an Kuang-tan and Ch'ien Yu-tien, 潘光旦, 等: 蘇南土地改革訪問記 *Su-nan t'u-ti-kai-ke fang-wen chi* (Report on land reform in Southern Kiangsu), 北京, 三聯書店 San-lien shu-tien, Peking 1952; Hsiao Ch'ien, *How the tillers win back their land*, Foreign Languages Press, Peking 1951.

[7] Ou-yang Tsai-wei, *op. cit.*

8 *Loc. cit.*

9 'Scholars and Land Reform', *People's China*, I, 8., p. 24. See ch. XV for Lei's later criticism of Communism.

10 Hsiao Ch'ien 蕭乾, 在土地改革中學習 'Tsai t'u-ti-kai-ke chung hsüeh-hsi' (Study in the land reform), 人民日報 *JMJP*, March 1, 1951.

11 Mao Tse-tung 毛澤東, 中國革命與中國共產黨 *Chung-kuo ke-ming yü chung-kuo kung-ch'an-tang* (The Chinese Revolution and the Chinese Communist Party), 1939. Cf. Teng Tzu-hui's speech, foot-note 1.

12 Nine of these editorials were reproduced in 反「白皮書」學習材料 *Fan 'Pai-p'i-shu' hsüeh-hsi tsai-liao* (Study material for opposing the White Paper) 天津, 中共天津市委總學委會 Chung-kung T'ien-tsin shih-wei tsung hsüeh-wei-hui, Tientsin 1949.

13 *JMJP*, August 23, 1949.

14 *JMJP*, September 5, 1949.

15 In 把抗美援朝運動推進到新的階段 *Pa k'ang-mei yüan-ch'ao yün-tung t'ui-chin tao hsin-ti chieh-tuan* (Push the Resist-America Aid-Korea campaign to a new stage), 北京, 人民出版社 Jen-min chu-pan-she, Peking 1951, p. 1-2.

16 'Self-propagating' means the propagating of a new religion free from imperialist influence and in harmony with the New Democracy.

17 'Chinese Christians announce New Direction of Endeavours', *The Shanghai News*, September 26, 1950.

18 Wu Yao-tsung 吳耀宗 has been one of the most active leaders of the Three-Self Movement. A former YMCA secretary, he came to the U.S. to study at the Union Theological Seminary in New York, Before the Communist victory, he was known as a radical thinker who had taken a deep interest in Marxism.

19 Wu Yao-tsung, 吳宗耀, 基督教新運動的新階段 'Chi-tu-chiao hsin yün-tung ti hsin chieh-tuan' (New stage of the new Christian Movement) *KMJP*, Jan. 14 1951.

20 See article by Lu Ting-i, 陸定一, 人民日報 *JMJP*, April 17, 1951.

21 *JMJP*, April 25, 1951.

CHAPTER V   [p. 30-36]

1 *Chung-hua jen-min kung-ho-kuo ch'eng-chih* 懲治 *fan-ke-ming t'iao-li*, published in the *JMJP*, February 23, 1950.

2 Even missionary schools at that time were told that they would be permitted to continue with only minor adjustments.

3 Italics are the author's.

4 Figures by Hua Kang 華崗, president of Shantung University, in *JMJP*, February 9, 1952.

5 Later, the number grew to 6,532 teachers from 24 higher institutions.

6 Ch'ien Chün-jui, 錢俊瑞, 高等教育改革的關鍵 'Kao-teng chiao-yü kai-ke ti kuan-chien' (Key to the reform of institutions of higher learning), *KMJP*, November 2, 1951. Also in *Hsüeh-hsi*, V. I, November 1951 and 人民教育 *Jen-min chiao-yü*, IV, 2, December 1951.

7 *Loc. cit.* (condensed).

8 *KMJP*, January 15, 1951.

9 The confessions of the intellectuals will be more fully discussed in ch. VIII.

10 *KMJP*, September 13, 1952; also *Ta-kung-pao* Hong Kong, September 11, 1952.

11 'Winter schools' are actually literacy schools established to enlist the adult peasant population in study during the winter months when the peasants are not busy with farming.

12 *JMJP*, November 13, 1951.

[13] Lin Yeh 重慶市中學教師的思想改造 'Ch'ung-ch'ing-shih chung-hsüeh chiao-shih ti ssu-hsiang kai-tsao' (Thought reform study of secondary school teachers) in the city of Chungking) *KMJP*, March 30, 1952.

[14] Ai Ssu-ch'i 艾思奇, 關於教育工作者的思想改造問題 'Kuan-yü chiao-yü kung-tso-che ti ssu-hsiang kai-tsao wen-t'i' (Regarding the thought reform problems of educational workers) 人民手册 *Jen-min shou-ts'e* (People's Handbook), 上海, 大公報 Ta-kung-pao, Shanghai, p. 98-100.

[15] 文藝工作者爲什麼要改造思想 *Wen-yi kung-tso-che wei-shen-mo yao kai-tsao ssu-hsiang* (Why literary and art workers must reform their thoughts) 北京, 中國人民文學出版社 Chung-kuo jen-min wen hsüeh ch'u-pan-she, Peking 1952, p. 1-8.

[16] *Ibid.*, p. 6-8.

[17] Yao Hua, 'The writers go to the People', *People's China*, February 16, 1953, p. 22.

[18] *Ibid.*, p. 23.

[19] *Ibid.*, p. 22-23.

[20] *Chinese World* (Chinese daily), San Francisco, October 1, 1952.

[21] Release of the New China News Agency, December 29, 1951. See *Current Background 123* (American Consulate General, Hong Kong), p. 37-38.

CHAPTER VI   [p. 37-50]

[1] *P'i-p'an Wu-Hsün-chuan* 批判武訓傳 (A critique of the story of Wu Hsün) 北京, 人民出版社 Jen-min ch'u-pan-she, Peking 1951, vol. I, p. 2-6.

[2] *TKP*, Hong Kong, May 29, 1951.

[3] Liu Ch'ang-lin, 劉昌臨, 鬥爭武訓與改造思想 *Tou-cheng Wu Hsün yü kai-tsao ssu-hsiang* (Struggle against Wu Hsün and ideological reform), Tzu-yu ch'u-pan-she 自由出版社, Hong Kong 1952, p. 53.

[4] *P'i-p'an Wu-Hsün-chuan*, 批判武訓傳 II, p. 71-72.

[5] *JMJP*, June 1, 1951.

[6] A non-Communist and member of the China Association for the Promotion of Democracy, a 'minority party'.

[7] Ma Hsü-lun 馬叙倫, 我過去表揚過「武訓」的自我檢討 'Wo kuo-ch'ü piao-yang-kuo Wu Hsün ti tzu-wo chien-t'ao' (A self-examination of my praise of Wu Hsün in the past), *Jen-min chiao-yü, III*. 3, July 1, 1951, p. 18.

[8] Fei Hsiao-t'ung 費孝通, 克服盲從 'K'e-fu mang-ts'ung' (Overcoming the habit of following blindly), 學習 *Hsüeh-hsi, IV*. 5, June 16, 1951, p. 23.

[9] Feng Yu-lan 馮友蘭, 關於武訓的批判 'Kuan-yü Wu Hsün ti p'i-p'an' (Criticism of the Story of Wu Hsün), *ibid.*, p. 24-25

[10] *Wu Hsün li-shih tiao-ch'a-chi* 武訓歷史調查記 (Report on a historical investigation of Wu Hsün), 北京, 人民出版社 Jen-min ch'u-pan-she, Peking 1951

[11] Hua-nan jen-min ch'u-pan-she 廣州, 華南人民出版社 (ed.): 武訓與武訓傳的批判 *Wu Hsün yü 'Wu-Hsün-chuan' ti p'i-p'an* (Criticism of Wu Hsün and the Story of Wu Hsün), Canton 1951, p. 9-29.

[12] Liu Ch'ang-lin, *op. cit.* in note 3, p. 55.

[13] *Loc. cit.*

[14] Hsü Te-li 徐特立, 武訓傳的討論是一個嚴重的政治問題 'Wu-Hsün-chuan ti t'ao-lun shih yi-ko yen-chung ti cheng-chih wen-t'i' (Discussion of the story of Wu Hsün is a serious political problem) 人民教育 *Jen-min chiao-yü, III*. 3, July 1, 1951, p. 17.

[15] Chung-kuo min-chu-t'ung-meng nan-fang tsung-chih-pu hsüan-ch'uan wei-vüan-hui (ed.) 中國民主同盟南方總支部宣傳委員會: 知識份子的思想改造問題 *Chih-shih fen-tzu ti ssu-hsiang kai-tsao wen-t'i* (The problem of thought reform of intellectuals), Jen-chien shu-wu 人間書屋, Canton 1952, p. 176, 179.

[16] The 'Four Big Families' were the families of Chiang Kai-shek, T. V. Soong, H. H. Kung, and the Ch'en brothers (Ch'en Kuo-fu and Ch'en Li-fu).

[17] The text of the letter was reprinted in *Chung-sai yat-pao* 中西日報 (a pro-Communist daily newspaper then published in San Francisco) September 29, 30, October 1, 1950. A translation of the letter appears also in Appendix I of Edward Hunter's *Brainwashing in Communist China*. It is interesting to note that young Hu, inspite of his denunciation of his famous father, did not escape being denounced as a Rightist in 1957. Did the Communists find evidence of insincerity by his over-reaching himself in his denunciation? We do not know.

[18] *TKP*, Shanghai, November 29, 1951.

[19] *Chin-pu jih-pao*, 天津, 進步日報, Tientsin, December 13, 1951.

[20] For a discussion of Hu Shih's ideas and why he is unacceptable to the Communists, see Chin Ta-k'ai, 金達凱, 中共批判胡適思想研究 'Chung-kung p'i-p'an Hu Shih ssu-hsiang yen-chiu' (A study of the Chinese Communist criticism of the thought of Hu Shih), 香港, 自由出版社 Tzu-yu ch'u-pan-she, Hong Kong 1956, p. 3-19. *Current backround 167* contains a number of the articles attacking Hu Shih and his ideas. The campaign against Hu Shih did not end at this time. It was revived again a few years later; see ch. X.

[21] Liang Shu-ming 梁漱溟, 兩年來我有了那些轉變 'Liang-nien-lai wo yu-liao na-hsieh chuan-pien', *KMJP*, October 5, 1951, reprinted in 舊金山, 少年中國 *Shao-nien chung-kuo*, San Francisco, March 10, 11, 1952.

[22] The article was reprinted in *Shao-nien chung-kuo* (Daily newspaper in San Francisco), March 13 and 14, 1952.

[23] 民盟廣州支部舉行大學教授座談會記錄 'Min-meng kuang-chou chih-pu chü-hsing ta-hsüeh chiao-shou tso-t'an-hui chi-lü' (Record of the discussion meeting of university professors sponsored by Canton branch of Democratic League), *Documents, III*, p. 30.

CHAPTER VII [p. 51-58]

[1] These were officially listed in the Resolution on Convocation of all China People's Congress adopted by Communist China Central Government on January 13, 1953, The argument was that these 'glorious victories' greatly strengthened the 'people's democratic dictatorship' and laid the necessary groundwork for the first five-year plan and for the convocation of the National People's Congress.

[2] See text in 人民週報 *Jen-min chou-pao*, January 6, 1952, p. 3.

[3] For a discussion of the number of offences exposed and the dismissals and purges that followed the exposures, see Theodore Hsi-en Chen and Wen-hui C. Chen, 'The three-anti and five-anti movements in Communist China', *Pacific Affairs, 26*: 3-26, March 1953.

[4] *Loc. cit.*

[5] The first five-year plan was inaugurated in January 1953 and the liquidation of private business was, in the main, accomplished by 1955.

[6] Cheng Hsiao-feng and Hsü Tzu-mei 鄭笑楓, 許子美: 從北京高等學校反浪費展覽會看資產階級思想對人民教育事業的侵蝕 'Ts'ung pei-ching kao-teng hsüeh-hsiao fan-lang-fei chan-lan-hui k'an tzu-ch'an chieh-chi ssu-hsiang tui jen-min chiao-yü shih-yeh ti ch'in-shih' (A look at the corrosion of the people's educational enterprises by bourgeois ideas from the anti-waste exhibit of Peking's institutions of higher learning), *Documents, IV*, p. 89.

[7] *Ibid.*, p. 92.

[8] *Current Background 182*, May 15, 1952, p. 15.

[9] *Ibid.*, p. 13.

[10] A translation of the article is found in *ibid.*, p. 3-7.

[11] *Loc. cit.*

[12] Cheng Hsiao-feng and Hsü Tzu-mei, *op. cit.* in note 6, p. 90.

[13] Tsinghua was founded in 1911 as a college with funds from the Boxer Indemnity which the U.S. Government returned to China for the promotion of education.

[14] Cheng Hsiao-feng 鄭笑楓, 記清華大學在反對資產階級思想鬥爭中的收穫 'Chi Tsinghua ta-hsüeh tsai fan-tui tzu-ch'an chieh-chi ssu-hsiang tou-cheng chung ti shou-hou' (Report on the results of the struggle against bourgeois ideology at Tsinghua University), *Documents, IV*, p. 97.

[15] *Loc. cit.*

[16] *Current Background, 182,* May 15, 1952, p. 13.

[17] Shen Jung 沈容, 記燕京大學「美帝國主義文化侵略罪行展覽會」 'Chi Yen-ching ta-hsüeh mei ti-kuo-chu-yi wen-hua ch'in-lüeh tsui-hsing chan-lan-hui' (Report on Yenching University's exhibit of evidences of American imperialistic cultural aggression), *Documents IV* p. 105-110.

[18] *Ibid.,* p. 106.

[19] *TKP*, Shanghai, March 31, 1952.

[20] Reports of the three-anti and five-anti campaigns in schools and universities in Central and South China may be found in *Current Background, 123,* October 1, 1952.

CHAPTER VIII   [p. 59-71]

[1] A partial listing of the confessions is found in Appendix B. A glance at the titles may give some idea of the nature of the confessions.

[2] Chou P'ei-yüan 周培源, 批判我的資產階級的腐朽思想 'P'i-p'an wo-ti tzu-ch'an chieh-chi ti fu-hsiu ssu-hsiang' (Criticism of my decadent bourgeois ideology), *Documents, IV*, p. 38-48.

[3] Ke T'ing-sui 葛庭燧, 批判我的崇美思想 'P'i-p'an wo-ti ch'ung-mei ssu-hsiang' (Criticism of my admire-America ideology) *Documents, II*, p. 19-20.

[4] Chung Hsin-hsüan 鍾心煊, 清算我的親美崇美思想 'Ch'ing-suan wo-ti ch'in-mei ch'ung-mei ssu-hsiang' (To liquidate my pro-American admire-America mentality), 教師思想改造文選 *Chiao-shih ssu-hsiang kai-tsao wen-hsüan* (Selected Documents on the Thought Reform of Teachers) 漢口, 中南人民出版社 Chung-nan jen-min ch'u-pan-she, Hankow, 1953, Vol. I, p. 47-52.

[5] Hsia K'ai-ju 夏開儒, 批判我的崇美思想 'P'i-p'an wo-ti ch'ung-mei ssu-hsiang' (Criticism of my admire-America mentaltiy), *Documents, V.* p. 24-25.

[6] Li Fang-hsün 李方訓, 批判我的政治思想 'P'i-p'an wo-ti cheng-chih ssu-hsiang' (Criticism of my political ideology), *Documents, V*, p. 69.

[7] T'eng Ta-ch'un 滕大春, 我對敵友認識的檢討 'Wo tui ti-yu jen-shih ti ch'ien-t'ao' (Examination of my understanding of friend and enemy), *Documents, II*, p. 59.

[8] See testimony by Hsia K'ai-ju, *supra.*

[9] T'eng, *op. cit.*, p. 56.

[10] *Ibid.*, p. 61.

[11] Huang Nien-t'ien 黃念田, 批判我的「人生如夢」的錯誤觀點 'P'i-p'an wo-ti "jen-sheng ju-meng" ti ts'o-wu kuan-tien' (Criticism of my erroneous viewpoint 'Life is a Dream'), *Documents, V*, p. 40.

[12] Chou P'ei-yüan, *op. cit.*, *Documents, IV*, p. 41.

[13] *Ibid.*, p. 44.

[14] Ch'en Yung-ling 陳永齡, 堅決丟掉我的名位思想 'Chien-chüeh tiu-tiao wo-ti ming wei ssu-hsiang' (Resolutely discarding my fame-and-position mentality), *Selected Documents on the Thought Reform of Teachers, op. cit.* in note 4, Vol. I, p. 80.

[15] Wang Yi-chai 王毅齋, 思想改造學習中的自我檢討 'Ssu-hsiang kai-tsao hsüeh-hsi-chung ti tzu-wo chien-t'ao' (Self-examination in connection with thought reform study), *ibid.*, p. 9.

¹⁶ Ts'ai Ch'iao 蔡翹, 和資產階級思想劃清界限 'Ho tzu-ch'an chieh-chi ssu-hsiang hua-ch'ing chieh-hsien' (Drawing a clear demarcation line from bourgeois ideology), *Documents, V*, p. 13.

¹⁷ Yen Kuai-yü 嚴怪愚, 批判我的個人主義和自由主義 'P'i-p'an wo-ti ko-jen chu-i yü tzu-yu chu-i' (Criticism of my individualism and liberalism), *Selected Documents on the Thought Reform of Teachers, op. cit.* in note 4, Vol. II, p. 25-26.

¹⁸ Chin Yüeh-lin 金岳霖, 人民日報 *JMJP*, November 10, 1951.

¹⁹ Chao K'e-tung 趙克東, *Documents, V*, p. 61-62.

²⁰ Chiang Yin-en 蔣蔭恩, *Documents, I*, p. 22.

²¹ Chang Chung-yi 張重一, *Documents, I*, p. 59.

²² Ts'ai Ch'u-sheng 蔡楚生, 改造思想為貫徹毛主席文藝路線而奮鬥 'Kai-tsao ssu-hsiang wei kuan-ch'e Mao chu-hsi wen-yi lu-hsien erh fen-tou' in 知識份子的思想改造問題 *op. cit.* in ch. 1, note 5; p. 151.

²³ Mao Tse-tung's official title when Chairman of the People's Republic of China.

²⁴ See J. A. M. Meerloo, *The Rape of the Mind*, World Publishing Company, New York, 1956.

CHAPTER IX　　[p. 72-79]

¹ Mao Tse-tung, *On Contradiction*, Foreign Languages Press, Peking, 1952.

² Mao Tse-tung, *Report of an investigation into the peasant movement in Hunan*, 1927. Republished in *Selected Works of Mao Tse-tung*, I, London, 1954.

³ Chou En-lai, 為鞏固和發展人民的勝利而奮鬥 'Wei kung-ku ho fa-chan jen-min ti sheng-li erh fen-tou' (The struggle for the consolidation and expansion of the people's victory), 新華月報 *Hsin-hua yüeh-pao*, II, 6, June 15, 1950, p. 1220.

⁴ Ai Ssu-ch'i 艾思奇, 從頭學起 'Ts'ung t'ou hsüeh ch'i' (To learn from the beginning), 學習 *Hsüeh-hsi, I*, 1 September 1949, p. 4.

⁵ Chen Ren-bing, 'New China's thought reform movement', *China Monthly Review, 122*, 2, February 1952, p. 128.

⁶ Quoted by Yang Hsien-chen 楊獻珍, 談談群眾路線問題 'T'an-t'an ch'ün-chung lu-hsien wen-t'i' (On the problem of the mass line), 學習 *Hsüeh-hsi, I*, 3, November 1949, p. 10.

⁷ *Chih-shih fen-tzu ti ssu-hsiang kai-tsao wen-t'i* 知識份子的思想改造問題 (Problems of thought reform of intellectuals), 廣州, 人間書屋 Jen-chien shu-wu, Canton 1952, p. 185-186.

⁸ Fei Hsiao-t'ung, 思想陣線的一角 'Ssu-hsiang chan-hsien ti yi-chiao', (One corner of the ideological battlefront), *Hsüeh-hsi, II*, 1, March 16, 1950, p. 17-19.

⁹ Reform through labour is legalized in Communist China by 'Regulations Governing Labour Service for Reform', promulgated in August, 1954.

¹⁰ Members of the Communist youth organizations are supposed to refer all their personal problems, even romantic and marital affairs, to the 'organization' for advice and decision.

CHAPTER X　　[p. 80-93]

¹ These phrases appear in the preamble of the Constitution.

² The translated text appeared months later in *People's China*, Nov. 1, 1955.

³ A part of the material for this chapter appeared in the *Far Eastern Survey*, 24: 177-184, December 1955.

⁴ Yüan Shui-po, 'Dream of the Red Chamber' *China Reconstructs*, Peking, May 1955, p. 22.

⁵ Li Hsi-fan and Lan Ling 李希凡, 藍翎: 走什麼樣的路 'Tsou shih-mo-yang ti lu' (Which way should we travel?), *JMJP*, October 24, 1954.

[6] Yüan, *op. cit.*

[7] Li Hsi-fan and Lan Ling, 評紅樓夢研究 'P'ing hung-lou-meng yen-chiu' (Comment on the study of the *Red Chamber*), *KMJP*, October 10, 1954, Translation in *Current Background, 315*, March 4, 1955, p. 22.

[8] Yüan, *op. cit.*

[9] Chung Lo 鍾洛, 應該重視對「紅樓夢」研究中的錯誤觀點的批評 'Ying-kai chung-shih tui *Hung-lou-meng* yen-chiu chung ti ts'o-wu kuan-tien ti p'i-p'ing' (We should stress the importance of criticizing the mistaken viewpoints in in the study of the *Dream of the Red Chamber*), *JMJP*, October 23, 1954.

[10] Yüan Shui-p'o 袁水拍, 質問文藝報編者 'Chih-wen wen-yi-pao p'ien-che' (Interpellating the editor of Wen-yi-pao), *JMJP*, October 28, 1954.

[11] *KMJP*, December 9, 1954.

[12] Wang Jo-shui 王若水, 清除胡適的反動哲學遺毒 'Ch'ing-ch'u Hu Shih ti fan-tung che-hsüeh yi-tu' (Liquidate the remaining poison of Hu Shih's reactionary philosophy), *JMJP*, November 5, 1954.

[13] Address at discussion meeting, Peking, October 24, 1954, published in *KMJP*, November 14, 1954.

[14] *Wen-yi-pao* 文藝報, March 15, 1955, as translated in *Current Background, 325*, April 5, 1955.

[15] Wang Jo-shui, *op. cit.*

[16] Hu Sheng 胡繩, 爲什麼要批判胡適, 俞平伯, 胡風的思想 'Wei shen-mo yao p'i-p'an Hu Shih, Yü P'ing-po, Hu Feng ti ssu-hsiang' (Why we have to criticize the thought of Hu Shih, Yü P'ing-po and Hu Feng), 學習 *Hsüeh-hsi*, April 2, 1955.

[17] *KMJP*, December 19, 1954.

[18] *Hsüeh-hsi*, March 2, 1955, p. 22.

[19] *Loc. cit.*

[20] Ho Lin 賀麟, 兩點批判一點反省 'Liang-tien p'i-p'an yi-tien fan-sheng' (Two points of criticism, one point of reflection), *JMJP*, January 19, 1955.

[21] Chang P'ei 張沛, 學者—政治陰謀家 'Hsüeh-che—cheng-chih yin-mou chia' (Scholar—political intriguer), *JMJP*, January 15, 1955.

[22] Wang Jo-shui, *op. cit.*

[23] Li Ta 李達, 胡適反動思想批判 '*Hu Shih fan-tung ssu-hsiang p'i-p'an*, (Critique of Hu Shih's reactionary thought), 漢口, 人民出版社 Hankow, Jen-min ch'u-pan-she, 1955, p. 73.

[24] *Ibid.*, p. 72.

[25] Jen Chi-yü 任繼愈, 胡適的實驗主義思想方法批判 'Hu Shih ti shih-yen-chu-i ssu-hsiang fang-fa p'i-p'an' (Critique of Hu Shih's pragmatic ideology and method), *KMJP*, December 1, 1954.

[26] Chin Ta-k'ai 金達凱, 論胡風問題 'Lun Hu Feng wen-t'i' (On the Hu Feng problem), *Tzu-yu chen-hsien* 自由陣綫 (Freedom Front), Hong Kong, *22*, 1, February 28, 1955, p. 9-11, 19.

[27] *Ibid.*

[28] *Ibid.*

[29] *KMJP*, December 10, 1954.

[30] Wang Yao 王瑤, 不能按照胡風的面貌來改造我們的文藝運動 'Pu-neng an-chao Hu Feng ti mien-mao lai kai-tsao wo-men ti wen-yi yün-tung' (We cannot reform our literary movement according to the likeness of Hu Feng), *JMJP*, January 31, 1955.

[31] Kuo Mo-jo 郭沫若, 反社會主義的胡風綱領 'Fan she-hui-chu-i ti Hu Feng kang-ling' (The anti-socialist principle of Hu Feng), *JMJP*, April 1, 1955.

[32] For example, *JMJP*, January 4 and 14, 1955.

[33] Mao Tun's 矛盾 article in *JMJP*, March 8, 1955.

[34] Tseng Yen-hsiu 曾彥修, 胡風反革命理論活動的過去與現在 *Hu Feng fan-ke-ming li-lun huo-tung ti kuo-ch'ü yü hsien-tsai* (Hu Feng's activities in opposing revolutionary theories: past and present), Jen-min ch'u-pan-she, Peking, 1956, p. 4.

[35] Chinese equivalent of 'stuffed shirt'.

[36] *JMJP*, May 13, 1955.

[37] *Young China* (A Chinese daily in San Francisco), May 27, 1955.

[38] *Chinese World* (A Chinese daily in San Francisco), June 16, 1955. Also *New York Times*, June 14, 1955.

[39] *JMJP*, July 14, 1955.

[40] *Ibid.*, July 3, 1955.

[41] Lu Wei-jan 雷嘼然, 胡風事件的前因後果 *Hu-Feng shih-chien ti ch'ien-yin hou-kuo* (The causes and effects of the Hu Feng episode), 香港南風出版社 Nan-feng ch'u-pan-she, Hong Kong 1956, p. 39.

[42] Articles denouncing him appeared in *JMJP* on April 30 and May 31, 1955.

[43] *JMJP*, July 22, 1955.

[44] *JMJP*, July 22, 1955.

[45] Ch'ien Tuan-sheng 錢端升, 堅決肅清胡風集團和一切暗藏的反革命份子 Chien-chüeh su-ch'ing Hu Feng chi-t'uan ho yi-ch'ieh an-ts'ang ti fan ke-ming fen-tzu' (Resolutely purge the Hu Feng clique and all hidden counter-revolutionaries), *JMJP*, July 19, 1955.

[46] *Survey of China Mainland Press 1113*, supplement.

[47] Both reports appear in *JMJP*, Feb. 1, 1956; also in *Current Background, 377*.

[48] See chapter VI.

[49] Wu Ching-ch'ao 吳景超, 批判梁漱溟的鄉村建設理論 'P'i-p'an Liang Shu-ming ti hsiang-ts'un chien-she li-lun' (Critique of Liang Shu-ming's theory of rural reconstruction), *JMJP*, July 11, 1955.

[50] Ch'ien Chia-chü 千家駒, 批判梁漱溟堅持中國落後反對工業化的謬論 'P'i-p'an Liang Shu-ming chien-ch'ih chung-kuo lo-hou fan-tui kung-yeh-hua ti miao-lun' (Criticism of Liang Shu-ming's misleading theory of insisting on China's backwardness and opposing industrialization), *JMJP*, August 10, 1955.

[51] *Hsüeh-hsi*, 8 August 2, 1955, p. 43.

[52] Jen Chi-yü, 向梁漱溟的反動思想展開鬥爭 'Hsiang Liang Shu-ming ti fan-tung ssu-hsiang chan-k'ai tou-cheng' (Develop the struggle against Liang Shu-ming's reactionary ideology), in 梁漱溟思想批判論文彙編第二輯 *Liang Shu-ming ssu-hsiang p'i-p'an lun-wen hui-pien* (Critique of Liang Shu-ming's ideology), 三聯書店 San-lien shu-tien, p. 19-29, *II*, Peking, 1956.

[53] Hu Ch'ing-chün 胡慶鈞, 梁漱溟是怎樣向馬克思主義進攻的 'Liang Shu-ming shih tsen-yang hsiang Ma-k'e-ssu-chu-yi chin-kung ti' (How Liang Shu-ming attacked Marxism), *ibid.*, p. 67-85.

[54] Liang's address was published in *KMJP*, February 7, 1956.

CHAPTER XI   [p. 94-103]

[1] A geneticist who had studied under Thomas Hunt Morgan at the California Institute of Technology was not allowed to mention Morgan in his teaching, but required to teach the theories of Michurin. See also Kao Shih-shan, 'A visit to the Department of Biology at Futan University', *People's China*, August 16, 1957, p. 34.

[2] Yüeh Ch'ien 岳騫, 大陸教育工作者的現況 'Ta-lu chiao-yü kung-tso-che ti hsien-k'uang' (The present condition of educational workers on the mainland), *Tzu-yu chen-hsien* (Freedom Front Weekly) *XIII*, 5, Feb. 27, 1953, p. 16-17.

[3] Lei P'eng 雷朋, 新型的北京大學 'Hsin-hsing ti Pei-ching ta-hsüeh' (The new Peking University), *KMJP*, July 16, 1953.

⁴ A. S. Chang, 'Communist influence on the Chinese language: notes on the latest economic, sociological and technical terminology', in *Contemporary China* Vol. I, Hong Kong University Press, 1956, p. 142.

⁵ Ma Yin-ch'u 馬寅初, 我也來談百家爭鳴 'Wo yeh lai t'an pai-chia-cheng-ming' (I also say a few words on letting hundred schools contend), *JMJP*, July 11, 1956.

⁶ Ch'iu Lin 丘林, 中國人民大學的教條主義表現在那裡 'Chung-kuo jen-min-ta-hsüeh ti chiao-t'iao-chu-yi piao-hsien tsai na-li' (In what forms doctrinarism is expressed in the Chinese People's University), *KMJP*, September 14, 1956.

⁷ Fei Hsiao-t'ung 費孝通, 知識份子的早春天氣 'Chih-shih-fen-tzu ti tsao-ch'un t'ien-ch'i' (The early spring atmosphere among intellectuals), *JMJP*, March 24, 1957.

⁸ Lin K'ung-hsiang 林孔湘, 我堅持自己的正確意見 'Wo chien-ch'ih tzu-chi ti cheng-chüeh yi-chien' (I held on to my correct views), *KMJP*, June 12, 1956.

⁹ *KMJP*, June 1, 1957.

¹⁰ An Ch'ao-chün 安朝俊, 更好的發揮技術人員的作用 'Keng-hao ti fa-hui chi-shu-jen-yüan ti tso-yung' (Increase the usefulness of technical personnel), *JMJP*, January 12, 1956.

¹¹ Chi Hsien-lin 季羨林, 我對知識份子問題的一些看法 'Wo tui chih-shih-fen-tzu wen-t'i ti yi-hsieh k'an-fa' (The way I look at the problem of intellectuals) *JMJP*, January 13, 1956. Another complaint about the disdainful attitude of young cadres toward mature intellectuals was voiced by the noted engineer Mao Yi-sheng 茅以昇, 我們年老的科學家的願望 'Wo-men nien-lao ti k'o-hsüeh-chia ti yüan-wang' (What we elder scientists hope for), *JMJP*, January 22, 1956.

¹² Interview recorded in *JMJP*, December 18, 1957.

¹³ Wu Ta-k'un 吳大琨: 讓教授們獨立講課 'Jan chiao-shou-men tu-li chiang-k'e' (Let the professors lecture independently), *JMJP*, August 19, 1956.

¹⁴ Yüeh Ch'ien, *op. cit.* in Note 2. All examples in this paragraph are from this source.

¹⁵ *Chiao-shih pao* 教師報, October 9, 1956.

¹⁶ The story of the persecution was published in *Chiao-shih-pao*, October 9, 1956.

¹⁷ This term refers to a number of minority political parties which the Communists have permitted to exist. Several of these parties draw their membership almost exclusively from the intellectuals; many of their charter members had before the Communist conquest been exceedingly critical of the Kuomintang or had held leftist views.

¹⁸ A brief summary of these parties appears subsequently in the next chapter in connection with a new drive for the initiation of intellectuals into Communist Party membership.

¹⁹ *KMJP*, December 3, 1955.

²⁰ *KMJP*, December 5, 1955.

²¹ Text of the speech published in *JMJP*, January 25, 1956, The English translation was later published by the Foreign Languages Press, Peking, under title *Report on the Question of Intellectuals*. Direct quotations are taken from the English text.

²² The term 'higher intellectuals' refers to those with higher training. The Communists in China estimate that these number more than 100,000: over 31,000 teachers of the rank of Lecturer and above, over 25,000 trained doctors, over 3,000 research scientists, some 6,000 top workers in the cultural fields, and about 5,000 other experts.

²³ Chou, *Report on the Question of Intellectuals*, Foreign Languages Press, Peking, 1956, p. 26.

CHAPTER XII   [p. 104-116]

[1] Fei Hsiao-t'ung, 知識份子的早春天氣 'Chih-shih-fen-tzu ti tsao-ch'un t'ien-ch'i' (The early spring atmosphere among intellectuals), *JMJP*, March 24, 1957.

[2] See, for example, Theodore H. E. Chen, 'Collective learning in Communist China's universities', *Far Eastern Survey*, *26*: 8-11, January 1957.

[3] Shih Hsi-min 石西民, chief of the Propaganda Department of the Shanghai Communist Party Committee, article in *JMJP*, May 23, 1956.

[4] *KMJP*, December 3, 1956.

[5] *JMJP*, January 12, 1956.

[6] This provision is contained in the Decision on the Reform of Wages adopted by the State Council on June 16, 1956. (see text in *JMJP*, July 5, 1956). In 1956, research scholars in the Academy of Sciences received a monthly salary of 330 *yüan* plus housing and other allowances. This salary made it possible to have a couple of household servants, each of whom would be paid about twenty *yüan* in wages. The official rate of exchange was 2·40 *yüan* to one dollar U.S. currency. Intellectuals were also given higher rations in food, especially meat, and they did not have to stand in long waiting lines.

[7] *JMJP*, July 9, 1956.

[8] *JMJP*, September 9, 1956.

[9] Shih Hsi-min, *JMJP*, May 23, 1956.

[10] *JMJP*, March 14, 1956.

[11] *JMJP*, July 15, 1956.

[12] *KMJP*, December 3, 1956.

[13] *JMJP*, July 3, 1956.

[14] *JMJP*, March 14, 1956.

[15] *JMJP*, March 14, 1957.

[16] *KMJP*, March 6, 1956.

[17] *KMJP*, March 23, 1956.

[18] *KMJP*, April 17, 1956.

[19] *JMJP*, August 12, 1956

[20] *KMJP*, August 28, 1956.

[21] *JMJP*, September 14, 1956.

[22] The three classes are always mentioned in this order, which represents the Communist evaluation of the relative importance of the three classes to the revolution.

[23] Interview reported in *KMJP*, July 2, 1956.

[24] Shen Chih-yüan, 沈志遠 'Long term co-existence and mutual supervision of parties', *People's China*, March 16, 1957, p. 5.

[25] *JMJP*, November 26, 1955.

[26] Liu Hsien-chou 劉仙洲, 我爲什麼加入共產黨 'Wo wei-shen-mo chia-ju kung-ch'an-tang' (Why I joined the Communist Party), *JMJP*, December 4, 1955.

[27] This term in Communist vocabulary may be translated as 'way of life'.

[28] *KMJP*, March 18, 1957.

[29] *JMJP*, April 2, 1957.

[30] *KMJP*, March 18, 1956.

[31] *JMJP*, July 1, 1956.

[32] *JMJP*, September 14, 1956.

[33] *JMJP*, May 15, 1956.

[34] *JMJP*, May, 29, 1957.

[35] *Survey of China Mainland Press*, *1306*, June 11, 1956, p. 3.

³⁶ *Chinese World*, July 24; also *China Daily News* (New York) August 4, 1956.

³⁷ *Wen-hui-pao* 文滙報, Hong Kong, September 29, 1956.

³⁸ *JMJP*, January 26, 1956.

³⁹ *JMJP*, August 22, 1956.

⁴⁰ *JMJP*, December 30, 1956.

⁴¹ *KMJP*, June 12, 1956.

⁴² *KMJP*, December 22, 1956.

⁴³ The Communists use this term to refer to other 'people's democracies' within the Communist bloc.

⁴⁴ 向科學進軍 Also translated by Communist writers as 'storming the heights of science'.

⁴⁵ *JMJP*, February 8, 1957.

⁴⁶ *Supplement to People's China*, July 16, 1957, p. 18.

Chapter XIII   [p. 117-126]

¹ *JMJP*, May 11, 1956.

² From Lu Ting-i's address, published in *JMJP*, June 13, 1956. English translation in *People's China*, August 16, 1956, *Supplement*.

³ The Communists use the term 'people' in a limited sence, to refer to those who support and are accepted by the new regime. As Chou En-lai once explained, the counter-revolutionaries, the landlords, and the 'exploiters of the people' are not 'people'; they are only 'nationals' of China, who have not attained the status of 'people'.

⁴ Kuo Mo-jo, 'Long live the policy—Letting diverse schools contend!' *People's China*, September 1, 1956, p. 5.

⁵ *JMJP*, June 19, 1956

⁶ Kuo Mo-jo, 演奏出雄壯的交響曲 'Yen-tsou-ch'u hsiung-chuang ti chiao-hsiang-ch'ü' (Play powerful symphonies) *JMJP*, July 1, 1956.

⁷ Lo Lung-chi 羅隆基, 我對目前高級知識份子問題的了解和意見 'Wo tui mu-ch'ien Kao-chi chih-shih fen-tzu wen t'i ti liao-chieh ho yi-chien' (My understanding and opinion regarding the current problem of higher intellectuals), *KMJP*, June 28, 1956.

⁸ *JMJP*, July 21, 1956.

⁹ English translation of *JMJP* editorial in *People's China*, Sept. 1, 1956, p. 13.

¹⁰ See report on a symposium organized by the branch organization of the Democratic League in Amoy University, *KMJP*, June 16, 1956.

¹¹ Reports on views of intellectuals who attended the National People's Congress as delegates, *KMJP*, July 10, 1956.

¹² *People's China*, September 1, 1956.

¹³ *Loc. cit.*

¹⁴ *KMJP*, July 9, 1956.

¹⁵ Ma Yin-ch'u 馬寅初, 我也來談談百家爭鳴 'Wo yeh-lai t'an-t'an pai-chia cheng-ming' (I also say a few words about letting a hundred schools contend), *JMJP*, July 11, 1956.

¹⁶ Chin Yueh-lin, 'The "hundred schools" policy as I see it.' *People's China*, June 16, 1957, p. 10.

¹⁷ The term 'Liberation' *chieh-fang* 解放, is used in Communist China to describe the Communist conquest in 1949.

¹⁸ Ou-yang Yü-ch'ien 歐陽予倩, 聽了毛主席的報告的幾點體會 'T'ing-liao Mao chu-hsi ti pao-kao ti chi-tien t'i-hui' (A few points of understanding after hearing chairman Mao's report) *JMJP*, March 19, 1957.

CHAPTER XIV   [p. 127-140]

[1] Dispatch from Warsaw, *New York Times*, May 1, 1957.

[2] Dispatch form Warsaw, *New York Times*, May 14, 1957.

[3] Associated Press dispatch from Warsaw, *Christian Science Monitor*, May 16, 1957.

[4] All quotations from Mao's speech are made from the officially released English translation. The full translated text appears in the *New York Times*, June 19, 1957, and also in the supplement to *People's China*, July 1, 1957, The Chinese text appears in *JMJP*, June 19, 1957.

[5] Quotations are from Mao Tse-tung, *On Contradiction*, Chinese Languages Press, Peking 1953. It was also republished in *Selected Works of Mao Tse-tung*, II, People's Publishing House, Bombay, 1954.

[6] Report of the forum in *KMJP*, October 24, 1956.

[7] Report of the forum in *JMJP*, November, 17, 1956.

[8] Ch'en Liao, 陳遼: 對陳其通同志的「意見」的意見 'Tui Ch'en Ch'i-t'ung t'ung-chih ti yi-chien ti yi-chien' (An opinion on the opinion of comrade Ch'en Ch'i-t'ung), *JMJP*, March 1, 1957.

[9] *JMJP*, March 18, 1957.

[10] Examples of student criticisms may be found in *KMJP*, July 4, July 8, August 18, September 4, September 9, 1956.

[11] China sent rice to India and Egypt, and the export of grain and oil bearing crops was a part of the economic agreement with the Soviet Union.

[12] The scarcity of goods and the long queues of housewives waiting to buy from the market were frankly admitted in an article on 'The state of the market' in *People's China*, May 16, 1957, p. 10-14.

[13] Said Chou En-lai in a report on June 26, 1957: 'The natural calamities that beset us in 1956 were not only the worst since Liberation, but also the worst in last few decades'. See Supplement to *People's China*, July 16, 1957.

[14] In an editorial urging greater attention to the 'ideological education' of workers, the *JMJP* frankly admitted that some workers were still 'sceptical or even opposed' to socialism. This is only another way of saying that they were opposed to the Communist Party.

[15] See Chapter XIII.

[16] Quotations in this section are taken from the officially released English translation of Mao's speech.

[17] This argument is quite in line with Mao's earlier exposition on the 'Peoples' democratic dictatorship'. Dictatorial methods, he said, must be used to 'suppress the enemies of the people and to 'compel' them to conform. Mercy, or 'bourgeois sentimentalism', would have no place here. But in dealing with the 'people', the democratic methods of 'education' and 'persuasion' are used and compulsion is avoided. See Mao Tse-tung, *On the People's Democratic Dictatorship*, 1949; also a speech in 1950 reported in *People's China*, July 1, 1950.

[18] Before an official text of Mao's speech was released, it was reproted that in his speech he had admitted the liquidation of 800,000 'enemies' between 1949 and 1954: see Warsaw dispatch in *New York Times*, June 13, 1957. A few months later Chou En-lai stated that in the suppression of counter-revolutionaries in 1952, 16·8 per cent had been 'sentenced to reform through labour', and 32 per cent 'put under surveillance'. See Supplement to *People's China*, July 16, 1957.

[19] Italics not in the original translated text.

CHAPTER XV   [p. 141-151]

[1] U.P. dispatch from Hong Kong, *Chinese World*, September 18, 1957.

[2] *Eighth National Congress of the Communist Party of China, Volume I, Documents*, Foreign Languages Press, Peking, 1956, p. 9-10.

[3] *Ibid.*, p. 75.

[4] *Ibid.*, p. 100-101.

[5] *Ibid.*, p. 132.

[6] *JMJP*, March 5, 1957.

[7] The official English translation authorized by the Communists used the terms 'bureaucracy' and 'anti-bureaucracy'. In the opinion of the author, 'bureaucratism' would be a better translation of *kuan-liao chu-i* 官僚主義.

[8] The text of the directive appears in *JMJP* May 1, 1957.

[9] *JMJP*, April 30, 1957.

[10] Text of directive in *JMJP*, May 15, 1957.

[11] *JMJP*, March 19, 1957.

[12] *JMJP*, April 22, 1957.

[13] *JMJP*, April 4, 1957.

[14] The text of 章伯鈞 Chang Po-chün's remarks appeared in *JMJP*, March 19, 1957.

[15] The text of 羅隆基 Lo Lung-chi's remarks appeared in *JMJP*, March 23, 1957.

[16] Fei Hsiao-t'ung, 知識份子的早春天氣 'Chih-shih-fen-tzu ti tsao-ch'un t'ien-ch'i' (The early spring weather of the intellectuals), *JMJP*, March 24, 1957.

[17] *JMJP*, April 20, 1957.

[18] Statement of 王贛愚 Wang Kan-yü in *JMJP*, April 22, 1957.

[19] Lei Hai-tsung 雷海宗, *loc. cit.* in Ch. IV, note 6.

[20] Statement of Wang Wei-chung, a professor of economics, made in a forum discussion in Shanghai, *Chieh-fang jih-pao* (Liberation Daily), Shanghai, April, 20, 1957.

[21] Yen Chi-t'zu 嚴濟慈, 尊重科學家, 改造科學家 'Tsun-chung k'o-hsüeh-chia, kai-tsao k'o-hsüeh-chia' (Respect the scientists, reform the scientists), *JMJP*, April 17, 1957; also Ma Ta-yu 馬大猷, 領導科學, 領導科學家 'Ling-tao k'o-hsüeh, ling-tao k'o-hsüeh-chia' (Leadership for science, leadership for the scientists), *JMJP*, April 25, 1957.

[22] T'ang Lan 唐蘭, 行政命令不能解決學術問題 'Hsing-cheng ming-ling pu-neng chieh-chüeh hsüeh-shu wen-t'i' (Problems of scholarship cannot be settled by administrative orders), *JMJP*, April 18, 1957.

[23] Ho Kuo-chu, 何國柱, 黨能領導那些不能領導那些 'Tang neng ling-tao na-hsieh, pu-neng ling-tao na-hsieh' (What the Party should lead and what it should not lead), *JMJP*, April 23, 1957.

[24] See report of a forum of Shanghai scientists in *JMJP*, April 17, 1957.

[25] Examples: May 4 is the anniversary of the Student Movement of 1919; May 7 and May 9 are the dates of the Japanese ultimatum for the acceptance of the Twenty-One Demands of 1915; May 30 is the date of the student demonstration in Shanghai which resulted in a number of deaths in 1925, and so on.

CHAPTER XVI   [p. 152-163]

[1] *KMJP*, May 9, 1957.

[2] *JMJP*, May 9, 1957,

[3] *KMJP*, May 22, 1957.

[4] *JMJP*, May 11, 1957.

[5] *KMJP*, May 11, 1957.

[6] *KMJP*, May 23, 1957.

[7] *JMJP*, May 9, 1957.

[8] Stalin made this statement in a speech mourning the death of Lenin, at the Second Congress of Soviets of the U.S.S.R. See *History of the Communist Party of the Soviet Union*, International Publishers, New York 1939, p. 268.

⁹ *JMJP*, May 9, 1957; *KMJP*, May 9, 1957.

¹⁰ *KMJP*, May 8, 1957.

¹¹ *KMJP*, May 17, 1957.

¹² *KMJP*, May 1, 1957.

¹³ *KMJP*, May 4, 1957.

¹⁴ *KMJP*, *loc. cit.*

¹⁵ *KMJP*, May 8, 1957.

¹⁶ *KMJP*, May 10, 1957.

¹⁷ *KMJP*, May 17, 1957.

¹⁸ *KMJP*, May 17, 1957.

¹⁹ See, for example, report of a forum of Chiu-san Society in *KMJP*, May 16, 1957.

²⁰ *KMJP*, May 8, 1957.

²¹ *KMJP*, May 11, 1957.

²² *KMJP*, May 15, 1957.

²³ *KMJP*, May 17, 1957.

²⁴ *KMJP*, May 19, 1957.

²⁵ *JMJP*, May 15, 1957.

²⁶ Interview with Prof. Ch'ien Wei-ch'ang 錢偉長 as recorded in *JMJP*, May 17, 1957.

²⁷ *KMJP*, May 21, 1957.

²⁸ Statement of Yen Hsi-shun 嚴希純 in *KMJP*, May 17, 1957.

²⁹ *JMJP*, May 13, 1957.

³⁰ *JMJP*, May 17, 1957.

³¹ *Chiao-shih-pao* 教師報 (Teacher's Journal), May, 31, 1957.

³² *KMJP*, May 23, 1957.

³³ A similar complaint of 'distance' was made in a forum by a secondary school teacher, who reported that Party members in his school addressed one another by such intimate terms as 'Old Chang' and 'Old Wang' but would call non-Communists 'Mr Chang' and 'Mr Wang'. See *Chiao-shih-pao* 教師報 (Teachers' Journal), May 14, 1957.

³⁴ *KMJP*, May 27, 1957.

³⁵ *JMJP*, May 26, 1957.

CHAPTER XVII   [p. 164-170]

¹ *KMJP*, June 2, 1957.

² Up to this time, no one had dared criticize the top Communist leaders by name.

³ Chu Teh, a veteran Communist.

⁴ As a transitional step in the liquidation of private enterprises, the Communists have changed them into joint public-private enterprises. In this transitional period, private capitalists put their assets under joint management and the 'leadership' of the state. In return the state agrees to pay the private owners a fixed annual interest. The payment of this interest is described by the Communists as a vestige of bourgeois exploitation, which is temporarily tolerated but will be eliminated in the era of complete socialism.

⁵ *JMJP*, June 5, 1957.

⁶ *JMJP*, May 24, 1957.

⁷ *KMJP*, May 31, 1957.

⁸ The word 'Han' refers to the dominant Chinese race in China, as distinct from the racial minorities in Mongolia, Tibet, Sinkiang, Southwestern China, and other areas.

[9] This summary is based on published criticisms of Lung Yün in the *JMJP* June 19, 1957 and *KMJP* of the same date. News dispatches concerning Lung Yün may be found in the *New York Times*, June 24, 1957 and *Christian Science Monitor*, June 15, 1957.

[10] *Survey of China Mainland Press*, 1563, July 5, 1957, p. 7. Italics not in the original.

CHAPTER XVIII   [p. 171-182]

[1] See Chapter XIII.

[2] *JMJP*, May 26, 1957.

[3] *JMJP*, June 10, 1957.

[4] *JMJP*, June 14, 1957.

[5] See Chapter XI.

[6] English text of Chou's report in the Supplement to *People's China*, July 16, 1957.

[7] Lu Ting-yi, 'Where we differ from the Rightists', *People's China*, August 1, 1957, p. 4-13.

[8] *JMJP*, June 8, 1957.

[9] *JMJP*, June 10, 1957.

[10] *JMJP*, June 9, 1957.

[11] Chang Yüan-shan 章元善, in *JMJP*, June 9, 1959.

[12] *JMJP*, June 20, 1957.

[13] *Ibid.*

[14] Hu Yü-chih, 'Right-wing coterie exposed', *People's China*, August 16, 1957, p. 11-17.

[15] Tseng Chao-lun 曾昭掄, vice-minister of Higher Education, *ibid.*

[16] The Rightists, according to the Communists, were 'anti-socialist, anti-people and anti-Communitst'.

[17] *JMJP*, June 19, 1957.

CHAPTER XIX   [p. 183-201]

[1] *JMJP*, June 14, 1957.

[2] *Loc. cit.*

[3] *JMJP*, June 18, 1957.

[4] *JMJP*, July 16, 1957.

[5] *JMJP*, July 16, 1957.

[6] Lo Lung-chi 羅隆基, 我的初步交代 'Wo-ti ch'u-pu chiao-tai', *JMJP*, July 16, 1955.

[7] *Ibid.*, July 14, 1957.

[8] *Ibid.*, July 15, 1957.

[9] This statement does not apply to anti-Communists who are branded as counter-revolutionaries. Many 'counter-revolutionaries' were arrested, imprisoned or executed during the period of the 'counter-attack'.

[10] Many intellectuals are being required to engage in physical labour in order to reform themselves.

[11] *JMJP*, September 10, 1957.

[12] According to a UP dispatch from Hong Kong which appeared in the *Chinese World*, October 25, 1957, Lung Yün had been sent to his home-town in Kunming to face trial for his anti-socialist views. He was probably being used as a 'living textbook' for the education of the people of Yünnan.

[13] United Press dispatch from Tokyo, in *The Young China* (Chinese daily in San Francisco), October 23, 1957.

[14] See report on sending students and intellectuals to farms, in *New York Times*, November 11, 1957. A later report stated that by the beginning of December, 810,000 government and Party workers and 10,000,000 students and local officials had been sent to farms and other labour projects. See *New York Times*, December 6, 1957.

[15] The recent scientific triumphs of Soviet science will probably swing the pendulum a little over to the Soviet side again, but it is doubtful that it will revert to the pre-1956 position. At any rate, Soviet scientists today are in communication with the scientists in the non-Communist countries much more than before, and Communist China is likely to follow the same trend as far as scientific research is concerned.

[16] 'Pao-wei che-hsüeh she-hui k'o-hsüeh ti tang-hsing', 保衛哲學, 社會科學的 黨性 (Protect the Party character of philosophy and the social sciences), *JMJP*, September 19, 1957.

[17] Articles attacking the proposal to revive the study of 'bourgeois social sciences' appeared in *JMJP*, September 9, 1957 (by philosopher Chin Yüeh-lin), and September 23, 1957.

[18] *JMJP*, September 19, 1957.

[19] Fei Hsiao-t'ung, 我這一年 'Wo che-i-nien' (My past year), in 我的思想是怎 樣轉變過來的 *Wo-ti ssu-hsiang shih tsen-yang chuan-pien kuo-lai-ti* (How my thought was changed), 北京, 五十年代出版社 *Wu-shih nien-tai ch'u-pan-she* Peking 1950, p. 71-77.

[20] Fei Hsiao-t'ung, 舊人物的改造 *Chiu jen-wu ti kai-tsao*, 通俗文化出版社 T'ung-shu wen-hua ch'u-pan-she, no date.

[21] Fei Hsiao-t'ung, 'Old friends and a new understanding', *People's China*, June 1, 1956, p. 12-17.

[22] Lin Yao-hua 林耀華, 'The treacherous and ugly Fei Hsiao-t'ung', *Current Background*, 475, August 28, 1957.

[23] *JMJP*, July 14, 1957.

[24] *JMJP*, July 14, 1957.

[25] Ch'ien Tuan-sheng 錢端升, 爲改造自已更好的服務祖國而學習 'Wei kai-tsao tzu-chi keng-hao-ti fu-wu tsu-kuo erh hsüeh-hsi' (Study to reform ourselves and to serve our fatherland better), *Documents*, 1, p. 44-49.

[26] Ch'ien Tuan-sheng, 'Our new state structure', *China Reconstructs*, February 1955, p. 2-5.

[27] *JMJP*, August 6, 1957.

[28] For example, at one time to push agricultural co-operative with too much hurry was condemned as 'blind adventurism', but a few months later the official policy was revised and those cautioning against hurry were condemned as 'Rightists' who were trying to hold back the wheels of progress.

[29] *Hsing-tao jih-pao*, 星島日報 August 8-9, 1957.

[30] Reported in *The Young China* 少年中國, November 26, 1957.

[31] *JMJP*, June 15, 1957; see also *ibid.*, June 11, 1957, reporting on the activities of the Democratic League.

[32] *Chinese World*, September 9, 1957.

[33] *JMJP*, July 13, 1957.

[34] *Survey of China Mainland Press, 1583*: 19, August 2, 1957. The fact that a large portion of the soldiers come from the peasant population and reflect the discontent of the peasants adds to the gravity of the problem in the army. Among Christians denounced as Rightists are the former president and one-time acting president of Hua Chung (Christian) University. Reported in the *China Bulletin* of the Far Eastern office, Division of Foreign Missions, NCCC/USA, September 30, 1957.

[35] *Survey of China Mainland Press, 1575*: 36, July 23, 1957.

[36] Disturbances reported in *New York Times*, April 21, 1957, and in the *Time* magazine, May 20, 1957.

[37] *JMJP*, August 6, 1957.

[38] 'Peking paper bares executions', *Christian Science Monitor*, September 25, 1957. According to a refugee who escaped from the Mainland to Hong Kong, the Hanyang Middle School demonstrations resulted in the execution of 70 persons, including a couple of teachers and the vice-principal of the school. See *Chinese World*, October 12, 1957.

[39] See reports in *The Young China*, June 29, and July 12, 1957.

[40] See *Chinese World*, August 26, 1957.

[41] 'Peiping now admits an uprising in July', *New York Times*, Sept. 18, 1957.

[42] 'Peiping reports plotters' arrest', *New York Times*, June 28, 1957; also *Chinese World*, June 28, 1957.

[43] 'Peiping reports new plot broken', *New York Times*, July 31, 1957; also *Chinese World*, August 2, 1957.

[44] 'Peiping arrests more anti-reds', *New York Times*, August 6, 1957.

[45] *Chinese World*, December 6, 1957.

INDEX

The numbers in italics refer to the Notes, *v.* for *vide*, see.
For abbreviations, see cross-references.

大陸知識份子之思想改造

版權所有

著者　　　陳世鐸
出版者　　香港大學出版社
承印者　　國泰印刷所
定價　　　港幣式拾伍圓
出版日期　一九六〇年三月